THE EXPERIMENTAL SUTTON HOO SHIP

Context and Design

Visitors to the ship in the Longshed in 2024.

THE EXPERIMENTAL SUTTON HOO SHIP

CONTEXT AND DESIGN

WRITTEN FOR THE
SUTTON HOO SHIP'S COMPANY BY
MARTIN CARVER

WITH ILLUSTRATIONS BY
CATHERINE HOY

THE BOYDELL PRESS

First published 2026
The Boydell Press, Woodbridge

ISBN 978 1 83765 3676

The Boydell Press is an imprint of Boydell & Brewer Ltd
and of Boydell & Brewer Inc.
website: www.boydellandbrewer.com

Our Authorised Representative for product safety in the EU is
Easy Access System Europe - Mustamäe tee 50, 10621 Tallinn, Estonia,
gpsr.requests@easproject.com

A CIP catalogue record for this book is available from the British Library

Book designed by Simon Loxley

CONTENTS

LIST OF ILLUSTRATIONS

Captions and credits

CHAPTER 3

CHAPTER 4

CHAPTER 5

PREFACE

Martin Carver

The building, launching and putting to sea of a full-scale reconstruction of the ship found in 1939 at Sutton Hoo under Mound 1 is an enterprise in which we invite wide participation. It has four main phases: the design, the build, the trials and the publication of the results of the experiment, which are expected to take about fifteen years between 2017 and 2032. We can be followed on social media and via our website at https://saxonship.org , and in films and YouTube broadcasts. The build is being carried out by the Sutton Hoo Ship's Company at Whisstocks Place on the waterfront at Woodbridge, Suffolk where visitors are always welcome.

Visitors like to take home a published account of what is being done, and since fifteen years is a long time to wait for it, we decided to publish consecutive short books to cover each of the three phases. The first book (the present one) covers the period in which the project was conceived and designed. The second, composed with Tim Kirk, Laurie Walker and Jacq Barnard, will take the story from the start of the build to the launch. A third, still a twinkle in the eye, will describe the ship's achievements on trials and its eventual retirement on display.

The present volume lays the basis for the project. It explores the early English society which knew the Sutton Hoo Ship, first in narrative of characters mentioned in surviving histories, pre-eminently that of Bede, and then by making archaeological visits to the graves of unnamed persons of the time, of higher rank and of no clear rank at all. Other key players are the artisans who left their inventive personalities encased in artefacts - metalworkers, textile workers and carpenters. We search for ideas in the minds of the ship-builders, detected in boats built both before and after the Sutton Hoo Ship and boats built and used around the northern seas, on the Continent and the Mediterranean. Having laid out the evidence for the ship and its context, the book turns its attention to the reconstruction project of the 21st century, how it came about, how it was set up, what it hoped to achieve, and why, how it was organised, how it fitted itself to serve the research and social agendas of our time. The story of a research campaign, its objectives, the decisions and the setbacks, tend to get lost or remain unshared. And yet they are not without interest, certainly to the many trustees, advisors and above all volunteers who made them happen, and not less to the future generations of students and enthusiasts who study and relish these projects - and wish they had been there.

ACKNOWLEDGEMENTS

This is not the definitive account of the Sutton Hoo Ship Reconstruction project which has to wait until the ship is built and exercised upon the water. In the meantime, I am very grateful to Witan member Catherine Hills for updating me on the latest Anglo-Saxon research and improving my text, and to Jacq Barnard, Andy Mills, Joe Startin, Damian Robinson, Angela Care Evans, Helen Geake and Natasha Symes for their very helpful correctives and comments, and especially to master shipwright Tim Kirk for sharing his expertise and insights while the ship was under construction. Andrew FitzGerald gave me valuable help for the history of the project in Chapter 5. The pictures were provided through the generosity of their originators as itemised in the list of illustrations, and the book enlivened by the evocative drawings in Chapter 1 and the brilliant rendering of tools in Chapter 5 by Ship's Company volunteer Catherine Hoy. Emily Boulting and her Time Team have provided inspired broadcasting of the project since 2021. Project Manager Jacq Barnard and publisher Richard Barber produced the book, which was designed by Simon Loxley. I am most grateful to Madeleine Hummler, Sarah Perkins, David Keeble and members of the ship's crew for their sharp-eyed proofreading. The earnings from the book are to be donated to the Sutton Hoo Ship's Company for its Reconstruction Project. We are especially grateful to the National Trust and the Sutton Hoo Society for their long-term interest and support.

INTRODUCING THE EAST ANGLES

Shadowy figures inhabit the seventh century - names without bodies, bodies without names. Their legacy comes from diverse sources, from rare conserved manuscripts and from numerous graves and artefacts buried under the ground. Pieced together from king-lists and Bede is a sequence of East Anglian kings, members of the Wuffinga dynasty that would endure until the mid-eighth century. In addition, thousands of men, women and children have been rediscovered in their graves, along with their dogs and horses. We can give names to none of them, although all were individuals. And there is a special group of people, seldom encountered in their burials but declared by their handiwork: gold and garnet weaponry, brooches of gilt bronze, necklaces of coloured beads, intricate animal patterns on the jewellery of humans, solemn human faces on the harness of horses. And there are Old England's placenames that survive in every part, and there are East Anglia's rivers which still flow, their tides still drawing steadily in and out. On a summer morning on the River Deben you can still see and smell and hear the same landscape with the same birds and same trees and weeds, and no more sounds of travel than a shout and the slap of a sail.

How daring can we be with words and pictures to remake the past? Can we capture its challenges, anxieties and exhilarations with any conviction? Can we ever reproduce, by rediscovering their swords and bridles, or the lines of vanished ship, a moment of ancient thrill or trauma or triumph that may come to life today? One way is to think one's way into such moments and imagine and write about them; but another is to relive them today. This book is an account of one such venture, the reconstruction of the 27m long ship that was buried beneath a mound of sand and turf at Sutton Hoo in about 625CE. In these chapters, the echoes of history and the glimpses of archaeology will alternate with the clatter of today's people building the ship, the hard-fought debates of design, the trials and errors of carpentry on the grand scale. The aim is to bring the community of the seventh century into dialogue with the twenty-first century crew of the Ship's Company, both of them performing on a common stage - the banks of the River Deben in south-east Suffolk.

This book is an attempt to weave the written information incorporated in Bede's History, with the evidence captured by archaeology. In this period the disciplines, equally entitled to their deductions, suffer from a rarity of precisely dated events and their detailed description. To make a narrative of this material, often surviving in small disconnected parcels, is certainly a challenge, but hopes to have some value in setting the context in which our ship was constructed. While some assumptions are made, for example that Sutton Hoo was the burial place of King Rædwald, it is accepted that, as always, new evidence may one day modify the story.

We begin by painting in the background, drawing on the earliest history to evoke the individual players in the seventh century: characters such as Rædwald, king of East Anglia, his astute but unnamed queen, his ancestors and descendants, what they did and when and why (Chapter 1). Then we meet key figures not mentioned in books, the many warriors and wise women who lie in seventh-century graves (in Chapter 2). Then the other players, and by no means the least significant, are witnessed neither on the page nor in the grave, but enshrined in the things they made. Chapter 3 celebrates these artisans showing that the birth of the Sutton Hoo ship coincided with a moment of significant innovation for the smiths, who made weapons and jewellery, the weavers who made clothes and the carpenters who made timber halls – and ships.

Having assembled our cast of characters we turn to the making of our own ship, an artefact that represents a high point in what kings, queens and artisans were achieving in the seventh century. First, we review what we knew about other ships that were sailed or rowed before our ship was made and after, its possible inspirations and models in the northern and Mediterranean seas (Chapter 4). Some of these can be counted as determinant, if not for them, certainly for us, and were folded into the process of researching and deciding the design of our ship, finding somewhere to build it, locating the materials, finding the work force and raising the funds (Chapter 5). We can share with the reader the hopes and expectations that are embodied in the plan, expose its workings and its prospects, and so create a platform for the project as a whole.

Sequels to this introduction are to be related in two more books: the first describing the triumphs and travails of the build, and the second the great adventure of trialling the ship on rivers, lakes and the sea. Of course, we cannot write these stories before they happen – but to wait until the project is finished in the 2030s would not suit the modern world at all, with its YouTubes and Instagrams and sound bites. But if all goes well, we too will join the digital mêlée by reporting each chapter as a podcast. Follow us too on http://saxonship.org. Our newsletters and broadcasts will let us share with you the events they happen. These books are both guides and souvenirs to the world of the earliest English boat-builders and seafarers that we hope to recreate.

THE EXPERIMENTAL SUTTON HOO SHIP

1 THE SEVENTH CENTURY ACCORDING TO BEDE

A summary

The Venerable Bede, England's first historian, lived and wrote in the early eighth century in Northumbria, a long way from the River Deben and a century later than the events I am about relate. But he was by no means ill-informed, taking evidence, as he tells us, from learned persons and the descendants of some of the main players. He was a champion of Christianity writing about pagans, and while he considered them to be wrong about the moral purpose of life and whatever was to follow it, he still gave them a history. His book would hardly have lasted if it had spoken inaccurately of the ancestors of his contemporaries. So he is at least a reliable purveyor of some of the widely held memories of his time. His *History of the English Church and People* was presented in thematic rather than consecutive sections (like a modern museum) and is reworked here into a plain narrative with an emphasis on places, people, travel and ships. The dramas are played out within and between British- and English-speaking communities, especially in the areas of Northumbria, Mercia, East Anglia, Kent and Wessex **(FIG 1.1)**.[1]

The chief characters are kings and monks, queens and abbesses - since the making of Christian England (Bede's theme) was considered to be in their hands. The names of the players present a considerable obstacle to an easy read since they often seem unfamiliar, unpronounceable, or even too like each other to tell apart. Most names of ordinary folk were acquired in early England based on what they did or where they were from: Cooper, Shipman, Baker, French, Dane, Moor. The Anglo-Saxon aristocracy had higher pretensions and named their children from a rather limited list of descriptors: aethel/noble, frith/peace. So: Æthelfrith = prince of peace; Rædwald = Wise ruler; Eadbald = Rich and bold; ruler and Freothwebbe = Peaceweaver - a woman winning peace through marriage to an enemy. Like our own surnames today, the names are more important than their meaning: Æthelfrith will hardly be seen as a prince of peace. (For a list of the names of the principal actors and a Timeline of their activities, please refer to pp.156-9.)

In this seventh century world, and Bede's view of it, politics is religion and vice versa. Among the immigrant English, kingdoms replace tribal groups, individual kings override communities, and the agenda is dominated by the great dilemma on alignment with the neighbours overseas - whether to stay close to pagan Scandinavia or ally with Christian Rome. In Britain, these

1.1 Map of Britain showing locations of communities and places mentioned in the book.

differences meant that supporters of both parties, whether military or spiritual leaders, whether kings, warriors, holy men or wise women, were in contention with each other for a hundred years. In this vigorous atmosphere our ship emerged.

AT THE COURT OF KING RÆDWALD

In the early seventh century, Æthelfrith, king of Northumbria was on the rampage. Bede describes him as 'most eager for glory... no ruler or king subjected more land to the English race or settled it having first either exterminated or conquered the natives'.[2] Æthelfrith belongs to the second or third generation of a large Germanic contingent who arrived in eastern Britain from northern Europe in the fifth century; his family settled in *Bernicia*, north of the Tyne. He disliked Christians and Britons and also the Scots, the other immigrants who are now arriving along the west coast from Ireland. At the battle of Degsastan (603CE) he is supposed to have driven these Scots out of Bernicia, the land between the Tweed and the Tyne, although archaeology shows they kept

1.2 At Raedwald's court, Rendlesham on the River Deben.

coming and three centuries later would create the kingdom of Scotland.[3] He also disliked Edwin, his brother-in-law and heir to *Deira*, the land between the Tyne and the Humber, land Æthelfrith wanted. Æthelfrith chased Edwin to the court of Rædwald, king of East Anglia, probably at Rendlesham where he took refuge in 613 - an indication perhaps of Rædwald's particular reputation as a powerful warrior **(FIG 1.2)**.

Æthelfrith soon tempted Rædwald, with three consecutive bribes, to have Edwin murdered. Edwin was apprised of the plot, but refused to flee: "I would rather die by his royal hand...what refuge remains for me who have already wandered for so many years in every corner of Britain trying to escape my enemies?" Bede pictures Edwin in a reverie sitting sadly alone, when he felt the presence of a stranger putting a hand on his head telling him to 'remember this sign' - the blessing of Christianity. More practical action, when she got wind of the matter, came from Rædwald's queen who took her husband fiercely to task for accepting the bribe: "It is unworthy of a great king to sell his best friend for gold and to sacrifice his honour for money" - and so the plan was dropped.[4] These words of a pagan woman to a pagan man were remembered for a hundred Christian years so presumably stayed in common knowledge, until Bede wrote them down. He must have admitted, if only to himself, that Christianity did not have the monopoly on morals **(FIG 1.3)**.

1.3 Rædwald told off by his queen.

This was a confusing time for religion. Columba (Columcille) had arrived in Iona from Ireland in 563 as part of the Scottish immigration, and died there in 597 - the same year that Augustine arrived in Canterbury to conduct a second Christian mission, this time from Pope Gregory who had seen some English boys for sale in Rome's slave market. Augustine had some initial success - in Kent it was easy, as King Æthelberht's queen was already a Christian. Sæberht king of Essex followed in 603. Conversion was a top-down project then, and both Kent and Essex reverted to paganism after their first Christian kings died. Æthelberht's successor, his son Eadbald, had an additional reason to revert: he married his father's second wife, now his widow.[5] Although not unknown among the pagan English, and presumably having social and economic advantages, the church did not approve of this transparent device for keeping things in the family.

Meanwhile, although he already had a wife and two sons in Mercia, Edwin had found time to woo Eadbald's sister Æthelburh known as Tata.[6] She was a Christian, but pagan Edwin promised his now pagan brother-in-law that he would allow her complete religious freedom. Rædwald had been to Kent to investigate Christianity and its possible political and economic advantages, getting himself baptised while there. He may have been pleased with this addition to his bargaining power, but it was his queen who once again

1.4 Æthelfrith of Northumbria confronting the monks of Bangor outside Chester.

pointed out the dangers of his actions - in this case for their existing alliances. Always pragmatic, Rædwald, added an altar to Christ in their temple (probably at the nearby palace of Rendlesham). Bede recounts the episode with disdain: Rædwald was "baptised in Kent but to little purpose - on his return home his wife and certain evil counsellors persuaded him to revert... so his last state was worse than the first." He adds "Like the ancient Samaritans he tried to serve both Christ and the ancient gods, setting up in his temple an altar to Christ alongside the one where sacrifices were offered to devils". According to Bede, a later Christian king of East Anglia, Ealdwulf, remembered seeing this temple still standing when he was a boy.[7]

As we have since learnt from archaeology, Paganism was a complex and multifaceted system of belief to which Christianity owed a great deal - in the northern seas as much as in the Mediterranean. These religions were embraced or disdained, but less on their teaching or morality and more on the outcomes of battles where the will of the gods was most evident. Loyalty to a victorious god also meant loyalty to the society of the victors; thus religion both determined alliances and caused wars. Wavering between religions destabilised the politics of the day - and no doubt these were among the concerns of Rædwald's astute queen.

THE BEAST OF BERNICIA

In his zest for conquering Britons, Æthelfrith, took himself to Chester in 616 to raise an army against the Welsh. Before battle commenced he discovered an immense company of monks from the monastery of Bangor in a safe place away from the old Roman city who were on their knees praying for victory over the English barbarians **(FIG 1.4)**. Æthelfrith announced that since "they were crying to their god against us, they are fighting us even if they do not carry weapons".[8] So he slaughtered twelve hundred of them, only fifty escaping, before going on to destroy the Welsh men at arms. Bede himself judged the Britons harshly - serve them right: they had rejected the true version of Christianity (his) so merited destruction. In preferring the pagan English over the Christian British, Bede revealed something of his political sympathies.

Meanwhile Rædwald had sensed the danger posed by Edwin's tormentor and prepared himself for war **(FIG 1.5)**. In 616/7 he and Edwin surprised Æthelfrith at Bawtry at the River Idle, and killed him before he had time to muster his full army.[9] Rædwald's son Regenhere was also killed in this battle. The East Anglian contingent had likely headed for the old Roman fortress of Lincoln and from there struck north-west along the Roman road that led from Lincoln

1.5 Rædwald, dressed for battle.

1.6 The River Derwent at Ellerton.

to York (now roughly the A57/A631) crossing the Trent at Littleborough, originally named *Tiowulfinga caestir* (the camp of the Wulfings, Rædwald's family). From there it was a short dash to the crossing of the River Idle at Bawtry where the battle took place. It could be that Rædwald's company made the journey to Lincoln by boat via the Wash and the Witham, but they could equally have reached Lincoln on horseback via other still viable Roman roads (i.e. the Great North road, now the A1).[10] Given the achievement of surprise, Rædwald's army probably assembled within the Roman city walls in secret and then marched or rode the 30 miles along the Roman road to Bawtry. Mustering one army and surprising another says something about good communications for Rædwald, but less for Æthelfrith who was caught south of the Humber and outside his home territory. Three important battles would be fought on this road, all of them at river crossings, which suggests that river traffic could have been significant, either for scouts or provisions, if not for transporting armed crews.

Rædwald died in about 625 and is thought to be buried in Mound 1 at Sutton Hoo, with which I believe we can make a legitimate equivalence.[11] The designer of this burial, with its multiple meanings, political and religious, was surely the work of his queen. His queen invites a similar equivalence with Mound 14 which covered the chamber of a woman who died in about 650. 'Equivalence' here means while the identity can be questioned, it is sufficiently credible to carry the story along for the time being.

Rædwald's ship was buried with him, so it might seem that its story ends there. However, what happened next in England, and in East Anglia, is important because the wars of words and of swords and spears and the travels of kings and holy men remain relevant in the whole kingdom-forming period up to the death of Bede in 735, if not until the arrival of the Vikings a century later. The years following the burial of the ship were marked by changing attitudes, pitched battles and overseas journeys, as England became Christian and was challenged by its former pagan allies. In them we will encounter many episodes located in time and space from which interesting inferences about travel and ships can be drawn.

A HAPPY COUPLE IN PERIL: EDWIN AND TATA

Following the battle of the River Idle, Edwin took the throne of Northumbria and in 626 he and Tata were happily married and living by the River Derwent in the East Riding of Yorkshire (FIG 1.6). On Easter day (20 April) in that year they were hosting Tata's spiritual counsellor, the sanctimonious Bishop Paulinus, when an assassin called Eomer arrived. He had been despatched by Cwichelm king of Wessex and carried a double-edged short sword, smeared with poison beneath his cloak. Unsuspected, he was allowed into Edwin's presence to deliver a supposed diplomatic message, but once close enough to Edwin, he drew the sword from beneath his mantle and leapt at him. The alert courtier Lilla, Edwin's trusted counsellor and close friend, threw his own body in front of the king and took the blow. It was delivered with such violence that it passed right through Lilla and into the body of the king, but wounding Edwin only slightly (FIG 1.7). The assassin was immediately attacked on all sides, and killed, but not before another of the king's men named Fordhere had met his end in the fight.[12] These events happened at the royal palace of Edwin's father Ælle, so not improbably at modern Ellerton (Ælle's *tun*) by the Derwent.[13]

That same day saw the birth of Eanflæd, daughter of Edwin and Tata. So, a day of rejoicing tempered by sharp anxieties. Paulinus was quick to credit the king's survival and his daughter's safe delivery to the blessing of Christ and urged him to convert. In common with the thinking of the day, Edwin wished to rate the new god in terms of the support he gave in battle, where chance rules, but dominant deities rule chance. Once healed of his wound and to test Christ's power, he mounted a revenge attack on the West Saxons killing or arresting all implicated in the plot. Christianity was now a serious option, but Edwin still had some deep thinking to do. Bede describes him as by nature a wise and prudent man, who often sat alone for long periods in silent conversation with himself, turning over in his inmost heart what he should do and which religion he should follow.[14]

1.7 ... an assassin called Eomer: The attempt on Edwin's life.

This was certainly a problem and one with major economic and political as well as spiritual consequences. Akin in our day to Brexit, and as finely balanced, the ancients wanted to stick with the old ways and guard the wealth of their landowning families, while the moderns were seeking the wider opportunities and alliances of the Christian continent. This first bout in the 1400-year cross-channel sparring match went to Europe. In some ways the Christian god was ahead in the polls, having secured the victory in Wessex, but the effects were marred by an impertinent letter from Pope Boniface bribing Edwin to convert, using a somewhat insubstantial premise: the Divine Majesty (Christian god) made the heavens and is adored by all the human race from the rising to the setting of the sun; "how can idols have the power to help you when they are made for you from perishable materials by the labour of your own subjects?" He was not oblivious to the power of fine artefacts himself. His letter was accompanied by a tunic with golden ornament and a cloak from Ankara. The pope also sent a nagging letter to Tata on her married life. "How can it be called a true union between you, so long as he remains alienated from the daylight of your faith by the barrier of dark and lamentable error?" adding that "the unbelieving husband shall be saved through the

1.8 Conversion: The sparrow in the hall.

believing wife." This letter was accompanied by a silver mirror and a gold and ivory comb.[15]

Paulinus put his hand on the injured Edwin's head and asked if he remembered this sign; and Edwin responded, characteristically, by taking counsel. He summoned his followers to Goodmanham on the Wolds, 14 miles east of Ellerton, where there was some sort of pagan sanctuary. Coifi, the chief pagan priest, urged the assembly to consider carefully the case for Christianity, commenting to the king, that "none of your followers has devoted himself more earnestly than I have to the worship of our gods, but nevertheless there are many who receive greater benefits and greater honour from you than I do and are more successful in all their undertakings. If the gods had any power they would have helped me more readily". Another of the chief men offered a less self-serving argument. He complained that their current religion offered little explanation of life outside its fleeting sensation, comparing it to the experience of a sparrow flying in one door of a hall and out of the other - a brief moment of warmth between two dark wintry storms. "Such is the life offered by our gods: of what went before or comes after we know nothing" (FIG 1.8). Coifi helpfully (or cannily) decided to support the Christian party and sug-

1.9 At Goodmanham: High priest Coifi spears his pagan shrine.

gested they desecrate and burn the temple and its shrines, adding that if the king would give him arms and a stallion he would throw the first spear himself; all of which duly happened[16] **(FIG 1.9)**. Of course, Bede's version might be slanted and we don't hear the kind of counter arguments that might have come from Rædwald, or his wife. But the conversion campaign had begun, even if it would need another half century to take effect in East Anglia.

WAR WITH MERCIA

In 627 Edwin was baptised at York in the church of St Peter on Easter Day (April 11). Also baptised were Edwin's children Osfrith and Eadfrith from his first wife Cwenburh, daughter of Ceorl, King of Mercians. His children with Tata were Eanflæd (daughter, baptised in 626), and later Æthelhun (son), Æthelthryth (daughter) and Uscfrea (son). Now it was safe to do so, Paulinus accompanied the royal family to Yeavering in Northumberland (territory of the late king Æthelfrith) and for 36 days baptised people from all the surrounding villages

1.10 Penda and Cadwalla ravage Northumbria and burn Yeavering.

and countryside in the River Glen, and - also in the presence of Edwin - at *Tiowulfinga caestir* on the Trent. The kingdom of Northumbria was opened up for travellers, creating unity and peace: "So peaceful was it in those parts of Britain under King Edwin's jurisdiction that the saying still runs that a woman could carry her new-born babe across the island from sea to sea without any fear of harm."[17] But the rose-tinted reign of Edwin was about to end.

The pagan Penda became king of Mercia in 626 just before his neighbouring kingdom to the north went Christian, and he was set to emerge as the next pro-pagan troublemaker of the formative English realm. In 633 in partnership with the similarly disaffected Welsh leader Cædwalla he ravaged Northumbria (FIG 1.10). There was terrible slaughter at their hands; although nominally a Christian, Welsh Cædwalla was bent on exterminating the English and removing them from the island. Tata took flight with Paulinus back to Kent, with her daughter Eanflæd, son Uscrea, Osfrith's son Yffi, and a sizable part of the royal treasure, escorted by the redoubtable warrior Bassus. Edwin headed south with Osfrith to meet the invaders at Hatfield near Doncaster on the Lincoln -York road where it crossed the River Torne, another tributary running north into the Humber. But Edwin and Osfrith were killed in the bloody encounter, after which Edwin's head was retrieved from the battlefield and taken to York, where it was placed in the church of St Peter.[18] He was 48 years old.

For the next 22 years, his descendants and his successors would fight Penda and Cædwalla, for the right to survive, and to maintain the cause of Christianity. Edwin's cousin Osric took over Deira, and Æthelfrith's son Eanfrith took over Bernicia. Within a year both were dead, Osric overwhelmed by a sudden sally by Cædwalla, while laying siege to him, and Eanfrith with all his bodyguard, after unwisely visiting Cædwalla to negotiate peace. Edwin's son Eadfrith was taken hostage but subsequently put to death by Penda in defiance of an agreement. Uscfrea and Yffi both died in infancy. Following Æthelfrith's death, his three sons, Oswald, Eanfrith and Oswiu had all been sent north of the Forth to Pictland or into Scotland where they converted to the Scottish-British brand of Christianity. After Eanfrith's death, Oswald became king of Bernicia and rallied his army in the name of Christ, planting a wooden cross in the earth at Heavenfield near Hexham on the Scottish side of Hadrian' s wall. Like the cross of Christ itself, it became a source of beneficial wooden splinters and innumerable miracles. Oswald managed to finally overpower Cædwalla, and kill him at Deniseburn, perhaps Rowley Water in Northumberland. But Oswald himself met his match in 642 giving battle at *Maserfelth* now Oswestry on the Welsh border.[19] There he was killed by the old adversary Penda. He was then 38 years old, and his sanctity, although it was of the northern un-English kind, remained widely valued.

ANOTHER GOOD MARRIAGE

Out of Æthelfrith's three sons, now only Oswiu remained and of Edwin's six children only his daughter with Tata, Eanflæd, had survived these 25 years of slaughter. The war had been about the survival of three kingdoms, Bernicia, Deira and Mercia, broadly located in Northumberland, Yorkshire and the Midlands, and the confrontation of three religions, paganism and the two Christian variants, Irish and Roman, with their not very different rituals and moral compass. The obvious way forward was for the surviving issue of the two families, Eanflæd , and Oswiu, to marry each other, thus uniting Northumbria and, eventually, the two kinds of Christianity. Meanwhile, there was Penda.

The old Mercian warlord continued his harassment of Northumbria for a further 12 years. Oswiu first tried to buy him off by amassing "an incalculable and incredible treasure as the price of peace".[20] This Penda refused, declaring that his intention remained to wipe out the whole Christian nation from the

1.11 "... an incalculable and incredible treasure" Gold and garnet objects from the Staffordshire hoard.

highest to the humblest of the land. Oswiu then sought the support of God by promising to give his daughter Ælfflæd (just one year old) to the church and by building 12 monasteries. As for the treasure itself, it most likely resembled the Staffordshire hoard, a heap of gold and silver bullion stripped from swords, crosses and at least one helmet (showing that both warrior and clerical classes had contributed to the whip-round) weighing in at 5 kilos of gold and silver, about equivalent to a king's ransom **(FIG 1.11)**. Whether or not the actual Staffordshire hoard, found near the Roman road into Wales (now the A5), was this the same incalculable treasure that had somehow gone astray, the two resembled each other in concept (see Chapter 2). God helped Oswiu, who finally disposed of Penda at the battle of the Winwæd, a river crossed by

1.12 Battle of the Winwæd,"fought in flooded fields, with water so deep that it was said that more warriors drowned trying to escape than were slain by the sword".

that same Roman road from Lincoln to York that appears to be something of a natural frontier between Mercia and Northumbria. It was a battle fought in flooded fields, with water so deep that it was said that more warriors drowned trying to escape than were slain by the sword[21] **(FIG 1.12)**.

Oswiu's next task was to agree the 'right' form for British Christianity; it was proving inconvenient at home, as he and his wife had to celebrate Easter on different days. There were other differences too: while monks of the Roman persuasion had a dinner-plate style of circular tonsure, the Celtic monks shaved their foreheads and wore their hair long in a mullet at the back, in the style of the pre-Christian druids. Although these liturgical battles seem trivial, they mattered, partly because they disguised the real issue - who was going to determine the ideological direction and alliances of the English Christians - the western Celts of Britain or the Continental Romans. The first was rooted in the long prehistory of the island and the second in imperial Europe. The husband-and-wife team in power were ideally suited to resolve this question, which was settled at the Synod of Whitby in 664.[22] They opted for modernism. The opponents, Wilfred for the Roman party and Colman for the west-

1.13 The synod of Whitby: battle of the tonsures.

erners, argued as only over-educated academics can, focusing on recondite topics such as the correct way of calculating Easter and the correct form of a monk's tonsure, and avoiding any temptation of pragmatism or compromise. Unprovable abstractions were posed, answered with ranting rage (Wilfred) or impenetrable piety (Colman) **(FIG 1.13)**. The matter was settled by Oswiu on unstated political grounds: we go with St Peter, Rome and Europe. To mollify the losing party, he increased investment in the northern monastery, a type of spiritual college that was the natural successor to the druids of ancient Britain. Oswiu built at least 10 monasteries notably at Hartlepool, Old Melrose. Tynemouth, Whitby and Coldingham in addition to his 12 foundations, each of 10 hides, promised to Christ before the battle of the Winwæd.[23] The new monastic movement combined royal and spiritual authority and would peacefully conquer the north and west of England, as well as Wales, Scotland and Pictland. The monasteries were beacons of culture and innovative farming, scholarship, literature, illuminated manuscripts, painted sculpture and fine metal work. In their art, orthodox Christianity incorporated and calmed the leaping and wilful animals that had so animated the pre-Christian treasures at Sutton

Hoo. Europe was where the money was; the axis of travel swung from the North Sea to the Channel and the Rhine; the new links with Europe's political and spiritual hierarchy would replace the Scandinavian kinsmen of the seventh century. That is, until the latter struck back as Vikings.

RETURN TO EAST ANGLIA

East Anglia toyed with Christianity after Rædwald. His son Eorpwald converted, but was then murdered by a pagan named Ricbert. His Christian successor Sigeberht had been exiled in France to avoid the hostility of Rædwald, and came back to convert more East Angles. He had no wish to rule on earth and handed over to his brother Egric before retiring to a monastery at Dunwich, now beneath the sea. When Penda attacked East Anglia in 635, Sigeberht was dragged out of his monastic hideaway and into battle. Enfeebled by piety he would brandish nothing more than a stick and was killed along with his brother Ecgric.[24] Their successor Anna, king from 644 and a dedicated Christian, was also killed by Penda.

However, although East Anglia, like most of England south of the Humber, had some named monastic establishments, no early sites have yet been found that resemble the ornate and busy central places of the north. East Anglian politics bought into aristocracy and 'magnate' farms and eventually trading places (wics) rather than communities of monks cultivating spiritual wisdom and answerable only to God. In consequence, the Vikings discovered some fellow feeling there and when their Great Army arrived in 866 they went first to East Anglia, where the East Angles made peace with them and supplied them with horses.[25]

The carnage of early English internecine warfare might seem a step away from the context of the Mound 1 ship, but its isolated splendour is underpinned by the military strength of the pagan Rædwald as a political actor, by a continuing interest in the Scandinavian homeland, and by the outstanding wealth of East Anglia which, as we will see, is affirmed by an archaeology that does not rely solely on burial. In addition, a theme of this book (developed in Chapter 3), is also that the creative achievements of manufacture can survive, and even feed off, the excessive gambles of the governing class.

TRAVEL OVER LAND AND SEA

Being where they were, at the junction of two maritime thoroughfares, the East Angles were never likely to give up travel overseas. In the time both before and after the arrival of Augustine at Canterbury, the frequency, length and speed of travel implied by Bede is impressive. On missions of vengeance, diplomacy or curiosity, kings and their companies moved from Northumbria to Chester, from Suffolk to Kent, from Yorkshire to Hampshire, from York to Pictland with seeming ease. Much of this relentless journeying must have made use of ancient trackways and the Roman roads that were still viable.[26] The horse was a frequently mentioned or implied upper-class icon, as in the tale of Coifi.[27] Everyone else walked or marched. What of boats and ships? The Romans had sea-going ships and came in numbers to all the shores of Britain on consecutive occasions. The Angles and Saxons arrived across the water in their turn. There was traffic along the east coast of Britain with its numerous estuaries as shown by the estuary locations of the principal monastic sites, but also by the coastal activity in East Anglia.[28] Sea travel from the islands of Britain and Ireland did not cease when the Roman government left. In the sixth and seventh centuries the early Christian Irish made journeys into the continent and founded monasteries there, and goods from the eastern Mediterranean and western France reached Irish and Pictish destinations. Many objects from Africa and India and from the Eastern Mediterranean have been found in pagan English graves, already in the fifth century, and by Rædwald's day his warriors were joining the Byzantine army.[29] In the seventh and eighth century the first Christian English made trips across the Continent and beyond.

Ships feature in Bede's history as a somewhat risky means of transport, and rarely as status property or a hero's ride. In 651 Utta, Abbot of Gateshead, was sent from Northumbria to Kent to fetch Edwin's daughter Eanflæd, as the wife for King Oswiu.[30] Utta decided to make the journey south by road and return with his larger escort by sea, so he went to Bishop Aidan to ask him to pray for a prosperous voyage. The Bishop blessed him and commended the passengers to God - and also provided a little bottle of holy oil to calm the sea when it got rough - which proved most effective: it saved the ship from sinking in a storm. Bede recalls an attempted voyage in the 690s when the monk Egbert and his companions waiting for a suitable wind saw their boat thrown onto the beach and broken up by a violent storm before they could set off.[31] Bede also relates how Arculf, a Bishop from France, had sailed the Mediterranean in *c.* 704, visiting Constantinople, the Holy land and Alexandria before turning for home.[32] Presumably on the Atlantic run to Bordeaux, he was driven by a violent storm all the way to Iona where he met Abbot Adomnan and drew him some diagrams of the Holy places. A few years later Bishop Wilfred of Northumbria took ship to Rome but was swept by a westerly wind to Frisia. It is stated or implied that, at least in Bede's day, ships were powered by sail and set out on voyages from the Tyne, the Humber, the Thames and the Hamble. It seems likely that they mostly used the tides to land and set off from beaches even in old Roman towns with docks - London's seventh century landing place was at The Strand (ie the beach), upriver from the Roman dock at Queenhithe. Navigation was by the sun and stars and governed by wind and tide. But it was not only the natural landscape, seas, and rivers that had to be navigated, but the social landscape too, with all its nuanced loyalties.

From Bede's *History* we can deduce that, in the period in which the Sutton Hoo ship was built, orders came from a king, but queens were powerful and steered or countered political decisions. The power of the gods, first pagan and then Christian, were strongly rated by their ability to win battles. Increasing powerful were the spiritual advisors of religions, old and new, who prophesised the future, interpreted dreams, pacified deities and advised leaders. These were the province of shamans, cunning women and then abbesses and bishops. Prominent, but less equal, was the warrior band, members of which could rise to the top through skill in battle, marriage or plain longevity. Considerable wealth was generated and expended on the principal goal - the dominance of the family. Add a taste for heroic poetry and heroic drinking and we can see the time of Sutton Hoo's principal burial ground as a transition period between a tribal to a heroic to a monarchical society, between loyalty to ancestors to loyalty to a single royal family to loyalty to a territory, between acknowledgement of a variety of divinities of both sexes, to a single overarching male god. The times were tied neither to pagan or Christian, Germanic or Roman convictions, but to a period of maximum creativity where all contributed but none overpowered - a period of potency and invention that springs from the fusion of strange and familiar ideas. The Christian commentators did not see it that way, especially in retrospect, and the period was not to last long; but the archaeology has preserved the moment, and that moment contained our ship.

2 REMEMBERED IN THE GRAVE

Warrior men and wise women

Bede has told us about the upper classes, reporting as a trusted commentator near in time and offering opinions on events, real or visionary. Archaeology, on the other hand, tells us about numerous individuals and individual actions, well located in both place and time. Their significance is not stated in words, but in materials and images with many possible meanings that must be deduced and decided by archaeological reasoning. The text is limited in scope and a record of one man's opinions; the archaeology is limitless in scope but more open to varied interpretation. Archaeologists also need to take care not to attribute cultural material too readily to the ethnic groups that Bede mentions - Angles, Saxons, and of course Britons - and to the speakers of the English, Welsh, Pictish and Irish languages that he recognised. Objects, and especially graves, have their own means of expression, that need not map onto these groups. The mixture of immigrants and indigenous people was well advanced by the later sixth century when British names are found among Wessex kings, and regions began to express their own identities. Since many of these regions coalesced into kingdoms at the time, and we know roughly where they were, I shall use these, and centuries, to indicate cultural regions and periods and 'Old English' for the language they spoke and wrote. Our own region is of course East Anglia, where the ship was found.

In our period neither text nor archaeology is the more senior account, just observations of the same world from different windows, and we shall be looking for ways in which they may converge. From archaeology we learn of the increasing investment by burial parties in the graves of individuals, the men in the late sixth-early seventh century and the women in the mid-seventh. These celebrations, which featured barrows, horses, boats and beds, were indicators of status, but also of spiritual powers developed on the road to Christianity, which was not itself institutionally effective outside Kent until the last quarter of the century. Especially relevant here was monumental ship burial, now suggested as a movement that began at Sutton Hoo and spread to Scandinavia (Chapter 4).[1]

PEOPLE WITHOUT HISTORY

Archaeology opens three pathways into a human society: its settlements where the people lived, their cemeteries where they were laid to rest, and their art and artefacts, the things they made. All of these have elements of reality - real timbers for building, skeletons in graves, ornamental metalwork and carved stone. Our main interest here is in ships, but to understand that task we need to get as close as we can to seventh-century shipwrights, the challenges that they faced and how they responded to them. Perhaps most influential in their lives, as in ours, was the society in which they worked, whether good or bad, the esteem or disdain from their peers, the opportunities or poverty of their kingdom, the strength or vacillation of its leaders, the political weather, its storms and the veering of its religious winds.

Our ship was originally constructed as the first kingdoms of England were forming, followed shortly by the radical switch of alliances both in heaven and on earth that was the Christian conversion. This was a period of a little over 150 years from the late sixth to the early eighth century, in which many assumptions and practices of early English society were revised.[2] The egalitarian-looking early villages of England with their sunken floored huts and short rectangular houses (like West Stow) were superseded by manorial type estate centres with grand prefabricated timber halls (like Yeavering) - the magnate farms in which large tracts of land were gathered and riches amassed and deities served in a temple.[3] The artistry, too, changed from animal magic performed by writhing jaws and disconnected limbs, to lively but ordered boars, bulls, hawks and pikes interlaced or standing proud (like Sutton Hoo).[4]

In the fields of the dead, hundreds of cremations in pottery urns decorated with a diversity of stamps were joined, and then superseded, by inhumations in rectangular graves, all containing grave goods, weapons for the men, notably the sword, and ornamental accoutrements for the women, notably brooches, necklaces and the *chatelaine*, a symbolic cluster of rods and rings suspended from a belt on light iron chains.[5] Spong Hill in Norfolk was the first Anglo-Saxon cemetery to be completely excavated, so revealing its whole sequence of use. The burial of cremations in pottery urns began in the first quarter of the fifth century, and spread into a cemetery of some two thousand urns. In the last quarter of the century they were superseded by a mixed cemetery of cremations and 57 inhumations, four under small barrows. A small settlement appeared at the same time, both cemetery and settlement enduring until the mid sixth century.[6] **(FIG 2.1)**

From the Germanic arrivals in the fifth century to the consolidation of kingdoms by their successors in the seventh, the cemetery was an important theatre, in which individual and communal identity was proclaimed. The cremated individuals manifested a shared culture, but expressed it in diverse ways in the decoration of the pots and their contents. The sixth century saw expression diversify still more and in greater detail: the rite of inhumation allowed

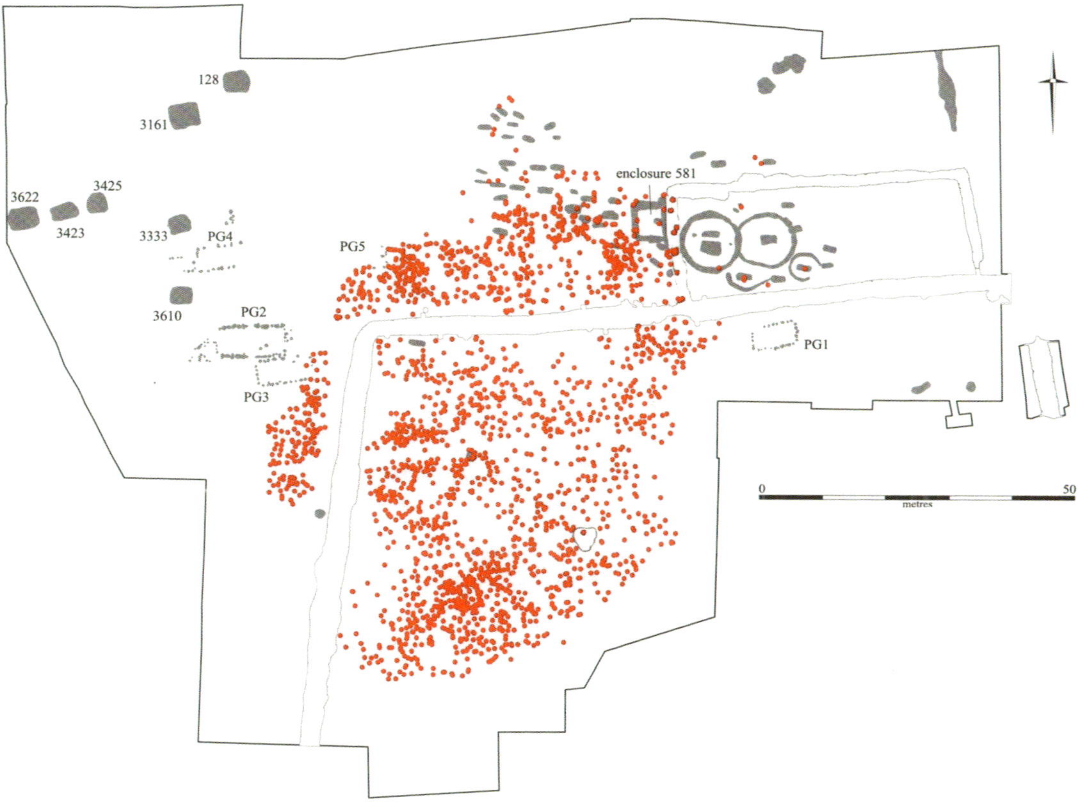

2.1 Changes in burial at Spong Hill, Norfolk, fifth to mid-sixth century. Red spots: cremation burials through the fifth century, joined in the first half of the sixth century by inhumation burials, barrows and settlement (in grey). Pre-Saxon ditches are indicated by thin lines (After Hills and Lucy 2013, Fig 1.15).

the better preservation of the skeleton and the artefacts, since they were not burnt on a pyre. The dead were clothed and their graves were furnished, with weapons or ornaments, proclaiming at one level a warrior or householder, but at another an individual, declared in brooches carrying lively patterns of limbs and heads and teeth, rich with reference, surely, to a complex system of belief, and in vivid colours of beads and textiles. This combination of communal and individual identity reveals a society of men, women and children surviving as so many thousand 'material biographies.' From the sixth through to the late seventh century, while the practice of pagan burial continued for most people at a modest level, the trend was towards investment in fewer, grander burials, both for men and women.[7] The examples given in this chapter are designed to show the variety of actors in sixth- and seventh-century society to help flesh out the society that built or knew the ship. We will meet some of the women first.

THREE ALPHA FEMALES

The village of Wasperton in Warwickshire had a cemetery that was completely excavated in advance of gravel extraction - and it gave us a window on a changing demographic that occurred by the River Avon in the fourth to seventh centuries.[8] Roman, British, Anglian and Saxon affiliations can all be recognised there. Its people began burying their dead in the last century of the Roman empire, commandeering a former animal enclosure as a cemetery and dividing it up into family plots. Some of the men and women of the Roman period were buried with hobnailed boots - equipped for the longest journey of them all. Some of the women had bronze neck-rings and bracelets. Some bodies had been decapitated and the head placed between the legs. This is what they did in Late Roman Warwickshire. After the Roman administration crumbled in the early fifth century, the graves became very simple, aligned east-west without any grave goods - but they could be lined with planks, and edged with lumps of stone, some pulled out of Roman buildings. This is the elusive world of the post-Roman Britons. In the late fifth century, a new people arrived - Angles, probably from Norfolk. They are easy to recognise, being cremated and buried in pots - and room was made for them in the cemetery - a small, fenced area, over to one side. In the early sixth century, the grave goods turned towards Wessex: spears and shields for the men, brooches and beads for the women.

Inhumation 24 must serve for all: a young adult woman wearing a wool twill cloak fastened at the neck with a large brooch with a square head. Under this, a linen garment fashioned from a diamond twill. This was fastened with a matching pair of round brooches, one at each shoulder, with a necklace of amber beads with a crystal centrepiece, festooned between them. Next to her head stood an earthenware pot, decorated with flower-like stamps. Unfortunately, there was very little left of her - only 20 crowns of teeth and a fragment of long bone - but enough to read from her isotopes of oxygen and strontium that she had been a local woman. She wore the traditional outfit of the early English - the *peplos*, secured at each shoulder by these small round brooches - the so-called saucer brooches, well known also among the people of the Thames Valley. These two had seven spirals so are later sixth century. A great square-headed brooch fastening the cloak came from further north or east and was made somewhat earlier - it was probably an heirloom. It is large and heavy, made of gilded bronze: a flat square plate joined to a trefoil plate by a great hoop. Its decoration is famously puzzling - little hints of beaks, claws, jaws, eyes and faces all jostling on the surface - giving a dream-like glimpse of the other world. These are rare and important trophies, this one no doubt belonging to a beloved grandma.

From the mid-sixth century, the people at Wasperton start to take a special interest in British prehistory - they re-used barrows from the Bronze Age, still visible next to the cemetery - and built a few new ones. An upper class was emerging it seems, one that wanted to proclaim its roots in the landscape. At the end of the century, as Augustine arrived in Canterbury to Christianise the English, a man of Mediterranean extraction was buried in a plot in the south-western corner of the Wasperton enclosure. This plot contained no Anglo-Saxon burials: owned, it seems, by a family that had stayed British and Christian all along. This little community on the frontier of a disputed Britain had rubbed along through restless times. But now, in the early seventh century, such varied burial ceases. The villagers adopted a new way of life, buried their dead at a new site - probably a mile or so up-river where today there stands a Christian church.

Not so far away from Wasperton, on the same river, lies Bidford-on-Avon. This village had its cemetery too, also sixth century: cremations and furnished inhumations shared the site - there were swords and shields and brooches left in graves, fixing the people's everlasting residence in the ground, as church and tombstone would do for a later generation. Among the men and women so determined to signal their sex and their identity, there was one woman who was clearly special to them all (FIG 2.2). She lay on her back with her head turned to her right, a young adult aged 18-20, about 1 m 60 tall (5 ft 4 ins), wearing a robe - her *peplos* - fastened by two brooches at the shoulder - and festooned between them a necklace of 39 beads, of red, green and yellow glass, gold foil and amber. She had a linen belt, decorated with beads of blue glass and amber and there was a shawl thrown over the top of everything, fastened under the chin with an iron pin.[9]

So far, well dressed and reasonably well to do. But she was curiously equipped. A leather bag had hung down by her right hip with iron and copper rings - used to close and suspend the bag. Inside it - the tip of an antler and a stud. Beside the bag hung a knife with a short blade and a long, decorated bone handle, resembling a surgical instrument. And then, slung behind her shoulder - but originally dangling in front over her chest, was a kind of leather bib, to which were sewn 12 tiny buckets with curved handles. This strange contraption had been suspended around her neck with leather thongs - their copper lace tags survived.

Nothing much survives inside these tiny containers, each of which would scarcely admit the tip of the tongue, except traces of thread or textile. In Eng-

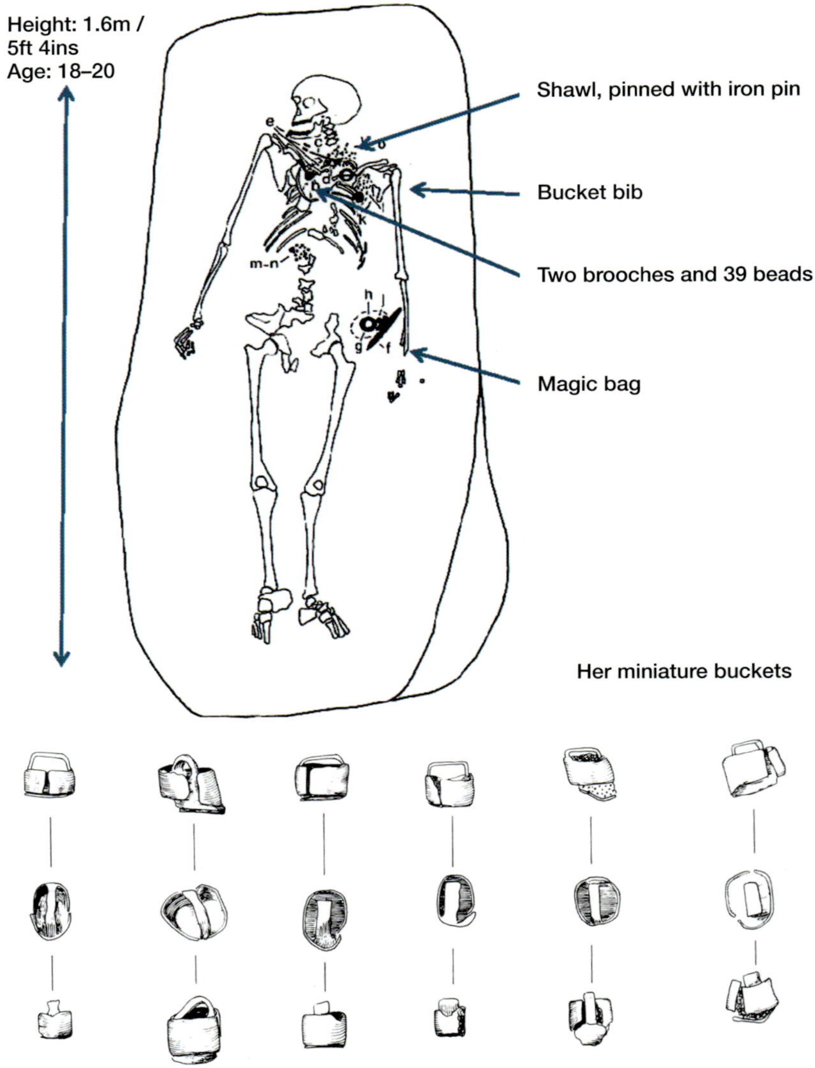

2.2 The Bidford-on-Avon *Cunning Woman*.

land, these tiny bucket-pendants have been found in burials mainly in the east from East Anglia to Northumbria, and in large and well-known cemetery sites: at the three adjacent burial grounds at Eriswell in Suffolk, seven graves contained them, one with 15 examples and 55 in all. Many more are known from the continent where aromatic and resinous substances have been detected with the traces of fabric.[10] In amongst all the material that the early English have left us, two experts on their dress, Tania Dickinson and Audrey Meaney, have discerned evidence for women of special powers, 'cunning women', and pronounced that the Bidford lady was one of them.[11]

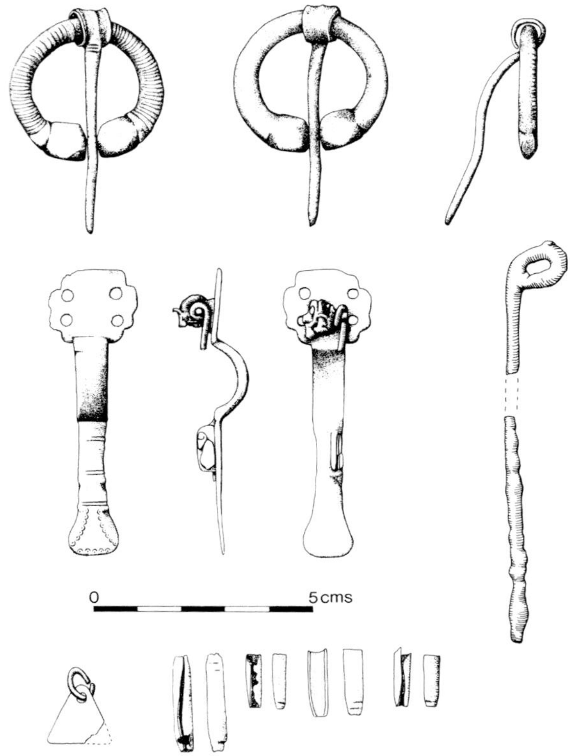

Her brooches

A mistress of the dark arts at 20 - a bit fanciful perhaps? Well possibly. But two generations later, men would be monks at 18 and priests ordained in their twenties. Besides, the arts can be learnt, especially from a practitioner mother. Less directly, since later, but more vividly, there's an echo of the Bidford cunning woman among the Vikings. The lady buried in a wagon in the grave known as Fyrkat 4, had silver toe-rings, a knife and whetstone, numerous silver pendants on chains, a bronze bowl and a miniature chair. By her side was a meat spit, a wooden staff and an oak box containing a pig's jawbone, seeds of henbane and owl pellets. Here surely is an example of the once famous and powerful female shaman, source of wisdom and reassurance, mistress of life and death, whose authority was to be challenged and eventually anathemised as witchcraft by institutionalised Christianity.[12]

Further west still, in a dominant position overlooking Wiltshire downland, we have a third encounter, this time with a Wessex young person in the seventh century **(FIG 2.3)**. She was buried in the later seventh century in a pre-existing Bronze Age barrow, beside an ancient ridgeway - now the A30 - on the skyline above Swallowcliffe, remembered as *Posses Hlaewe*, Possa's mound.[13] She was between 18 and 25 years old and 1 m 60 in height, with excellent teeth, and accompanied by a mass of costly things. She was buried in a box-

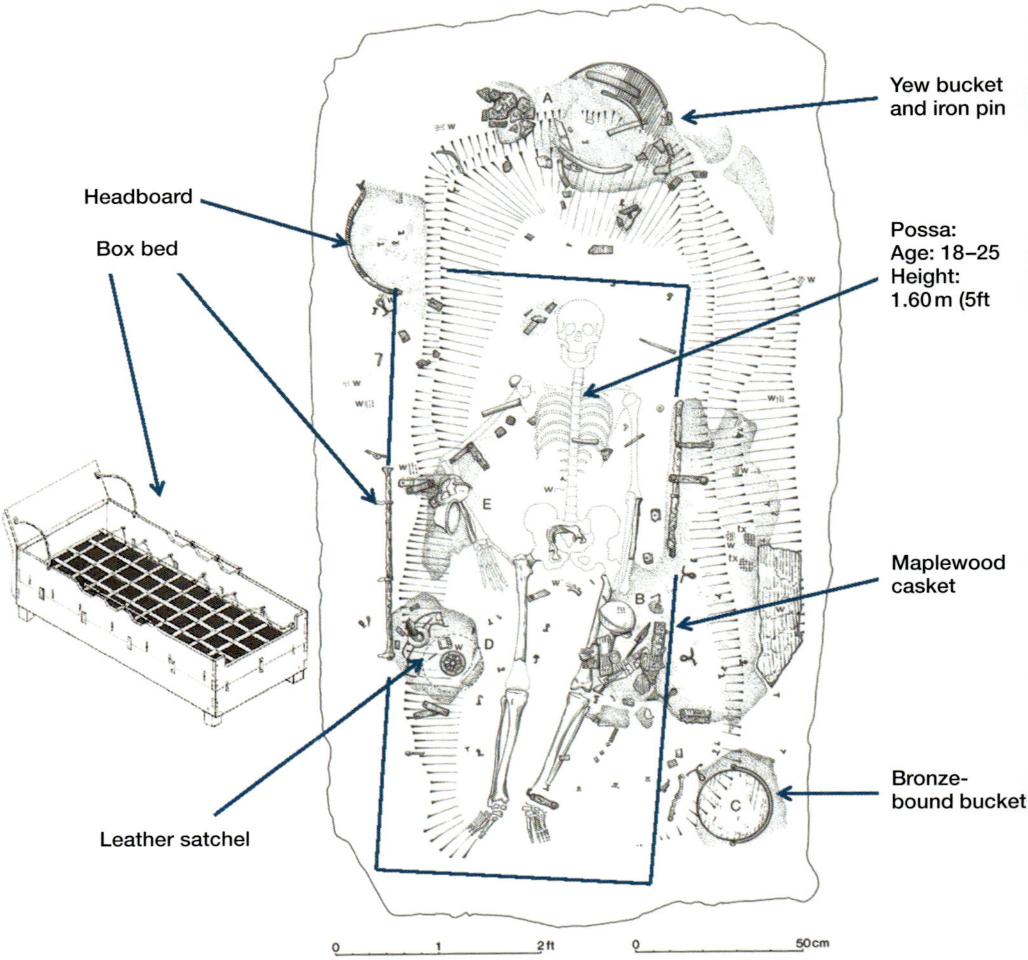

2.3 Alpha female bed burial at Swallowcliffe Down, Wiltshire. After G. Speake 1989,fig 19, 81.

bed made of ash wood, conjured up by archaeologist George Speake from 50 small iron fittings - which is all that was left of it. It was 6ft long and 2ft 9ins across - a single bed then. The sides were of two planks joined edge-on by metal cleats; there were short iron rails on each side; and there was a sloping head-board at one end supported by iron hoops. The mattress was missing, but its support was made of ash strips, probably woven crisscross to make a lattice with a little tack securing each crossover point. It appears to have been suspended inside the box frame using eyelets and cord. There's no doubt that this was a real bed with a real person laid upon it - maybe even her own bed. Tiny fragments of wool and flax and braid preserved on the nails give a hint of the bedclothes.

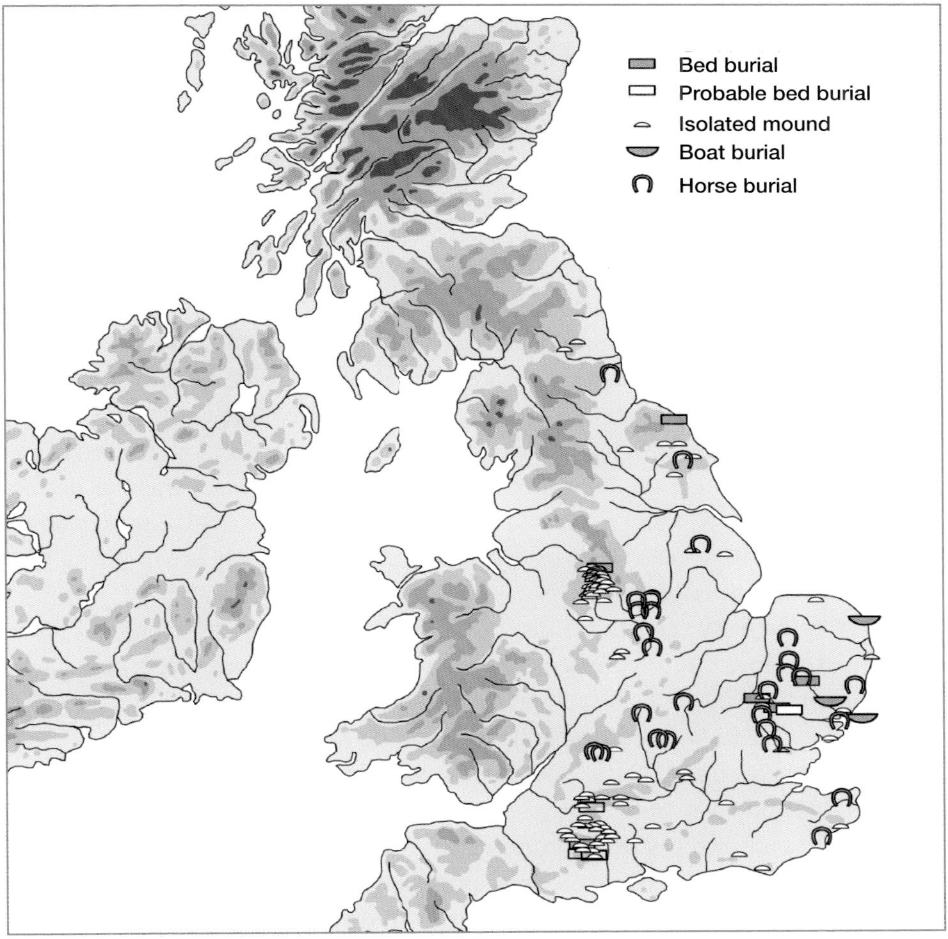

2.4 Locations of high status seventh-century themed burials: mounds, boat burial, bed burial, horse burial. Carver 2019, fig 4.67.

On the bed beside her left thigh was a maple-wood casket shaped like a miniature trunk with a curved lid and bronze hinges and a lockplate. Inside was a silver gilt spoon, four silver brooches like safety pins, two beads, two knives and a comb. And there was a bronze sprinkler: it took the form of a sphere with lots of little holes in it attached to a long hollow tube. Something you could dip into a bucket of rose water and sprinkle around the room or over yourself. All this was tucked into the casket on the bed - a make-up box in fact. On the other side of her lay a beautifully ornamented leather satchel, stiff-sided and shaped like a sporran, made to contain something precious and flat. Then there were the supplies: at the head end of the bed an iron-bound yew wood bucket and an iron pan. At its foot a bronze-mounted bucket; these would contain wine or beer or milk or butter or apples. And on the bed, close to the right forearm, two little shallow glass cups of a bluey-green colour, a sign perhaps of desperate remedies administered during a last illness.

Other bed burials are known from East Anglia and Wessex, showing that they are intended for high-ranking women in the mid to late seventh century - that is during the period of Christian conversion.[14] Possa's sprinkler gives a hint of the time she lived in: sprinklers were originally used in Roman villas to lay dust and perfume rooms. They were taken on by the Christian church to sprinkle the chancel and congregation with holy water at the beginning of the mass, accompanied by the chant *Asperges me*. This one is likely to have reached Wiltshire via some Christian Britons. But other things she has are Frankish or Byzantine - e.g. the spoon, the glass vessels. Of course, it says nothing about whether the Swallowcliffe woman was a Christian. Archaeologists used to call these graves final phase or proto-Christian; but we now see them as neither the end of a phase nor as Christian in the institutional sense. The rich chamber graves of the seventh century, especially those of women, are originals with their own messages to convey.

In the early seventh century, amongst the upper classes there was a rise in the repertoire of burial, innovatory and diverse, and often marked by mounds: in the early decades it was horse burial and boat burial for the men, and in the middle decades, bed burial for the women and chambers for both **(FIG 2.4)**. These high-status 'themed' burials were most in evidence in the parts of England away from Kent where Christianity had already made its landfall at the end of the sixth century; it was a newer, richer mortuary language, not completely decoded, but indicating an association with pagan communities in Scandinavia, and their similar rites and artefacts, and hinting at similar beliefs and ambitions for their people. The changing focus of men to women under mounds is a change from celebrating warriors to celebrating women, possibly for their wisdom, perhaps for their spirituality, or plausibly for their land and its inheritance. On the continent a new Roman Christian Europe was under construction, and churches and stone sculpture were slowly superseding earth barrows. The successors of cunning women would emerge in the last decades of the seventh century as abbesses of Christian England.[15]

Like people everywhere, the personality of those celebrated in burial is a combination of what they are, what they claim to be and how others see them. The archaeologist is like a doctor, partly undertaking numerous scientific tests, by sticking needles into the patient, and partly listening to what they have to say. It is the skeleton that tells us whether it's a man or a woman, what age they died and sometimes what of. And today's science goes further than that. Analysing isotopes of carbon, nitrogen, oxygen and strontium in the bone and teeth can indicate a person's liking for fish and where they grew up - and so, how far they had moved from their childhood home. Eventually DNA will show us their ancestry and how they are related. Meanwhile, the objects tell a parallel story. They represent a choice, the choice of what people took with them into eternity or what was chosen for them - the community's commentary on their lives. It doesn't say German or Danish or pagan or Christian - it is much more interesting than that. Every grave is a little biography, the memory of an individual life, an expression of what that life meant to their heirs.

2.5 Sutton Hoo. Burial ground of a warrior community.

The three alpha females were three characters from communities of southern England, 14 centuries ago. All young, as it happens, each with a different persona: wife, wizard, socialite. They mattered a lot to those they left behind - so much so that precious bronze and gold objects were buried with them - without any intention of retrieving them when times got hard. The objects told their story and expressed their ideas, and they give them a place in English history as potent as any prince.

SUTTON HOO: BURIAL GROUND OF A WARRIOR COMMUNITY (FIG 2.5)

Our search for the personality of those we find in furnished graves now leads us to the burial grounds at Sutton Hoo.[16] While the range of burial in early England provides a window on its many people, the Sutton Hoo cemetery is the most immediately relevant, in terms of attitude, philosophy, principles, command, social control, artistry and craft, to the ship being built beside the river Deben. Much care has been taken to establish the range and sequence of burial at Sutton Hoo, and to explore its context. In the area selected for excavation, the events of every period were brought to life. The result is to situate the Sutton Hoo sequence in deep time, some 5000 years from the Neolithic to today (FIG 2.6). The royal burial ground was certainly a high point in the story of this piece of England, but the inhabitants themselves, although descended

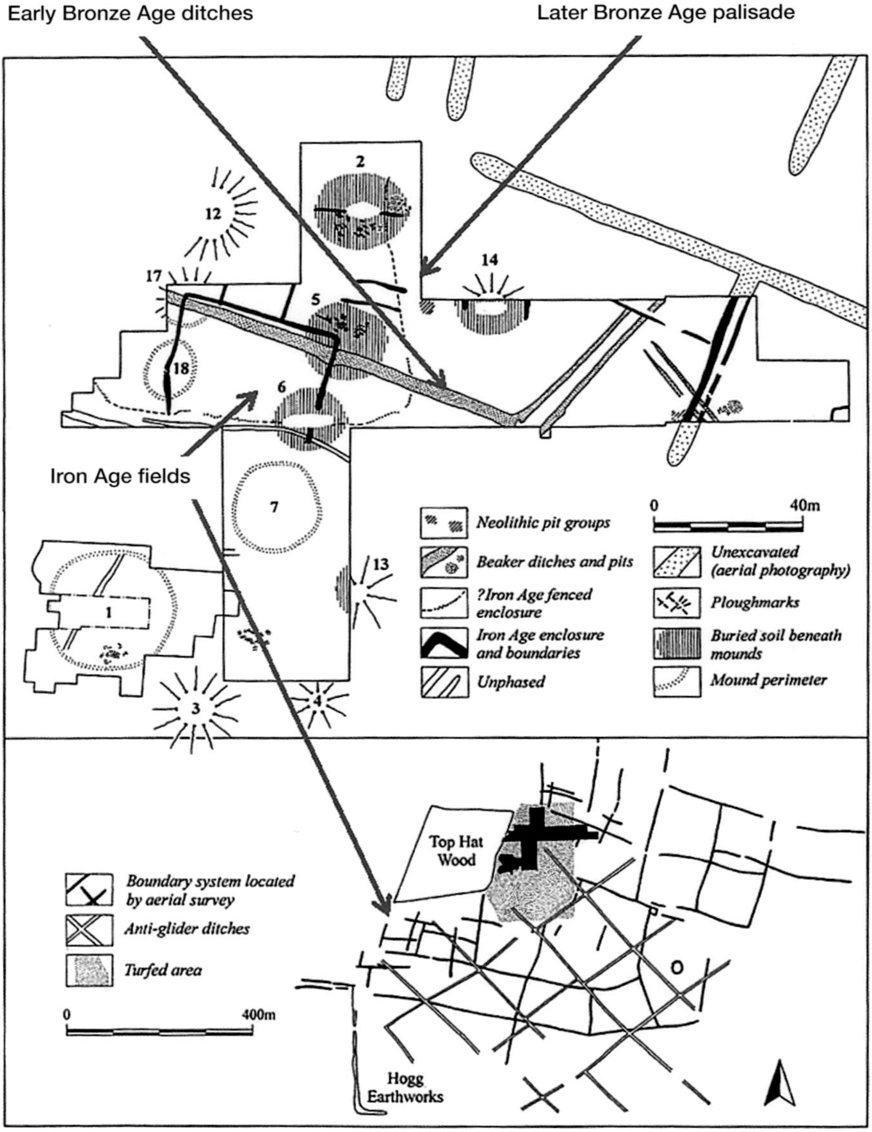

2.6 The prehistoric sequence under the royal burial ground, and (right) prehistoric finds from Sutton Hoo: Neolithic and Beaker period projectiles and Beaker period pottery.

from immigrants, became increasingly aware of the island's prehistoric past, as many studies have shown.[17] At Sutton Hoo they were aware of their predecessors and looked for ways of integrating themselves with the land; they reused Bronze Age mounds for burials and placed their monumental mounds at the junctions of Iron Age field boundaries. Two centuries, perhaps eight generations, had passed since the English immigrants arrived and they had

become integrated with the British population. By the early seventh century the families living by the Deben had developed a complex history and mythical memory. This invites us to dig deep into the way they thought and acted, and the way the politics changed.

The Sutton Hoo excavations have revealed a sequence of three cemeteries at adjacent locations with varied burial rites. The earliest of the three, dating between the fifth and sixth centuries, was discovered when the Sutton Hoo visitor centre and car park were being constructed in 1999 **(FIG 2.7)**.[18] In an area 30x30m were 13 cremations and 19 inhumations, arranged in two groups. The first group, dating to *c.*520-550 included five cremations in urns, one in a bronze hanging bowl and five furnished inhumations including one in a log-coffin.[19] In a second group, dated *c.*550-580, seven cremations with animal offerings, one wrapped in cloth and placed in a bronze bowl, were clustered around a pre-existing Bronze Age barrow or under smaller new-made barrows. Another cremation was placed in a bucket of hammered brass originating in the Byzantine empire. It was a key import to sixth-century Sutton Hoo and we will return to its story below **(FIG 2.8)**. The investment in cremation in copper alloy containers recalls burial practices among the Germanic people of the second century living on the Roman frontier or in Scandinavia.[20] And certain indications - the mounds, the log-coffin and the cremations in bronze bowls - give a pre-echo of what was to come. This group may represent the families that were to launch the mound cemetery 300m to the south.

This cemetery of 18 mounds manifested status of the highest order - a princely burial ground. It began in the late sixth century with cremations in bronze vessels buried under Mounds 18, 5, 6, 7, 3 and 4 **(FIG 2.9)**. Next came the

Cremation 8

2.7 Plan of the Tranmer House cemetery, showing the two family groups, the location of cremations (black dots), with Cremation 8 in a bronze bowl under excavation; and inhumations (lozenges), and the shield from Inhumation 21.

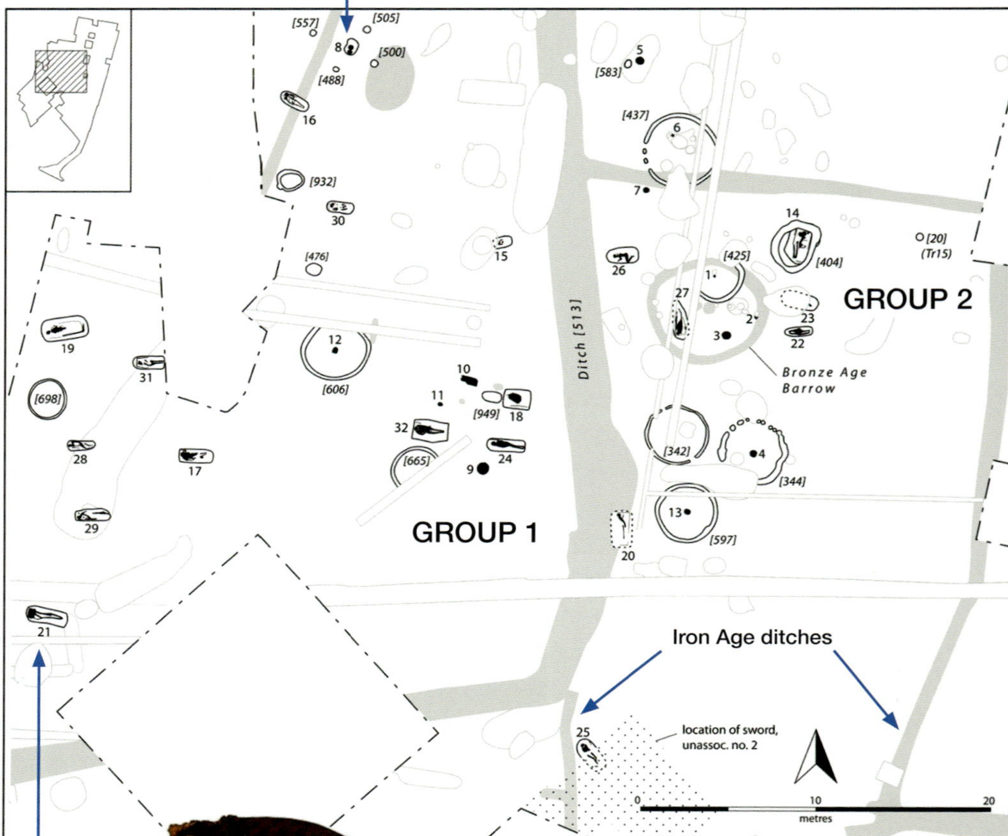

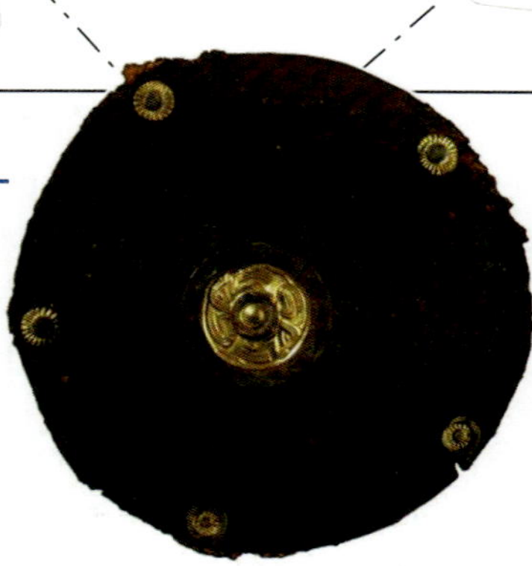

Inhumation 21

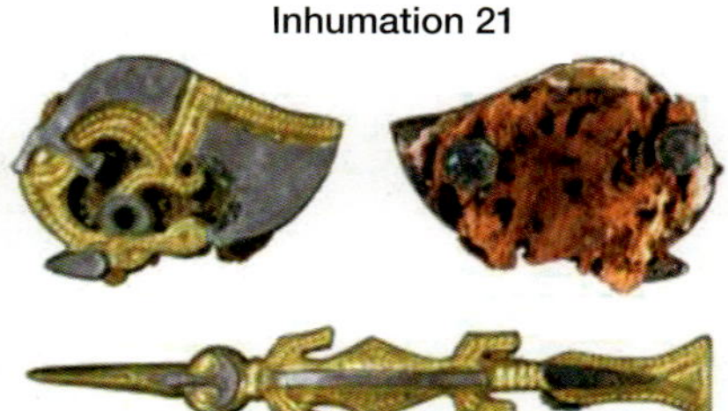

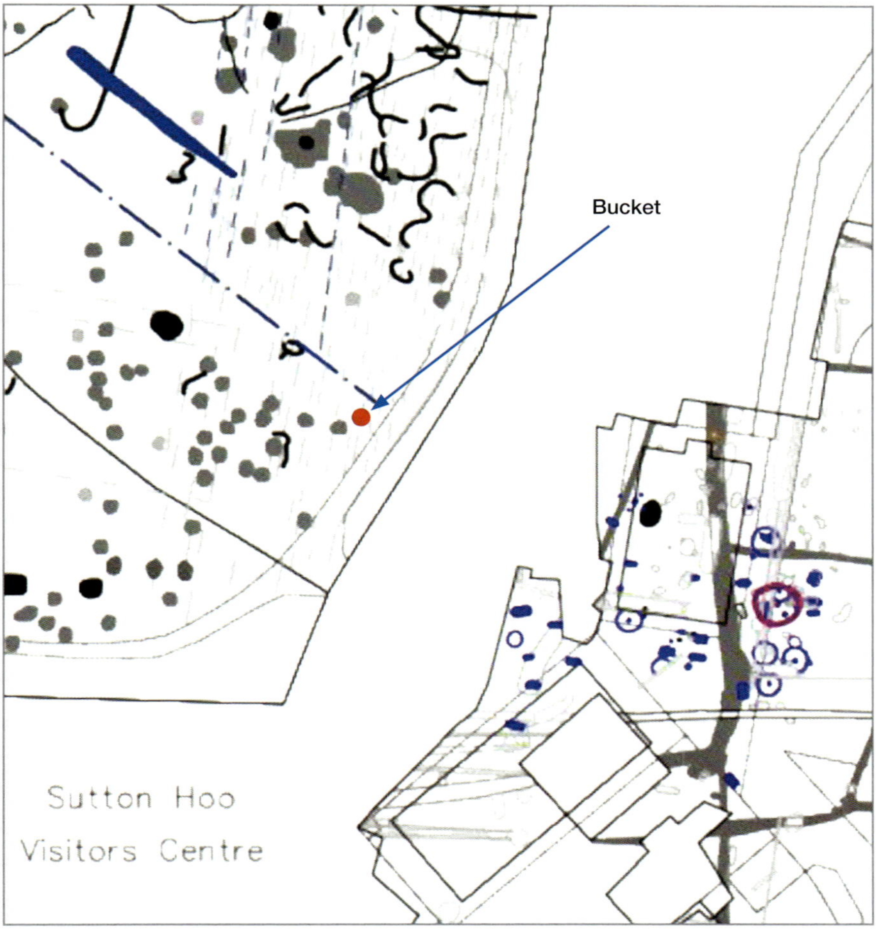

c)

2.8 Byzantine bucket from Sutton Hoo. (Above left) Find spot of the Sutton Hoo bucket in relation to the Tranmer House cemetery, (right). Below: a) A fragment of the inscribed rim of the Sutton Hoo bucket depicting a hunt and the inscription *Use this in good health, Master Count, for many happy years*. b) A similar bucket in the Ashmolean Museum, Oxford.

a)

b)

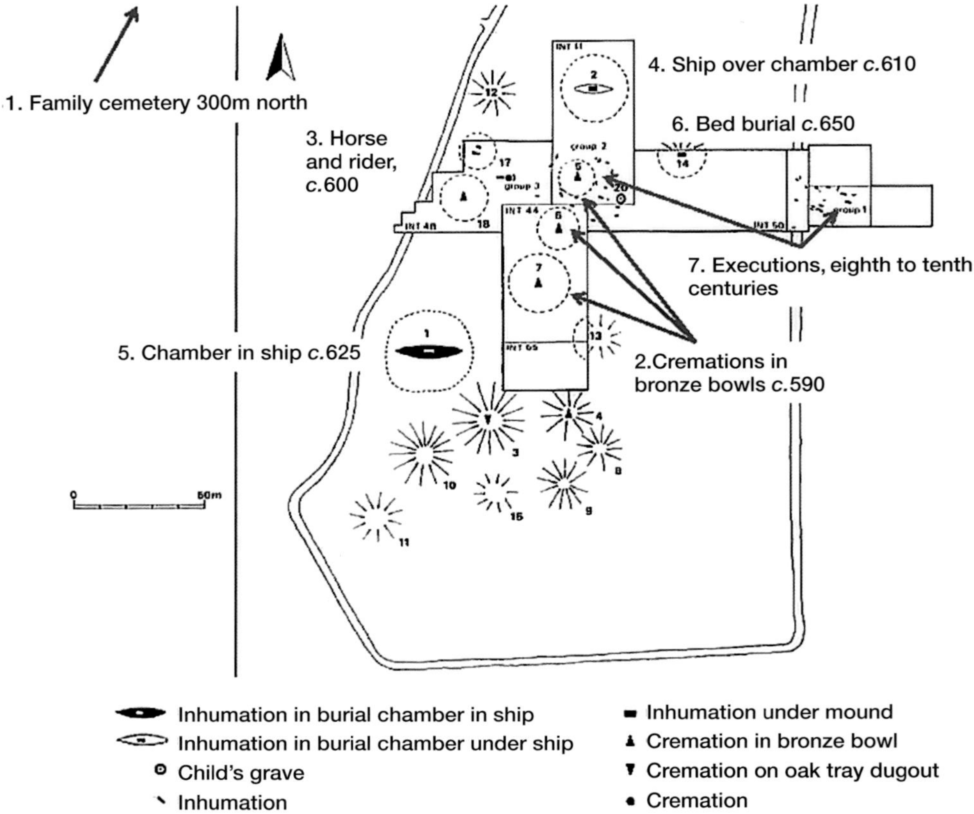

2.9 The sequence in the royal burial ground.

grave of a young man buried in a tree-trunk coffin, with his horse in an adjacent grave, dated by radiocarbon to the early seventh century **(FIG 2.10)**. Armed with a sword, a shield and two spears and equipped with a bucket, a small cauldron and a 'picnic', he was presented as ready for a campaign. Mound 2 came next in the excavated sequence, where the dead man, accompanied at least by a sword, shield, drinking horn, blue glass jar, bucket, and a copper alloy cauldron, possibly with an iron chain, had been laid in a deep underground chamber, sealed on top by a 20 m long clinker-built ship **(FIG 2.11)**. This mound, undoubtedly once rich, had been dug over in the seventeenth and nineteenth century and again by Basil Brown in 1938, the ship rivets scattered and the grave goods reduced to a few fragments. Its form - ship over chamber - is puzzling although not unknown in later Viking times.[21] The ship may have been an addition, in which case it could be viewed as a part of the grave goods, or have symbolic value for the dead man. In either case, the ship, like the horse, was a powerful part of his biography or origin.

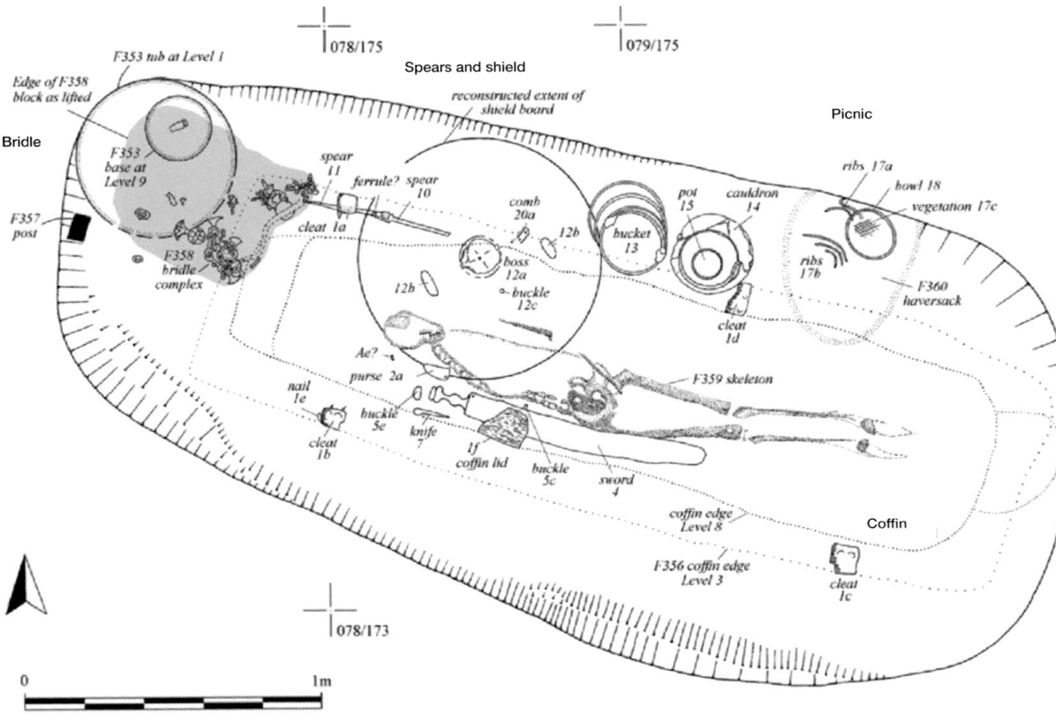

2.10 Sutton Hoo Mound 17: a young man and his sword buried in a tree-trunk coffin.

Then came the great ship burial under Mound 1, its chamber preserved more or less intact - not by a miracle, but through an understandable mistake by tomb robbers, who missed that the western end of the mound had been interfered with later, and drove their shaft downwards too far east. Archaeological investigations at Sutton Hoo into the 21st century have shown with a greater clarity how the Mound 1 ship burial may have taken place.[22] A huge trench was dug E-W, and the ship, 27 m long and 4.5 m wide amidships was dragged up the hill from the river and rolled into it **(FIG 2.12)**. A burial chamber was built in the centre of the ship - a gabled hut made of massive timbers. Within the area of the chamber floor were objects of gold, silver, copper alloy, iron, wood, pottery, textiles and fur - all disturbed by the eventual collapse **(FIG 2.13)**. The cluster of objects in the centre of the chamber suggest that this was the location of the buried person, but the exact arrangements are difficult to ascertain in the collapsed chamber. One interpretation is that the dead man was buried in a giant tree-trunk coffin about 3 m long and possibly squared

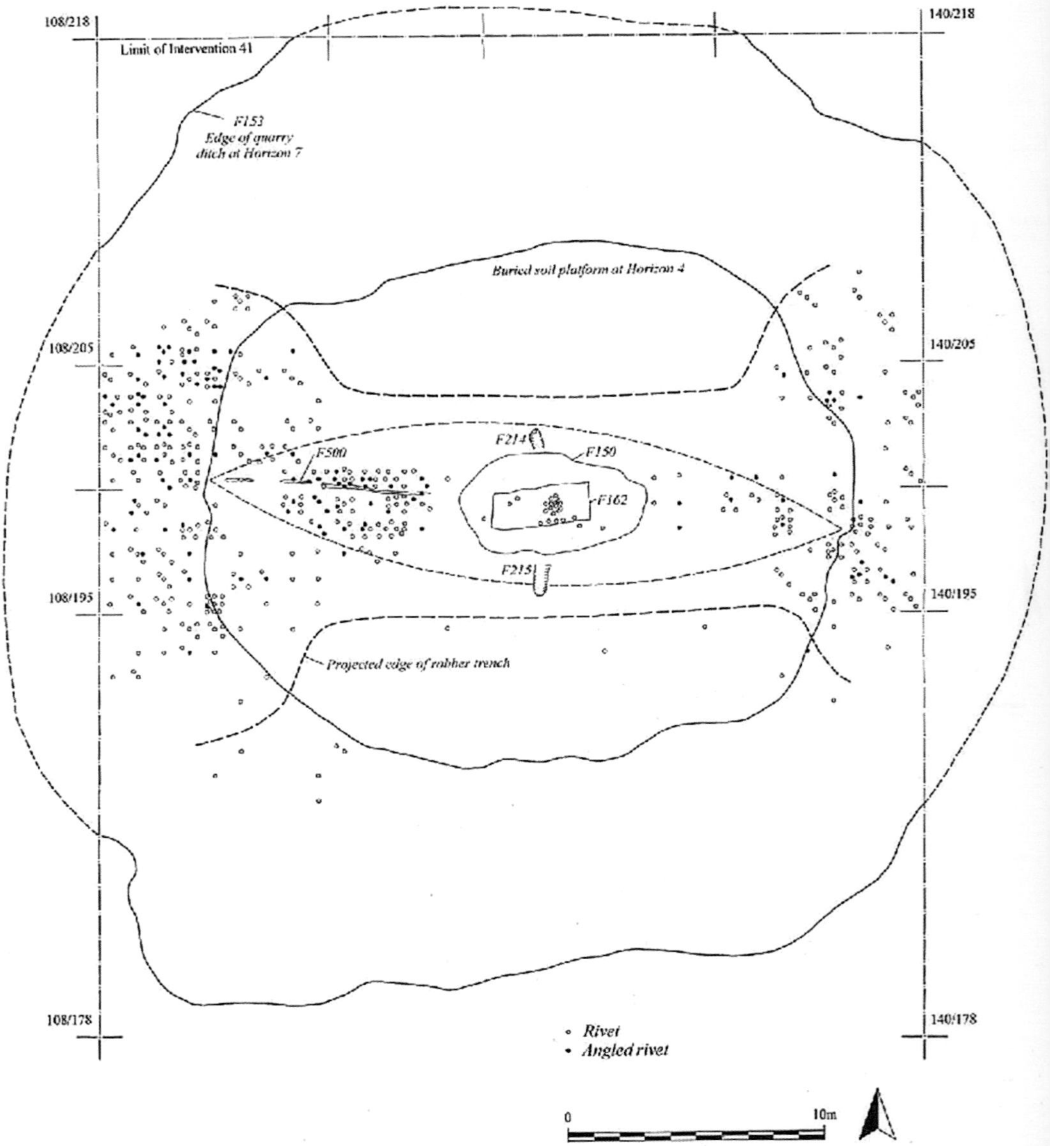

2.11 Mound 2 (Left) The limit of the mound, with the burial chamber (centre), the outline of the ship placed over the chamber and its scattered rivets. (Right, above) Form of chamber and burial and position of ship. (Right, below) Locations of vanished body and finds using chemical mapping.

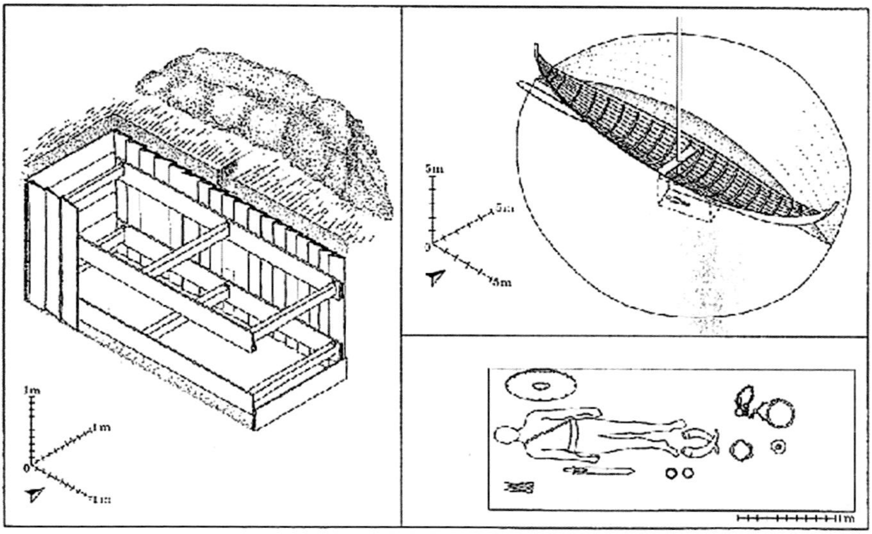

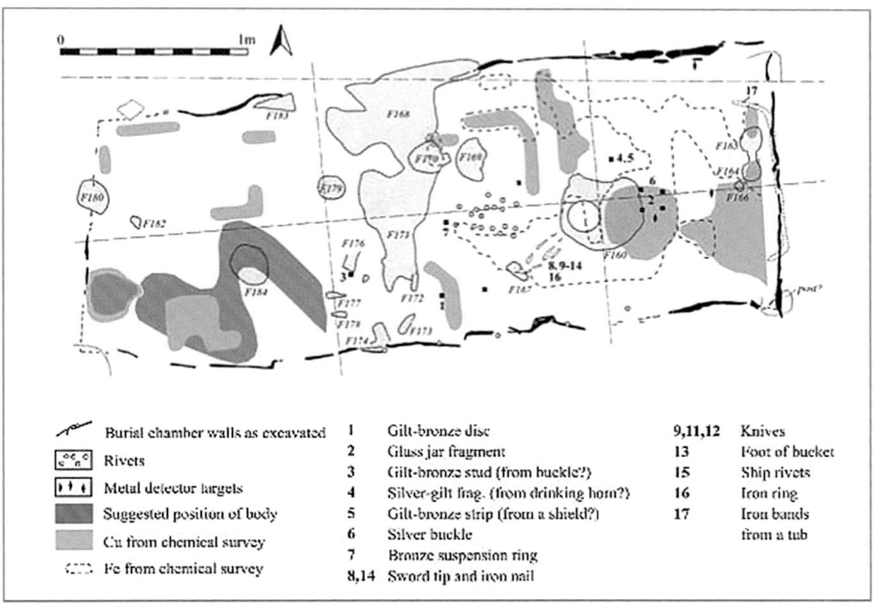
0
1m
Burial chamber walls as excavated
Rivets
Metal detector targets
Suggested position of body
Cu from chemical survey
Fe from chemical survey
1 Gilt-bronze disc
2 Glass jar fragment
3 Gilt-bronze stud (from buckle?)
4 Silver-gilt frag. (from drinking horn?)
5 Gilt-bronze strip (from a shield?)
6 Silver buckle
7 Bronze suspension ring
8,14 Sword tip and iron nail
9,11,12 Knives
13 Foot of bucket
15 Ship rivets
16 Iron ring
17 Iron bands from a tub

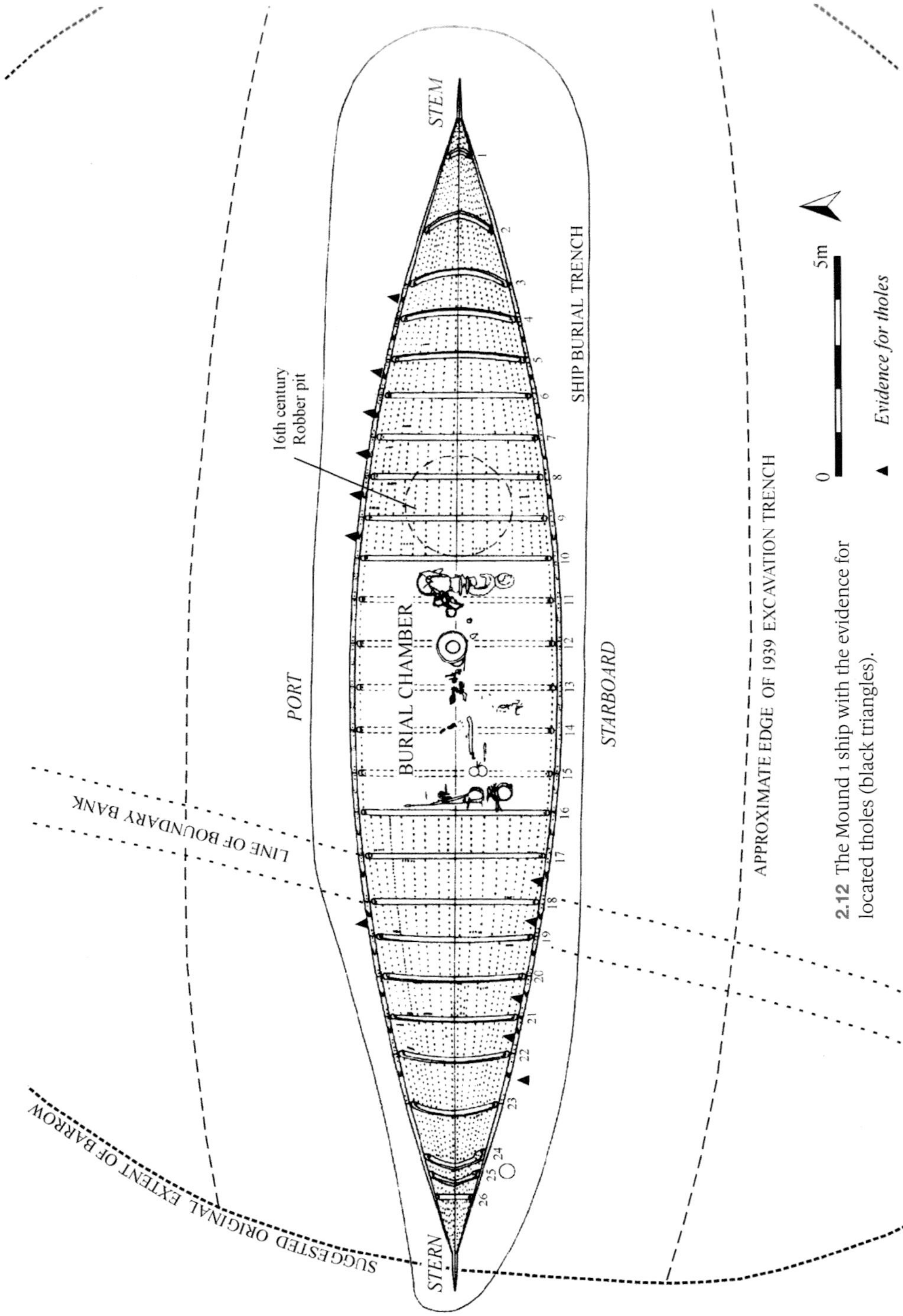

2.12 The Mound 1 ship with the evidence for located tholes (black triangles).

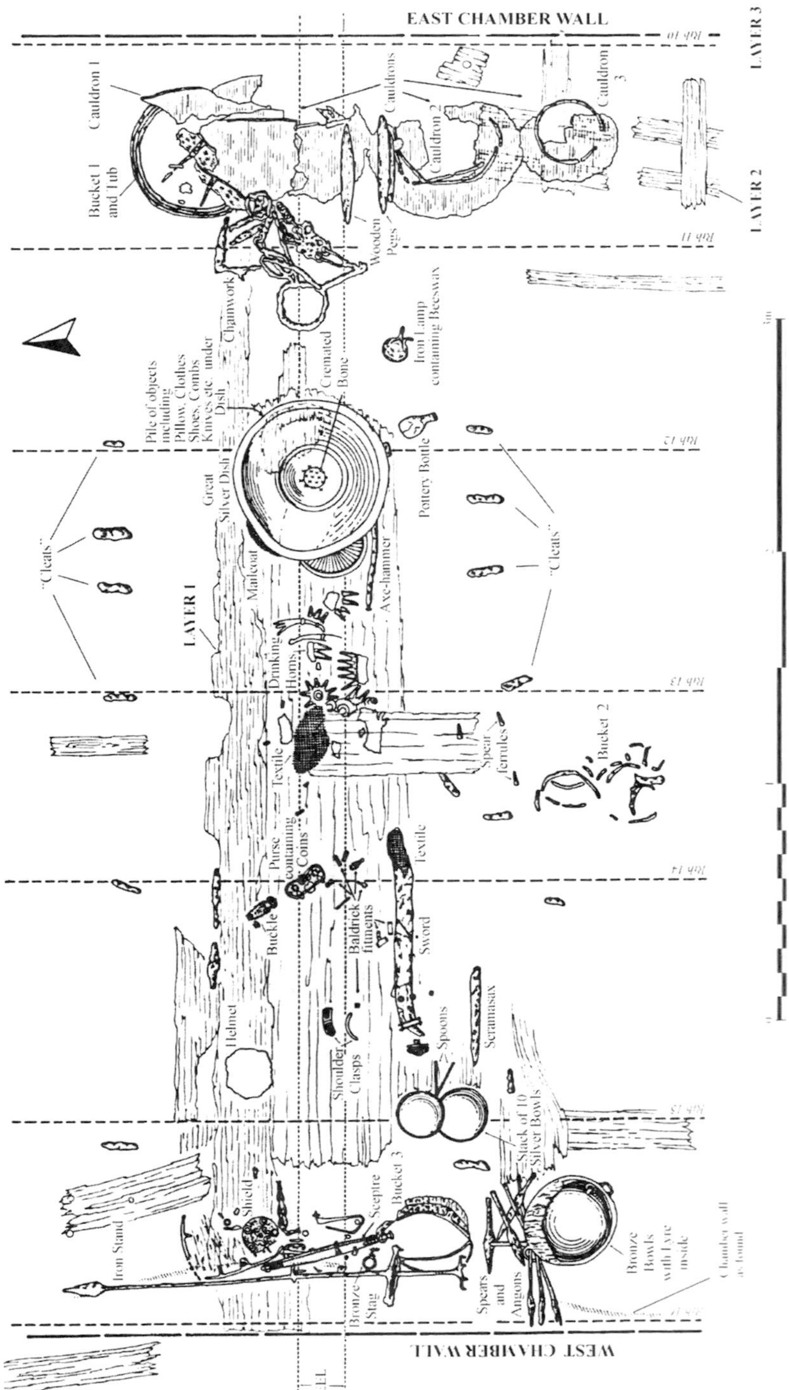

2.13 Plan of the Mound 1 chamber after Phillips 1940 and Bruce-Mitford 1975, figs 111 and 112 (redrawn as a composite by Elizabeth Hooper)

off at the top lid to display objects.[23] The body lay inside it, and in a space at the foot-end was placed a big heap of private things: a leather garment, two pairs of shoes and a pillow; clothes, a fluted bowl containing burrwood bottles, four knives with horn handles and combs - an upmarket toilet set. Once the lid was on the coffin, it was secured with 12 curved iron clamps on either side. Now we move into a more public domain. A yellow cloak was thrown over the coffin at the head-end and on this was placed the regalia and parade gear: an iron helmet, a sword, glittering gold and garnet shoulder clasps, an ornamental purse lid and a solid gold belt-buckle. Further along towards the foot-end, the lid was laid like a table for a feast with maple wood bottles and drinking horns and a great silver dish. Then more equipment for feasting: a lyre for the minstrels, three cauldrons, one with a long iron chain, buckets, bronze bowls, silver bowls, silver spoons, a maple wood drinking bottle, horns of aurochs, also for drinking. These precious objects on display during the burial emphasise the bid for immortality of the dead man, as does of course the ship itself.

At the west end, outside the coffin and against the chamber wall, was placed an iron pole with a square cage on top with an iron bull's head at each corner. This is thought to be a standard, for carrying trophies on parade. Beside it a whetstone, as long as your arm, was carved each end with faces - some with beards and some without. On top of it a little bronze stag of Celtic manufacture; at its foot a kind of upturned saucer that fits on the knee: this was the celebrated "sceptre", so far unique in England. Sceptre, standard, helmet, feasting, and extravagant clothing dyed in different colours; this was seemingly the burial of a warrior king.[24]

Among the visitors who made their way to see the discovery, was the eminent scholar of migration-period northern Europe, Hector Munro Chadwick, professor emeritus at Cambridge, author of *The Heroic Age* and the *Origins of the English Nation*. Nobody knew the literature better than he did, and he had a fondness for archaeology. He came chugging over from his summer hideout in Wales in his Austin 7, driven by his wife at his self-imposed speed limit of 20 mph. When he eventually arrived, he saw the lines of the ship, the dark depression of the chamber, the piles of silver bowls and the gold buckles and connectors packed in moss in tobacco tins. "It's Rædwald", he said as he took his leave; "It's Rædwald, I'm sure of that".

This identification has never been convincingly challenged, but the rationale for the burial has continued to provoke debate. For some, this is "the typical burial of an Anglo-Saxon king" - and there's an end to it. Others say it's typically pagan, others that it *can* be Christian. Others see it as the reality behind *Beowulf*, that most celebrated Old English poem, with its scenes of feasting in the hall, its cremations, its burials under barrows and in ships, its kings and heroes and dragons. But these attempts to place everything we find into some sort of norm doesn't do justice to the contents and performance of a burial like that in Mound 1. We know that he wasn't sent off with everything he possessed - the treasury was a lot bigger than that. These objects were selected, like words are selected from a general vocabulary; each object speaks to us, each has its own tale to tell; the burial is not a reflection of a poem like Beowulf, *it is itself a poem*, a palimpsest of allusions, performed by a people expressing their hopes and fears at a crucial moment in their shared lives.[25]

With imagination we can evoke the scene. The performance took several days, a trail of salutation winding up to the edge of the ship: the eldest son, the youngest grandchild, the oldest friend, the companions in arms, the captain of the fleet, the deckhands of the Royal ship, the visiting dignitaries from Denmark and France, eager for the old or a new alliance; Edwin of Northumbria or his envoys; the diplomats of enemies discreetly come to hear the rumours and sense the political wind; a bishop from Canterbury, a priest from Rendlesham, a cunning woman from the fenland, local farmers, huntsmen, horse traders, erstwhile lovers with lost status. The whole cast of characters is here to say good bye and claim a stake in the future. Each registers their attendance and maybe offers a gift, until it's time to close up the roof and then, or probably much later, build up the mound. The Mound 1 burial, with its diverse and intriguing grave goods, not only illuminates the man, but the community that contained him.

Other unnamed figures haunted Raedwald's court: ostlers, seafarers, poets and musicians - all were famous in their day, but only a few were granted personal memorials. The Sutton Hoo Ship burial contained a maplewood lyre, and in another cemetery not far away we have a memorial to an artist who played such an instrument. He lay accompanied by the remains of a shield, buckle, knife and bowl and, cradled in his arms, the remains of a six-stringed lyre: a bard and a warrior, therefore, who sang and played and was also ready to join battle. His grave was excavated at Snape near Aldeburgh where, fourteen centuries later, Benjamin Britten was to write his *War Requiem* incorporating words by Wilfred Owen, another soldier poet. Such bards were probably numerous. Three more examples of lyre burials have been excavated in the cemeteries at Eriswell, one a splendid tableau of the musician buried with the lyre held between hand and knee.[26]

Sutton Hoo's warrior king was an international player, as is clear from the provenance of the objects that accompanied him in the grave, from Italy, Syria, Byzantium. Objects from the eastern Mediterranean reaching Sutton Hoo include the Coptic bowl and silverware from Mound 1 and the lime-

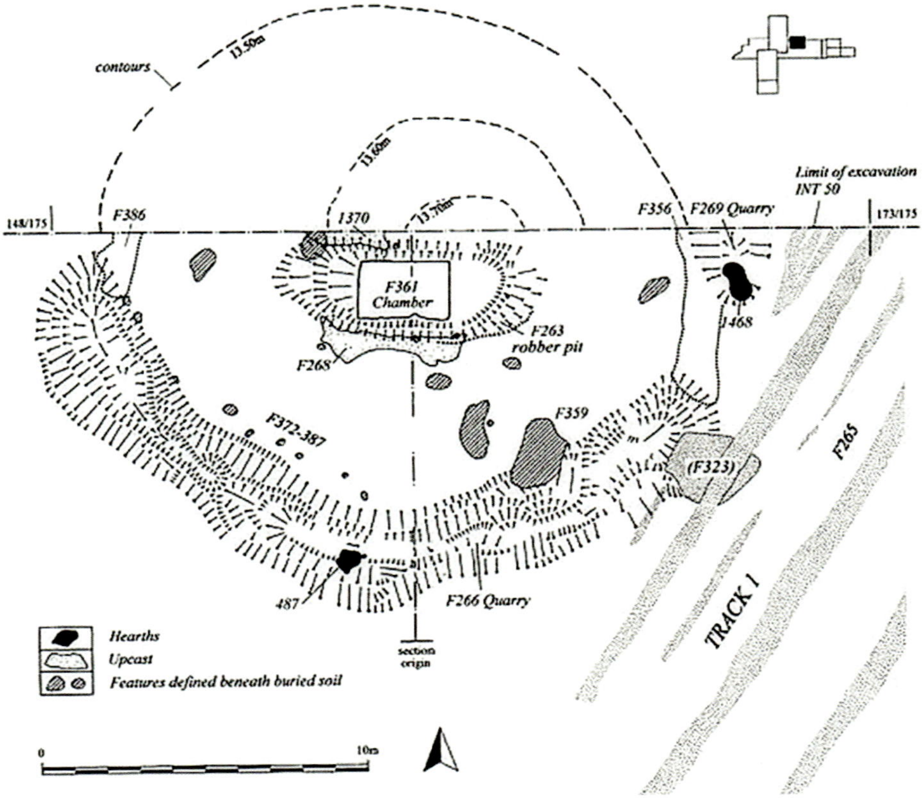

Her chamber grave

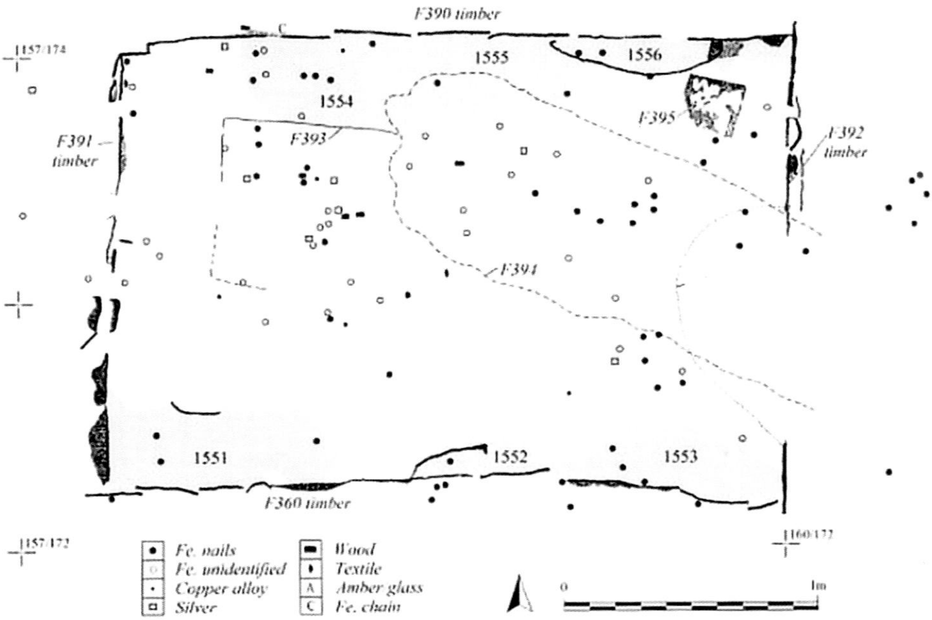

2.14 Mound 14. Burial place of Rædwald's Queen? Above left: the chamber in the mound. Below left: he shadows of the rectangular chamber, the couch and the robbers' trench. Above right: the distribution of nails and other finds.

stone plaque and ewer from Mound 3. These objects might have arrived with merchants or delegations, but the contacts implied by the Mound 1 finds and others like it, may have been direct and personal. Were these gifts from distant kingdoms or empires? Or had the man himself made journeys to the eastern Mediterranean? Support for the second idea is a found in a range of Byzantine imports not confined to Mound 1. The Byzantine bucket reused for a cremation in the Tranmer House cemetery belonged to a small group of buckets with similar decoration, inscription and hunting scene, dated epigraphically to the mid-sixth century (FIG 2.8). The Byzantine expert Marlia Mundell Mango wrote: "It has been suggested that [the buckets] formed part of officers' kit and were produced at state arms factories; indeed, their decoration is close to that of a sword sheath excavated at Sardis, site of a state weapons factory. Despite their small number, their wide distribution, including Mesopotamia, Caesarea in Palestine, Spain, three sites in Britain (Sutton Hoo, Southampton, Isle of Wight) and Kuwait, could be explained by travel home by mercenaries in the Byzantine army".[27]

Recently excavated to the south of Sutton Hoo, at Prittlewell in Essex was a richly furnished chamber grave, containing Byzantine imports and dated to the late sixth century (575-605), the earliest of the dated English mound-burials so far.[28] Amongst the objects beside the body (that lay in a plank coffin) was a folding camp stool, drop handle basin and a flagon also seen as emanating from Byzantine workshops, and also thought to have been carried home by pilgrims or mercenaries.[29] Subsequent studies by Helen Gittos have emphasised this late sixth-century link, of great significance for Sutton Hoo's warrior class, since in spite of their numerous opportunities for local battles they may have experienced Byzantine warfare (and Byzantine ships) in person.[30] These were exciting, enterprising and, as we will see, inventive times on the banks of the Deben.

AN EAST ANGLIAN QUEEN

Of those furnished mound burials examined at Sutton Hoo - the project design did not include all of them - only one was later than Mound 1, and only that one contained a woman. Mound 14 covered a wooden chamber made with thin vertical planks broken up by tomb robbers who made a catastrophic pudding of its contents. The fragments recovered from the mud included upholstery tacks and fragments of a silver chatelaine; suggesting a rich woman, buried on a couch in the mid seventh century. In this particular, she belongs to the phase of female celebration we have just visited **(FIG 2.14)**.

If the identity of Raedwald as the subject of Mound 1 is a forgivable conjecture that has understandably endured, assigning historical persons to the other mounds is still a risky business. Wuffa (d. 578) could have been the occupant of Mound 5, the earliest according to the archaeological analysis, and Mounds 6, 7, 3, 4 are also cremation burials and likely his warrior descendants. Raedwald's son, Regenhere, who died at the battle of the River Idle in 617, may have been the young man laid to rest with his horse in Mound 17 or perhaps celebrated more lavishly in Mound 2, so close to Mound 1 in content. My own indulgence is to put Rædwald's widow into Mound 14, dating to the mid-seventh century, 25 years after her husband. The Venerable Bede did not vouchsafe her so much as a name, but in spite of himself, he revealed her to be an astute and principled politician (Chapter 1). And who else, if not his queen, would take control of her husband's obsequies and compose and orchestrate his funeral? And what a composition it was: it referred to countries far and near, it saluted the ancient gods, it nodded to the oncoming Christians. It looked to victory in battle, prominence in wealth; it hailed origins from over the sea and put roots into the land. It sent him off to eternity in a ship, laden with a great feast, a floating mead hall, where ancestors, dead heroes and rivals could be welcomed in and plied with drink and hear themselves praised or satirised in long incantations to the lyre. And at the centre, was a man - a public figure still active in the hereinafter. On display was his royal finery; but stowed down below were his washing and shaving kit and a change of warm clothing. Here was someone equipped to proclaim to the mourners the independent future of the new kingdom of East Anglia, to send a message to whoever was pulling the strings of seventh-century Europe. All this seamlessly combined with personal affection for a remembered husband.

It is not necessary to people the Sutton Hoo burial ground with historical figures - except as an aid to the imagination. We can say that the mounds, as we know them so far, were used to commemorate at least eight male warriors and one woman, buried over a remarkably short period of time from the late sixth to the mid-seventh century. This was a period of great wealth and great achievement, one that featured the construction of the largest known ship of its time. It's as well to remember that the ship itself was an artefact with a story to tell. Those attending were the first - and the last - to know that saga.

Even more anonymous, but equally significant burials were those that marked the demise of the royal burial ground. A number of individuals were buried there whose position in the grave indicated that they had been executed by hanging. They were mostly young men, but some mature men, women and couples were also identified. There were two groups, one surrounding Mound 5 and one outside the mound cemetery to the east, beside an ancient routeway. Here there were traces of a gallows (FIG 2.15). Dating to the eighth to eleventh centuries, these unfortunates have been interpreted as malefactors, dissidents or non-conformists who offended against the tenets of institutional Christianity. They were disposed of by the new Christian kings, in and near the burial ground of their forebears who had practised the old religion.[31] The conversion period must have been deeply stressful for many, involving the suppression of former beliefs and allies and acceptance of new. It was noted by Bede at the time, describing a crowd on Tyneside mocking a group of monks being swept out to sea: "nobody is going to help them - they have done away with the old ways of worship and now nobody knows what to do".[32]

SOCIAL CHANGE AND HIGH INNOVATION

The levels of investment in these graves of women and men reveal an increasing emphasis on rank, the more richly furnished graves assumed to mean the burials of influential people. The process of posting more wealth in fewer graves accelerated during the late sixth and early seventh century. The formation of kingdoms increased the power of their leaders and began to diminish the agency of the majority, at least as expressed in cemeteries. There were three phases in this trend: first in the sixth century, men and women are equally honoured in the grave. Then in the early seventh century the emphasis is on

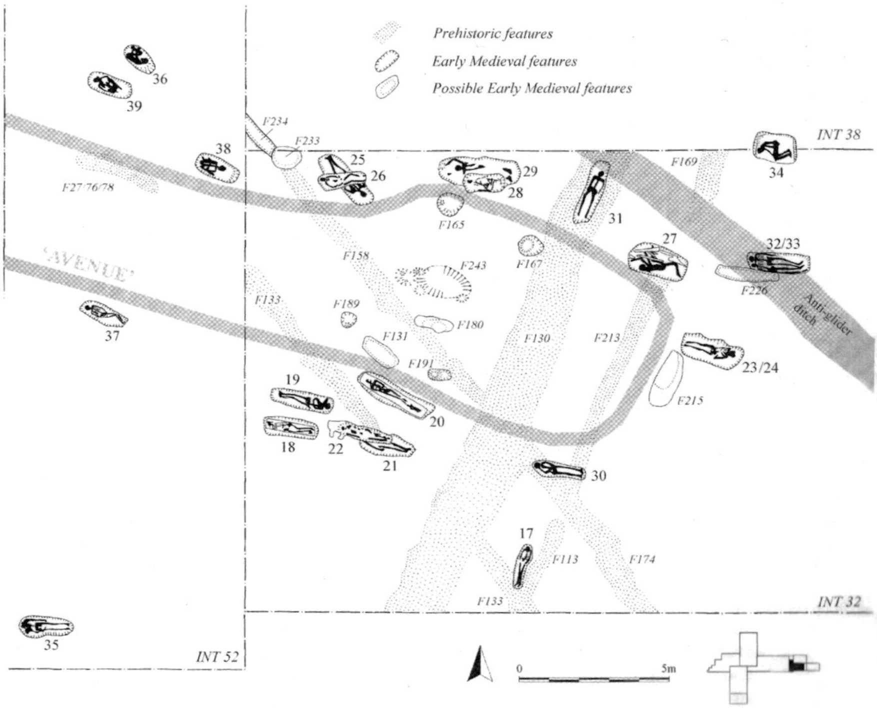

2.15 From the privileged to the damned: victims of regime change at Sutton Hoo: 8-11th century. (Left: below) Plan of Group 1 burials and posts of the gallows. (Right) Images of the positions of the buried victims.

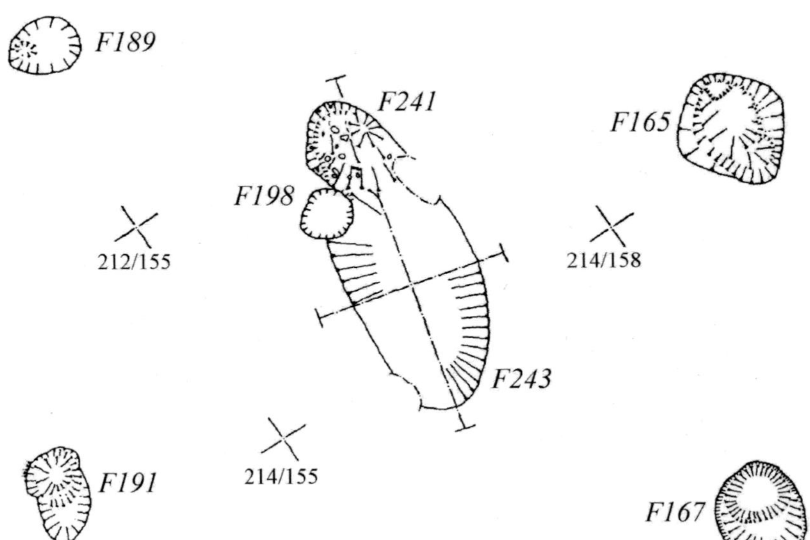

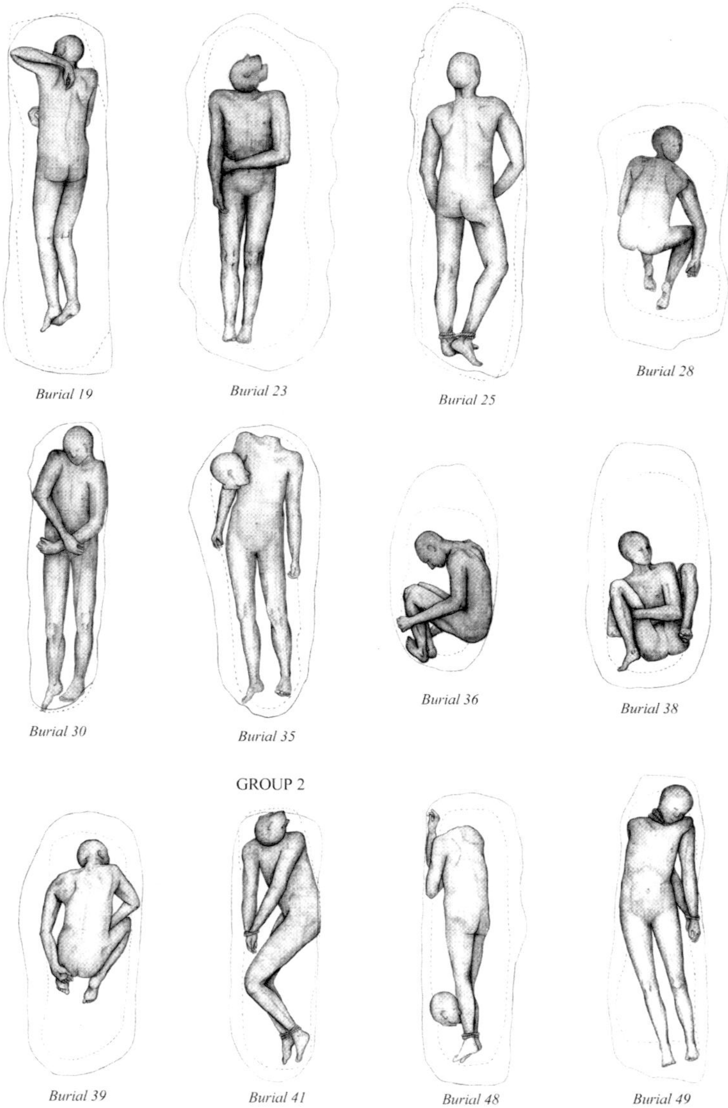

the men, celebrated as members of a warrior class and buried under barrows. In the mid-seventh century, the emphasis is on the women also buried under barrows and celebrated as spiritual specialists and guardians of inheritance. Towards the end of the century, grave goods disappear, and the vast majority of the dead are now unaccompanied and memorialised in other ways, such as burial in churches or beside them.

The burials show us that, after the period of migration, the English identified themselves with broad areas: Angles facing the North Sea, from the

Orwell to the Tyne and beyond, Saxons in the south, facing the Channel, with Kent in the corner nearest the continent. Within these regions, at least, there were large cemeteries that served communities that might include a bard and a cunning woman. Associated, from the sixth century, with community territories that bumped up against each other, they became increasingly competitive, electing or acquiring or suffering the protection of belligerent families and their warrior leader, the king.[33] In whatever order these trends occurred, the result was the late sixth- to early seventh-century arrival of kingdoms bearing names that were long remembered: Wessex, Mercia, East Anglia, Northumbria. The gods too were adapted to this social turning point, the more masculine and martial increasingly in charge. Christianity, with its vision of one all-powerful male god served by a male hierarchy, was about to have its moment, and the Christian kings would weaponise its influence in turn as an instrument of social control.

The archaeological narrative has important implications for our ship. It was not made for the Mound 1 burial since it had been repaired. Nor was it the first ship to be buried at Sutton Hoo; that was in Mound 2 and followed a different ritual – the ship placed on top of the chamber. The 14 m long Snape ship has been dated between 550 and 650 leaving the question of its relation to Sutton Hoo uncertain. But a conservative estimate would say that these ships, including Snape, were launched around Rædwald's reign *c.* 599–624/5. This was certainly a wealthy and inventive period involving the formation of a kingdom with no one model to follow: we can see the signs of multiple Germanic and Roman contacts, in weapons from the Rhineland and Sweden, coins from Gaul, hanging bowls from the Celtic north, and more besides.

The cargo of the Mound 1 ship and the contents of the other burial mounds give powerful signals of the range of contacts enjoyed by the community of those remembered at Sutton Hoo or living in Rendlesham. The iconic properties of the upper-class hall, horse and ship, the objects fashioned locally in gold and copper alloys, the silverware and valuable cloaks imported from the Byzantine east, leave little doubt that the early seventh century was a peak moment in the creation of an English kingdom that had yet to sign up to the imperial Christian alliance. When the warrior class was not employed in local wars, it found employment as freelance soldiers in other armies, notably those of the Byzantine emperor. In the Mediterranean, they not only enjoyed the benefits of imperial armament, acquiring souvenirs and the latest fashion accessories for their feminine companions back home, but they must have seen ships too, warships and cargo ships and transports with oars and rudders and sails, cabins and holds.

The archaeology also shows that the innovations of the period were not the prerogative of the upper classes. The carpenters, weavers and metal smiths were themselves innovators, building halls, making grand clothes and designing ornaments carrying intricate and brightly coloured symbolic schemes that adorned men, women and horses. It would be strange if the high status wooden structures of halls - and ships - were not also brightly ornamented. The combination of hand and eye implied by this creative work could not easily be commanded or controlled by a bystander.

In 668 Bishops Hadrian and Theodore were sent to Britain, arriving in Canterbury via Marseille, Arles and Quentovic, and set about touring the English kingdoms. Their mission: to accelerate the conversion and to reform England's infant Church, instituting episcopal control over the network of devotional monasteries. Their ministry began the end of furnished burial in England, to the great loss of personal memory - and of future archaeology.[34] It has made it a more difficult task to chronicle the character of individuals, whether of low or high estate, into the eighth century and beyond.

The agents of the conversion period reached deep into seventh-century society, demanding acceptance of numerous behavioural changes, not always welcomed by old or young. Many dissenters met their ignominious end at Sutton Hoo at the end of a rope. But others, more valued or less defiant, left a legacy independent of the grave, in the form of thousands of individual crafted artefacts. These are the metalsmiths, weavers and carpenters whom we are about to meet.

3 ENCOUNTERED IN THEIR WORKS
Artisans and innovators

Warriors and wise women were celebrated - as we learn mainly from their burials - primarily the men in the early seventh century and, around the mid-seventh, the women. The farmers and foot-soldiers left less of a footprint, but there is one cadre of early English society who earn our respect and whom we yearn to meet and learn from: they left their mark in every cemetery and settlement and enriched no small part of the splendour of the greatest of them. These are the artisans, those that made and assembled the regalia, stitched and dyed the apparel and built the burial chambers and halls. The great and the good did not do these things. Our artisans earn admiration at every turn; they not only designed and manufactured the artefacts that defined their society, but in every object they bequeathed something of their own expertise and personality. We will know them through their art. If we need to see their idea of perfection, and something of the way they saw the world - it is the things themselves that relate them. Through their artefacts we will meet makers of precious metalwork, creators of vivid clothing, and, most importantly, the carpenters. Of all the active artisans of the early seventh century, it is the creators of buildings who were most closely associated with those building its ships. We will see that the time of Sutton Hoo was a peak of productive creativity, with all the crafts contributing to an age of advanced invention.

THE SMITHS

The debris of workers in precious metals includes slags, small crucibles and moulds, and is best documented in the monasteries of Northumbria, Pictland, Scotland and Ireland. But although their workshops are elusive, early English smiths practised similar processes of casting gold, silver, copper, tin and zinc for two centuries or more before Sutton Hoo. They were notable for their ingenious and inscrutable ornament, depicting animal and human motifs, and met a continual demand for knives, spears and swords and brooches from the earliest years of the English settlement, and by the early sixth century, the range of dress fastenings and accessories was diverse **(FIG 3.1a)**. Glass beads were notable for their bright colours, some of which were imported, while others like the "traffic light" beads were made in England and - since they needed heat to work and wind the glass - their makers could have shared a

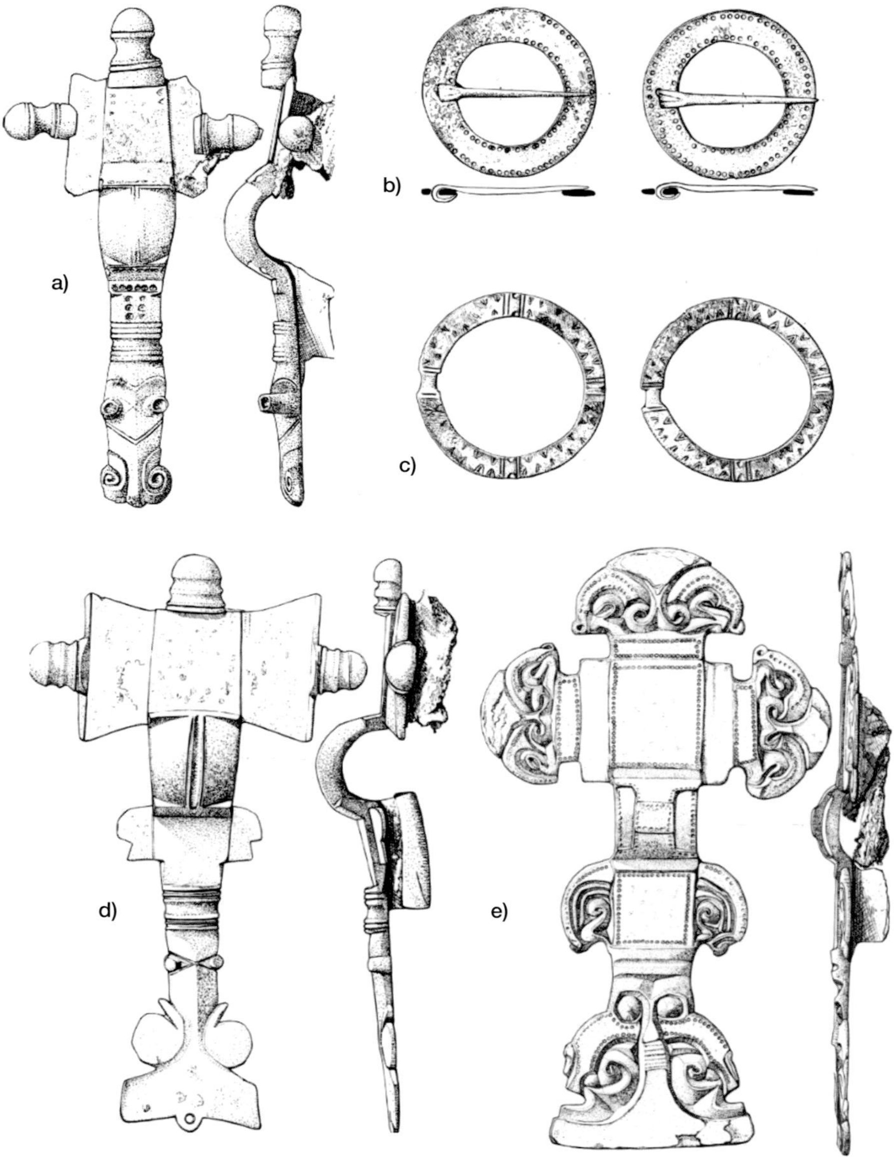

3.1a Early Anglo-Saxon metalwork. Examples of brooches from Spong Hill inhumations, Norfolk (From Burials 22(a), 56 (b), 29 (c), 39 (d), 57 e) .

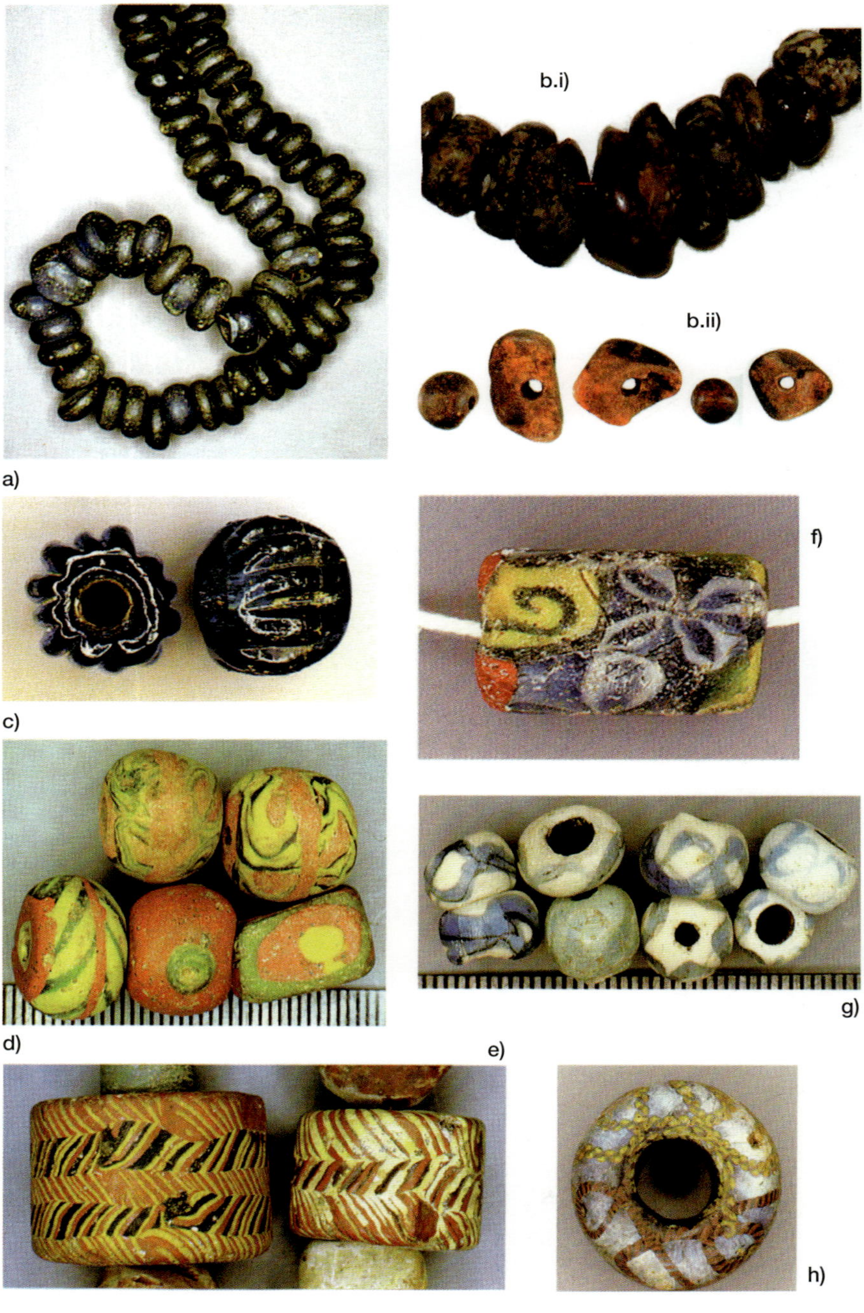

3.1b Early Anglo-Saxon multi-coloured glass beads from early Anglo-Saxon cemeteries: Wasperton (a), Petersfinger (bi), Scorton (bii), Compton Apple Down, melon bead (c), Morningthorpe traffic light beads (d), Sarre reticella beads (e), Buckland mosaic bead (f) Morningthorpe imported beads (g) and (h).

hearth, as well as a clientele, with the metal workers.[1] Vessels made from raw glass originating in the Mediterranean were already reaching England in the fifth century and are found in numerous cremations at Spong Hill (FIG 3.1b). [2]

In the late sixth and early seventh century, the animal ornament becomes more individual, more expressive than decorative; over the seventh century, the serpent-like zoomorphs known across Europe are superseded by quadrupeds.[3] The themes worked in miniature include varied fauna - a sea eagle chasing a fish, horses folded into spaces and quadrupeds forming chains linked by teeth and tails, here and elsewhere offering some attractive images for decorating our ship (FIG 3.2). The horse buried under Mound 17 had a bridle with gilt-bronze strap-distributors with dangling axe-shaped pendants, all featuring interlaced patterns. And while the horse's owner may have had animal ornament on his objects, the horse's bridle had gilt-bronze strap ends, featuring rather demanding humans. The horse also had a body harness with small silver axe-shaped pendants.[4] Similar items of horse harness found at Sutton Hoo, Portmahomack in north-east Scotland, Mote of Mark in Dumfries and Galloway and Dunadd in Argyll suggest a widely shared usage, serving members of an island-wide equestrian class that made use of the extant routes of Roman roads for ease of riding and direction.[5]

The recent research at Rendlesham up-river from Sutton Hoo featured an intensive survey by metal detector that recovered coins of copper alloy, silver and gold, and over a thousand metal fragments of which 58% relate to dress accessories.[6] Not only was this a rich assemblage denoting a special place, but the fragments themselves gave an indication of the technology of production. In the fifth-seventh century, copper alloy objects, including buckles, pins and bag catches, were made of recycled gunmetal (copper, tin and zinc) probably arriving as Roman coinage. Measurement of lead isotope signatures showed that the parent ores emanated from Germany (with some from the Aegean). The Rendlesham objects had been made with piece moulds (as opposed to 'lost wax') with many *sprues* (excess metal fragments) remaining. In the seventh century, some brasses (zinc and tin) arrived, together with objects in silver, gold and garnets. Copper, silver and gold were worked in the same areas, the objects showing a range of proficiency that suggested dispersed workshops, served by metalworkers under a master craftsman. Fragments of gold and garnet objects parallel those found at Sutton Hoo: could the Mound I shoulder clasps have been made here? The expert verdict was measured: "none of the gold and garnet pieces from Rendlesham is as well-constructed as the cloisonné master pieces from Sutton Hoo, but this does not rule out the possibility that the Sutton Hoo masterpieces were made at Rendlesham".[7]

The period of high value gold manufacture coincided with the appearance

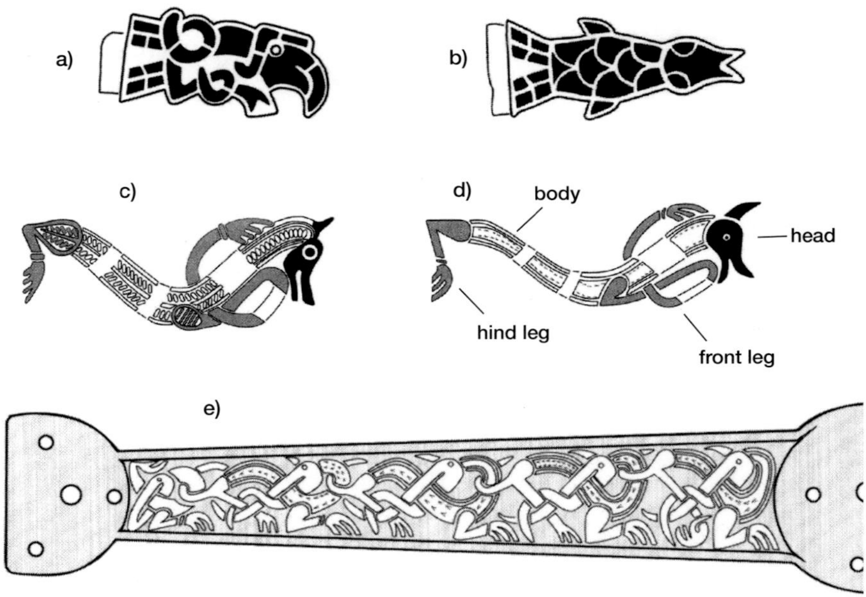

3.2 Animal themes from the Staffordshire Hoard: (a): Fern et al. fig 5.11, no 512 'sea eagle'; (b): Fern et al. fig 5.11 no 513 'fish'; (c) Fern et al. fig 6.3 (Sutton Hoo cup-mount); (d) Fern et al. fig 6.3 Staffs great cross 539; (e) Fern et al. fig 2.74 (cross-mount).

of a hall and the rise of Rendlesham as a central place in a wide area.[8] As expressed in coinage, its status developed in two stages during the seventh century.[9] Between 550 and 640, all coins came from overseas and mostly from southern and western France, with copper coinage from Byzantium indicating direct contact with the Mediterranean. In East Anglia the coins are restricted to coastal sites and some special places notably Rendlesham and Coddenham. In the early seventh century the source shifted to eastern France. This aligns with both the idea of East Anglian warriors on mercenary service in the Byzantine army in the later sixth century, and a more political focus on kingdom building in the early years of the seventh. Coins found in Rendlesham but not elsewhere suggest a royal status for the site. Between 640 and 680 there was a further shift. Coins came from north-east France and the Low Countries, and some were restruck as English products. There was little evidence of contact with the Mediterranean in East Anglia, and here the coinage struck (for example at Rendlesham, Coddenham and Hoxne) indicates a link with the elite secular power, rather than the coming Christian Church.[10]

The creators of the Sutton Hoo Mound 1 assemblage reached matchless levels of artistry, setting red garnets cut to precise three-dimensional shapes to be clutched by cells of gold (*cloisons*). Some show the 'mushroom' shape that was thought particular to Sutton Hoo but is now seen to be spread more widely.[11] The 'mushroom' shape has been recently defined by Noel Adams as depicting a helmeted warrior, and an object with a group of such cells, such as the curved dummy buckle or the T-shaped mount, as exhibiting a cohort.[12] The shoulder clasps feature racing 'ribbon' animals, and stately wild boars guarding the wearer. The great gold buckle features at least four entangled quadrupeds, arranged asymmetrically to give the impression of movement – they are alive! Heraldic images of a man between two animals and a hawk capturing a bird are laid on the lid of the purse. On the shield, the hawk and its victim are presented together with a flying dragon – now accorded individual freedom to defend, attack, inspire or interfere. These freestanding beasts may have meanings which are, so to speak, totemic figures recalling sayings or epigrams well known to a non-literate community.[13] The art of Mound 1 is a material celebration of a people in thrall to the spiritual forces of the animal kingdom.

The silverware came predominately from Byzantine workshops, as the form and inscriptions and symbolism make clear: the great silver salver inscribed for the Emperor Anastasius, the silver finger bowls inscribed with crosses, and the Roman 'conversion' spoons inscribed with *saulos* and *paulos*, all belong to that cultural milieu. The four copper alloy hanging bowls with enamel and glass decorated escutcheons were probably obtained from the Pictish north by gift or plunder. The smiths of East Anglia knew what was happening in their metier elsewhere. Those who created the Mound 1 regalia have been claimed as directly tutored by the smiths of Byzantium.[14] But foreign influence and local agency deserved to be distinguished: what mattered was the statement made by the burial in north-west Europe. Here the craftsmen blended the local skills of their previous century with the activities of their contemporary international forum – and emerged as ground-breakers.

The Staffordshire Hoard, comprising 3.9 kg of gold and 1.7 kg of silver, represents a major sample of the metalsmith's work (see Chapter 1, **FIG 1.11**). It was recovered mostly in a myriad of tiny pieces, but thanks to meticulous examination by Chris Fern and his team has been divided into consecutive phases of manufacture dating between *c.* 570 and 650, with a deposition date around 650–675. The main candidates for the regions of origin were Northumbria and East Anglia, with many of the key objects of the third phase strongly linked with East Anglia or workshops under East Anglian royal patronage.[15] Unsurprisingly, this part of the assemblage belonging to the conversion period contains both warrior gear, such as the pieces of helmet, a cloisonné *seax* hilt and a putative saddle mount, and ecclesiastical finery, a processional cross and a headdress mount.[16] Northumbria, Kent and East Anglia are places where later seventh-century military and ecclesiastical potentates might have rubbed shoulders. Sharing the high-status symbolism between the secular arm and the clerical cohort would provide more work for smiths, and emphasising the power and grandeur of the soldiers of Christ the King would have been an essential part of the conversion strategy.

The gold and silver had been stripped of their iron mounts or blades with tongs, so the extracting of bullion from those that had it was intended by authority and executed by smiths.[17] The experts have been reticent about signalling a historical context for the burial in Mercia of this remarkable treasure. But its alignment with the 'incalculable and incredible treasure' offered by Oswiu to Penda to desist his aggression is a tempting solution to the puzzle. Penda refused it and was killed by Oswiu at the Battle of the Winwaed in *c.* 654, which fits with the likely deposition date of the Staffordshire Hoard.[18]

The inventive progress of the early seventh century was to have a future after the age of Sutton Hoo, but in other media. Their lively representatives of the natural world ran, paw in mouth, into the ornamental pages of the early insular Gospel books. The animals, birds and fish tell visual jokes and set puzzles, like the riddles and kennings in Old English poetry - layered meanings that keep you guessing and coming back for more. There are other legacies too: the animal chains are so elegant and repeated so often that we can feel entitled to use them to decorate our ship (as the Vikings were to do later).

Smiths were not remembered with the same degree of extravagance as their sponsors, but they were certainly valued. The grave of a seventh-century metalsmith has been found at Tattershall Thorpe on the River Bain (a tributary of the Witham in Lincolnshire) and is a reminder of the range of skills required of these professionals.[19] His grave contained a 1 kg iron anvil with iron spike for driving into wooden blocks; iron snips for cutting off nail points, a draw plate for making wire, a file with an alder handle, iron tongs, three hammerheads with parts of a wooden handle, a punch, and a bell made of sheet iron riveted at the join. There were lead models for making clay moulds, hinges, a hasp and staple and fragments of copper alloy and lead. Some of these tools e.g. the hammer, the tongs and the snips would have been in action for the forging and installing of iron nails and rivets. The date of the grave was implied by the objects: a miniature bronze spoked wheel of a type known otherwise in the sixth-century upper Rhine area, four ornamental mounts dated to the mid-sixth century and later, and a glass jar dated to the seventh century.

Iron, too, played a role in the metalworking uplift in the age of Sutton Hoo. Smiths, like the person buried at Tattershall Thorpe, made iron blades forged by hammering with increasing amounts of carbon to achieve steel of greater hardness. By combining metal rods with different carbon content, a sword could be made both sharp and springy. The result of forging the twisted bundles of rods together and polishing them up was a sword blade with a characteristic herringbone pattern. The swords in both Mound 1 and Mound 17 were pattern-welded.[20] Another advance detected in England in this period is perhaps in the sources of iron. Recycled iron or bog ore were sources likely to have been used long term, but the study of slags from the sixth–seventh century at Quarrington and the eighth century at Flixborough (Lincolnshire) have shown high signatures of sulphur and phosphorous that should have come from the use of geologically bedded-iron (ironstone), and historical evidence suggested similar activity in Kent.[21]

The objects of high quality (some outstanding) in the Staffordshire Hoard belong to "the peak period of expert manufacture in seventh-century England, when paradoxically the opposite was true of production on the Merovingian continent".[22] This peak period in East Anglia with its upsurge in craft, skill and expression is echoed in both textiles and carpentry. It is not too fanciful to propose a community of seventh-century artisans on the banks of the Deben who were fluent in the language of contemporary art, with its vocabulary of animal aggression and strength in field and woodland, air and water: the bull, boar, hawk and pike. But this atelier contained also smiths of rare talent, who broke new ground, artistically and technically. They also formed a virtual community with their companions in craft, the weavers and needleworkers and carpenters, who clothed the leaders and built their halls.

TAILORS

Traces of numerous garments with a range of qualities, as might be expected, have been found in the graves of early England and recovered, analysed and reconstructed by specialists in cloth and clothing. The main tools were the spindle, of which the spindle whorl (a pottery or glass spheroid perforated to admit the spindle) is the usual archaeological survival and the upright loom, with vertical warp and horizontal weft threads interwoven with a shuttle, to make a variety of patterned weaves (Fig 3.3). Spinning and weaving skills were passed down through the women, and survival of evidence for a Roman inheritance e.g. 2/1 twills, or Scandinavian influence is present but patchy.

The impact of appearance relies also on accessories such as brooches, necklaces, knives, spears and swords, so there is an unstated synergy with metalworkers. Colour was an important part of the language of appearance, as is clear from the beads, the red and gold and blue and schemes on metal accoutrements (FIG 3.1). On clothing it was no doubt as important but liable to disappear in the ground, its discovery often dependent on chance

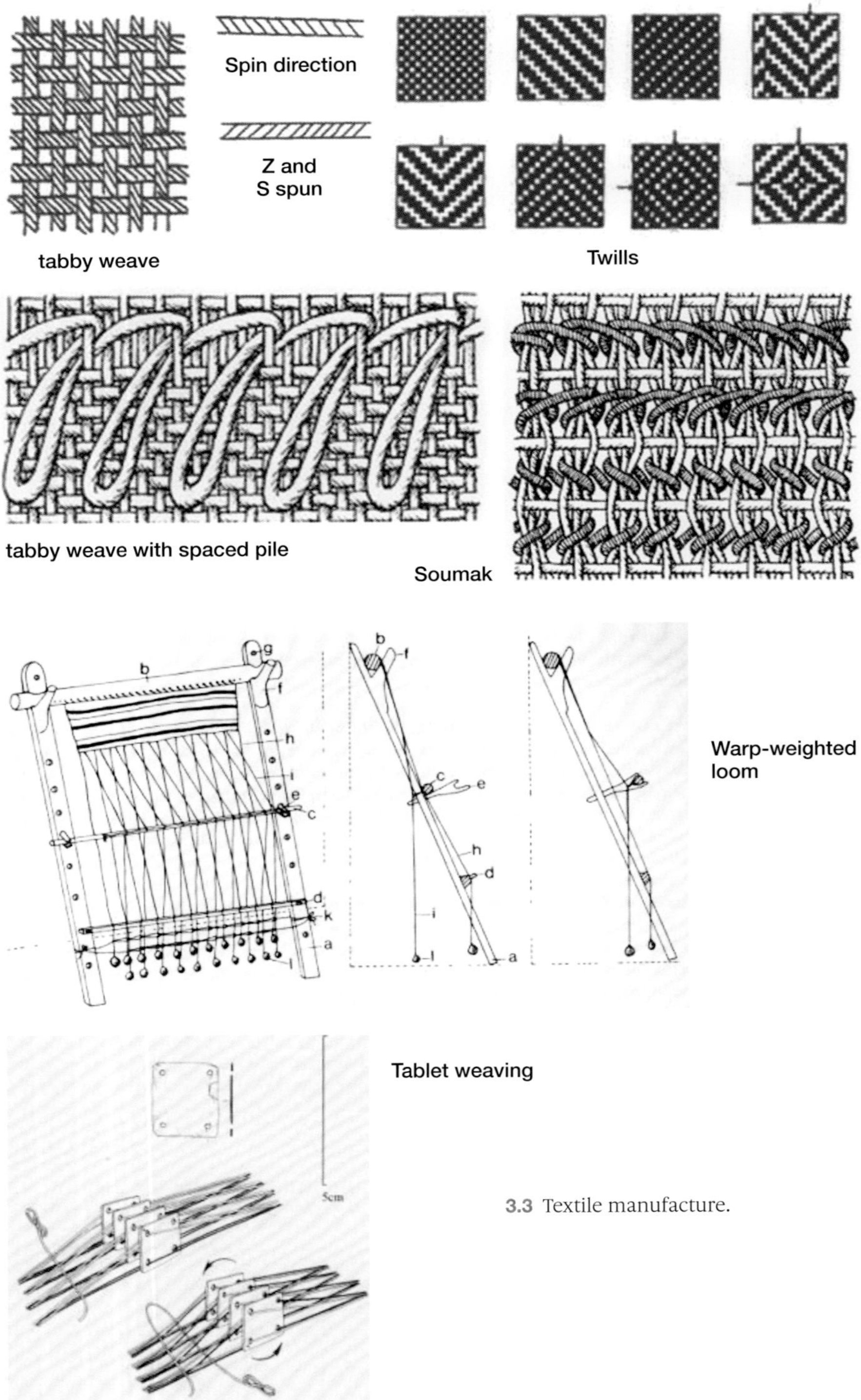

3.3 Textile manufacture.

3.4 Early English men, farmers, workers, soldiers.

preservation owed to contact with a metal object. Natural dyes used on clothing include shades of blue, green, brown and yellow; woad was used at Kempston and blue and green (yellow plus blue) at Uncleby. The yellow piled cloak from Mound 1 (SH10) is thought to be one of three imported from the east Mediterranean (Syria). Yellow dye is extracted from weld *Reseda luteola* L. and *Genista tinctoria* L., Red from *Rubia tinctorum* L. (e.g. Sutton Hoo Mound 1 textile SH5).[23] Once again the seventh century is a peak period for high impact clothing, although the full glory of early artisan colours has to wait until manuscript production in the later seventh and into the eighth century.

Not everyone was grandly dressed, not only because they were people of slender means but also because their work was mucky. Rank and file spearmen wore a belted tunic and leggings, or possibly leather trousers; riders wore cross garters. In later calendars, farmers are depicted sporting all-in-one tunics ending above the knee with a belt and wearing leather shoes.[24] Other men are inferred as sleeveless and with bare feet – this would suit seamen, on deck hauling, rowing or dodging ropes – remembering that they only set out to sea in spring, after the cuckoo first calls **(FIG 3.4)**.

Women displayed individual versions in a common language in clothes, brooches and beads, suggesting at least a need to be identified, by wearing

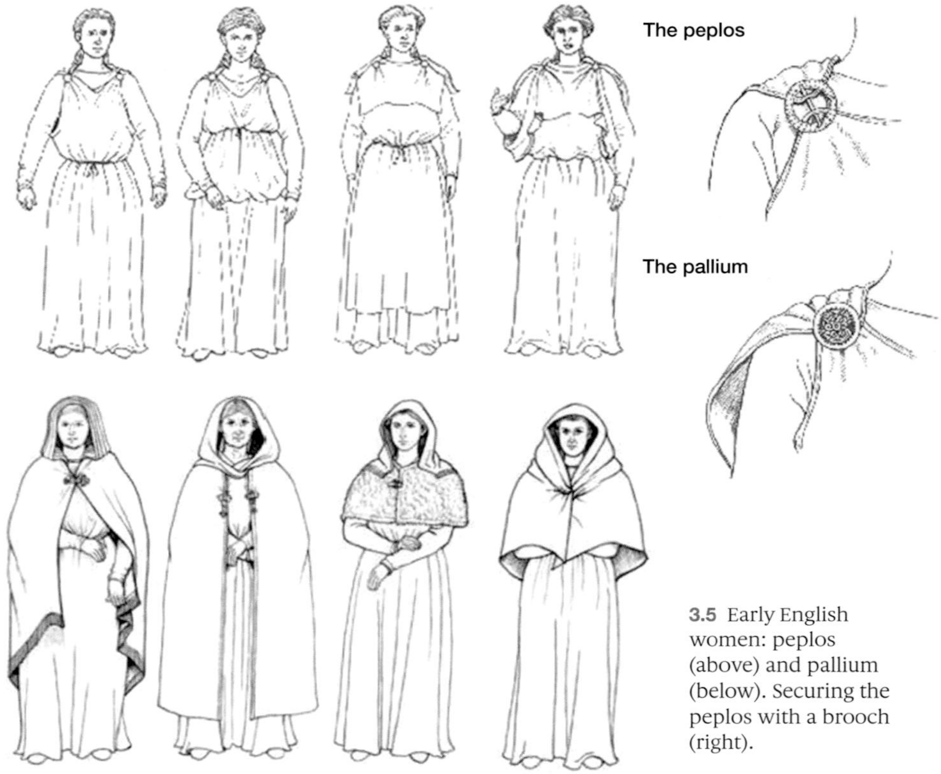

3.5 Early English women: peplos (above) and pallium (below). Securing the peplos with a brooch (right).

objects of spiritual and social meaning as well as of economic value. The sixth-century brooches were designed to secure the simple dress that was the peplos, or the cloak (pallium) that would cover it (FIG 3.5). Some exotic materials were also reaching England from the earliest years of the immigrations: coverlets of eastern Mediterranean origin and bag handles made of African ivory were among the materials found in early female graves.[25]

CHANGING APPEARANCE FOR MEN

By the later sixth century both men and women were wearing costumes different from those of the earlier period. Both wore their politics on their bodies, challenging the weavers, tailors and seamstresses to ever higher levels of quality and display. Some forty-two kinds of textile were detected under Mound 1, used both to decorate and furnish the chamber, and to dress a warrior of the highest rank.[26] The body in Mound 1 was not preserved, but widely distributed inside his coffin were diamond twills coloured red, blue or undyed; a textile cap trimmed with otterskin, two pairs of shoes one with tablet-woven bands for gartering; two leather garments, a number of pillows and one or more piled yellow cloaks. Other than some imports, like the cloaks, the Sutton Hoo textiles drew on the specialist products of a protected local industry, featuring both typical Anglo-Saxon weaves and specialist weaves in which native and imported technology was combined. On the other hand, the use of silk in English products, even at Sutton Hoo, is rare and arrives only with Christianity.[27]

An appreciation of Rædwald's apparel is helped by that of a contemporary buried at Taplow. Here the lines of gold-brocaded edging could be interpreted as a long-sleeved jacket with large flaps that folded one over the other and were secured by a belt. This is the "warrior jacket" or surcoat, ultimately derived from the dress of the early Mongolian horsemen and referred to on a stylised pair of spear-brandishing warriors on the Mound 1 helmet **(FIG 3.6)**. The significance of this type of jacket is that it appears in Persian graves and artwork during the period of the Sasanian empire (third–seventh century CE). Its appearance at Sutton Hoo and in other late sixth /early seventh century

3.6 Alpha males. Artist's impression of a spearman from Morningthorpe (Norfolk) (left) and the Taplow warrior (right) dressed in a Persian surcoat, the "warrior jacket"; Top right: the dancing warrior image from the Sutton Hoo helmet.

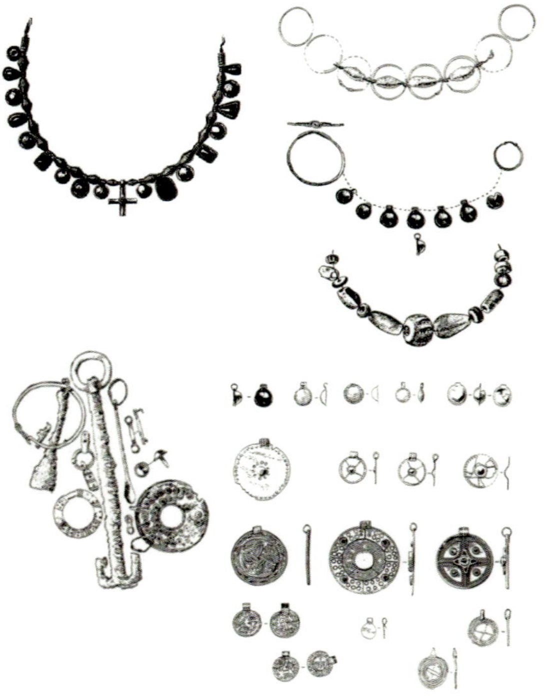

3.7 Alpha women celebrated 630–670 in Byzantine fashion; (Left) necklaces, pendants and a chatelaine. (Right) the Empress Theodora (d. 548) depicted on a mosaic in the Basilica of San Vitale Ravenna, sometime style leader in Constantinople.

burial mounds is another important indication of the early English affinities with eastern Mediterranean warrior apparel in the ongoing struggle against the people of Asia, in which the Byzantine army was the front line, and with which adventurous East Angles may have thrown in their lot.

CHANGING APPEARANCE FOR WOMEN

In the late sixth and early seventh century women begin to imitate more directly the fashions of Byzantium. Pairs of large, heavy brooches and long strings of beads went out of fashion, to be replaced by garnet-inlaid jewellery and choker-length necklaces of slender wire rings and small monochrome glass beads.[28] As in Byzantium itself, the ornamental repertoire included pendants, necklaces of imperial fashion and (more rarely in England) pendant crosses **(Fig 3.7)**.[29] The peplos was superseded by a brightly-coloured long gown worn over a long-sleeved garment and under the cloak. The buckled belt was replaced by a linen belt with strap ends. The practice of carrying

3.8 Female head-dress before (above) and after conversion (below).

tools and trinkets at the waist continued briefly into the Christian period and was then superseded by a bag or satchel like Swallowcliffe.[30] In later documents women were chided for sporting extravagant colours and silks - a sure sign that they did so,[31] no doubt annoying the new Christian hierarchy that regarded such things as their prerogative. As in burial, regional styles were superseded by an emphasis on class distinctions.[32] Perhaps in tune with the higher ranks of the church, upper class women lengthened their veils (Fig 3.8).

The person laid to rest in Mound 14, here suggested to be Rædwald's dowager queen, was wearing three layers of clothing: a cloak over a gown of fine linen, over an inner gown of medium weight linen against the skin - all (including the skin) preserved through contact with metal accoutrements. The textiles featured linen embroidered with woollen yarn to make a saltire pattern and tablet-woven cords used to make borders. Penelope Walton Rogers, to whom

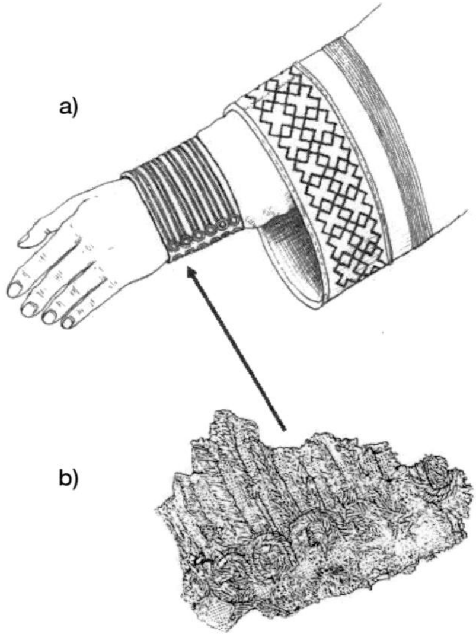

3.9 The Mound 14 lady. (a) Her outer sleeve with wide cuff tablet-woven band and inner sleeve with button-like sleeve clasps. (b) Scandinavian representations in textile of buttons or sleeve-clasps.

we owe this research, deduced that the woman wore an inner chemise with long sleeves and cuffs made of ultrafine linen, with embroidery imitating a row of metal fastenings of a type known from Sweden. Over this was another garment of fine linen, also with long sleeves but with wide embroidered cuffs bordered by tablet-woven bands **(FIG 3.9)**. Such wide ornamental cuffs were preserved on the forearms of the Merovingian Queen Arnegunde buried in a sarcophagus at the church of St Denis in *c.*590, while similar embroidery was worked into the tunic of Bathilde the Anglo-Saxon widow of Clovis II who died in 680/1. The Mound 14 lady lying on her couch in her wooden chamber belonged in royal company. The objects of her silver and iron *chatelaine* rested against the sleeve and between the outer garment and cloak that they had helped to preserve. The ornamental cuffs anticipated the gold brocade bands worn by the churchmen of the next generation. This detective work by an exceptional scholar leaves no doubt that the dressing of upper-class women was a major, perhaps *the* major signal of status and wealth in seventh-century East Anglian society. The intricate weaving of flax and wool, the neat symmetrical patterns and contrasts created, and the subtle stylistic references had plenty to inform ambassador and courtier alike.[33]

Such investment in identity was worthy of a queen, but the Mound 14 burial had suffered such a violent ransacking that only scraps of the expected jewellery remained. We can get an idea of this lost ornamentation from other graves of similar date: a late seventh-century burial from Lower Brook Street, Winchester sported 30 rings of silver wire, with two strings of beads, six bullae and a gold ring, together forming a collar. A dozen tiny beads found scattered around the neck were evidence of a tight-fitting necklet as worn by two of

Empress Theodora's attendants depicted on the Ravenna mosaic.[34] Objects (like crosses) that are supposed indicators of affinity to later religions should not be seen as determinant. People wear fashionable tokens for a variety of reasons, not necessarily retaining their exotic liturgical messages. We should not forget that, in addition to deep rooted prehistoric beliefs, the widespread relics of imperial Rome, and the emergence of a Romanised Christian Europe, from 622 there was also the eruption and rapid expansion of Islam, with its new approach to deity and sanctity, human images and the control of women, which certainly affected behaviour in the Byzantine world. In 638, before Christianity had been accepted in East Anglia, Muslims had already conquered Jerusalem and the Holy Land.

Women took an active part in building the new kingdom and in turning its face towards a future synergy with Europe and the Mediterranean. But there was a price to pay, the loss of spiritual authority to a younger generation of male priests and dogmatic bishops, and the loss of village morality to a book of rules that claimed to be universal. As the executions at Sutton Hoo showed, those who suffered for non-conformity were mainly young men, but women were also caught up in the web of new dogma. At artisan level, the clothing industry was depicted as mainly engaged in the formulaic dressing of kings and prelates, until the images of real people came alive in the manuscripts of the eleventh century.[35]

So much of the clothiers' trade has not survived, but the little we have shows that, notwithstanding their simple equipment, seventh-century East Anglian spinners and weavers and designers used patterns as intricate as the metalworkers. Those engaged in making patterned textiles will have worked with the smiths and may have inspired them. Clothing was equally in the front line of display, and its development at the time of Sutton Hoo reveals that the international and imperial stirring displayed in metalwork was felt in clothing too. In female fashion, the knowledge base reaches into the court of the Empress in Constantinople. The styled warrior jacket worn by men has been proposed as being brought back into north Europe, along with other prize objects, by Germanic warriors fighting against Persia in the Byzantine army. All this is significant for the ship being built in Woodbridge. East Anglian warriors serving in the Byzantine army or imperial guard in the later sixth and early seventh century would have seen for themselves the varied boats and ships that travelled the French rivers and sailed between France, Italy, Byzantium and the Levant. In Chapter 4 we shall see some of these and ask how far they may have affected the design of the Mound 1 ship.

CARPENTRY: ARRIVAL OF THE GRAND HALL

Workers in wood were always members of prehistoric, Roman and early medieval communities, even if their work is often hard to observe in detail. Our third group of artisans, the carpenters, designed and built structures using joinery, especially in oak. They created their own early seventh-century professional high point, emerging from a centuries-old craft. David Wilson and Kevin Leahy listed the tools available to the carpenter as deduced from hoards, graves and early illustrations.[36] These are all assigned to the world of early Britain, even if precise dating is difficult. The conservatism of craft and the fact that most of the tools were known in the Roman empire, permits us to throw wide the net of possibility. Before the Norman period we can cite axes for chopping and splitting, the adze (a transverse axe) for shaping timber, the T-shaped axe for trimming, draw knives for shaping spokes, the axe hammer, spoon bits for drilling holes, gouges (spoon-shaped chisels, e.g. for making grooves), the plane (one from Sarre in Kent), pole lathes and cutting tools for use in turning. Saws are known from Thetford and Icklingham, but so fine they are likely to belong to bone workers who used saws to cut antler. The range of woodworking tools suggests that pegged joints using predrilled holes for treenails, scarf joints, tongue and groove joints were already, or soon became part of the English carpenter's repertoire. The structure of the ninth century mill at Tamworth employed mortice and tenon joints. But most of the inferences about how carpentry developed between the sixth century and the eighth are owed to the meticulous excavation of burial chambers, houses and halls, and here a great deal has been revealed.

WOODWORKING UNDERGROUND

Nailed coffins or planks were present in inhumation graves of the Roman, British and Anglo-Saxon phases (fifth-seventh century) at Wasperton on the Warwickshire Avon.[37] More heavy-duty mortuary construction appeared in the sixth century and took the form of tree-trunk coffins, beds and chambers. Tree-trunk coffins were made in the same way as log boats - oak was split longitudinally and the two halves dug out to make a bearer and a lid often fastened with curved iron clamps.[38] Chambers at Sutton Hoo include Mound 1 where the chamber was constructed with hefty rafters bearing on the gunnel providing 'beaked' roof supports like Oseberg, with end walls of horizontal or more likely vertical planks tenoned into frames 10 and 16.[39] The chamber beneath the boat in Mound 2 was cut into the subsoil and seemingly constructed with revetments of overlapping vertical planks standing against the cut face on all four sides, held in place with horizontal walers and struts. No diagnostic iron fastenings were found.[40] In Mound 14 the ransacked woman's

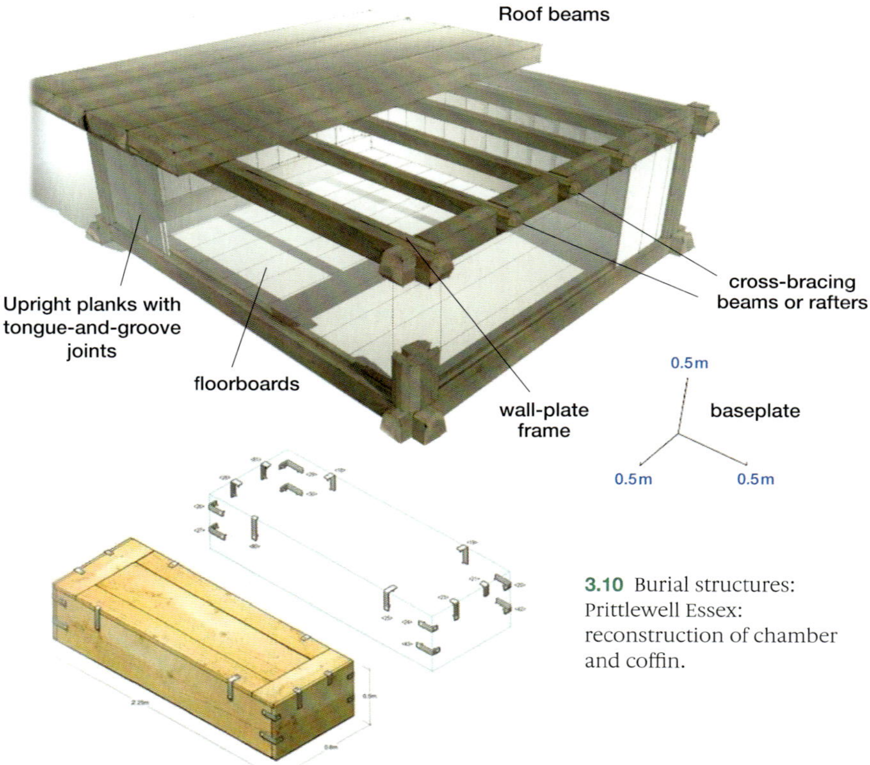

3.10 Burial structures: Prittlewell Essex: reconstruction of chamber and coffin.

grave was in a chamber constructed with thin vertical planks. Inside were traces of an upholstered couch in the form of a wood stain and numerous tacks. Other burials, such as that at Swallowcliffe Down (Chapter 2) give a more detailed account of the construction of a wooden bed.

Sophisticated beds and burial chambers were already being constructed in the continental Iron Age and some late examples may have fed into the early carpentry of early England. The chamber under the mound at Pilgramsdorf (East Prussia) dated third-fifth century was constructed 'log-cabin' style in a jointed square over a plank floor with wide slots for vertical planking on the upper part of each log.[41] Under Mound 2 at Högom, Medelpad on the east coast of Sweden, was a man's bed-burial richly furnished with weapons, horse tack and furs in a chamber measuring *c.* 5 x 2 m. The chamber walls were constructed of horizontal logs or coarse planks, with no sign of corner posts. A roof of logs was covered with at least two layers of birch bark; most of the floor and bed were covered in bear furs. The bed was *c.* 2.6 m long by 1 m wide, made of two planks 3-4 cm thick set on edge and bridged by seven planks 1 m long set at uniform intervals and attached by pegs. The chamber was interpreted as a two-room structure - a bedroom with the bed, and a reception room containing weapons and horse tack and a table laid for two persons. The Högom mounds were dated between the third and the sixth century CE.[42]

These show something of the northern European Iron Age traditions of mortuary woodwork which Anglo-Saxons could inherit.[43] The techniques were applied fully fledged in our earliest dated mound burial (575–605), that at Prittlewell in Essex which we have already met. The chamber here was in a pit measuring 4.35 × 4.00 m, 1.4 to 1.5 m deep, containing a timber-framed square room with a flat roof of horizontal beams. The chamber was robustly built – the wood had gone but the architecture and dimensions of the chamber were deduced from the direction of wood grain preserved by metal objects hung on the walls. It had been constructed with radially cleft oak planks measuring up to 5.3 cm thick, set upright on end **(FIG 3.10)**. The base of the planks had left no marks on the ground, so they were likely set in grooves in the upper course of a log foundation, as at Pilgramsdorf, and it was conjectured that the planks were joined edge to edge by tongue and groove.[44] A thin grey deposit on which objects sat was interpreted as the remains of a wooden floor, perhaps originally covered in matting. A roof was detected as organic stains up to 60 cm wide originally horizontal, so supported by beams. These carefully gathered clues were best explained as due to a timber frame structure with a square foundation and wall plate supported by squared corner posts grooved to lock into vertical planks and cross braced with horizontal rafters supporting heavy roof beams. The deceased lay in a wooden plank coffin held together with angle irons, with cloaks draped over it.[45]

WOODWORKING ABOVE GROUND – FROM HUT TO HALL

The first few generations of East Angles made buildings that survive as shallow rectangular pits, with posts at the corners or centred at the short ends probably joined by a cross piece, like the ridge pole of a tent. These *sunken feature buildings* (SFBs) supported a roof of heather or thatch with rafters resting on the grass or on a low wall of turves **(FIG 3.11)**. The excavator Stanley West suspected they had suspended wooden floors over the pits, and subsequent experimental reconstruction of West Stow over five decades have developed the idea that these SFBs not only had floors, but plank walls founded on sill beams and thatched rooves supported by rafters.[46]

The SFBs were often accompanied by rectangular houses surviving as rows of postholes at ground level, holes originally containing circular posts of similar diameter set vertically at intervals in the ground. The spaces between the posts were infilled with planks or wattles coated with daub -wet clay that hardened in the sun which often declares its presence in broken pieces. Such constructions could be made with minimum tooling using basic natu-

3.11 West Stow: reconstructed buildings.

ral resources to hand and served the earliest English settlers as working and living space for many centuries.

By the end of the sixth century, towards the age of Sutton Hoo, buildings north and south of the Humber began to reflect a new hierarchy and social prescription, just as that seen in the more lavish and more visible mound burials reserved for an upper class. The carpenters' focus was now on larger buildings, seated in foundation trenches, framed with squared-off and jointed beams - the house became a hall. We can follow the developments in carpentry that brought us to this point, by inspecting the increasingly ambitious construction techniques in two long-lived sites - one in the north (Yeavering) and one in the south (Cowdery's Down). For our purposes, the important thing to note is the way that carpentry evolved to the point that something as ambitious as the Mound 1 ship could be built.

SEVENTH CENTURY IN THE NORTH

The remains of hall buildings rarely include preserved timbers but have been studied from their ghost foundations preserved as shadows in the soil - perhaps nowhere with such meticulous observation and imaginative interpretation as in Brian Hope-Taylor's classic excavations at Yeavering.[47] Guided by a cropmark, he exposed the gravel surface beneath the plough and coaxed the form of the walls and buttresses by brushing and watering and observing the drying patterns until he could see directly the outlines of the grand halls and noted how some succeeded each other on the same footprint

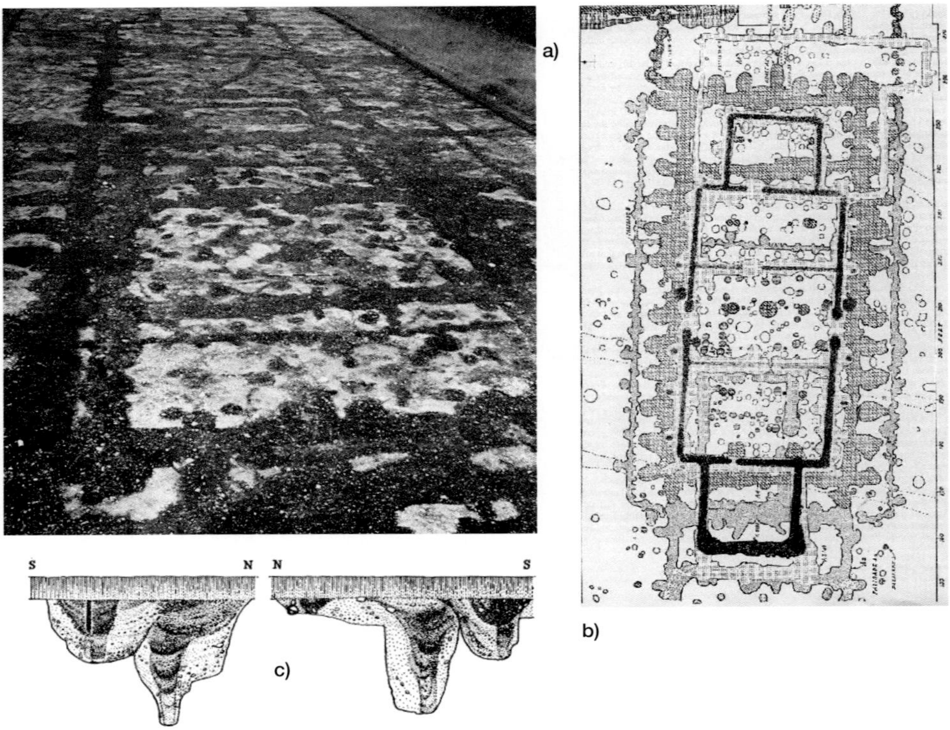

3.12 Yeavering: (a) hall buildings defined in the primary horizontal section. (b) the succession of superimposed halls A3, 4, 5 in Area A, A3 uppermost and (c) the sequence of wall shadows in section, wall of A3 cutting wall of A4.

(Fig 3.12). To gain the sharpest contrast in the ground, he worked in autumn. He then began to study the wall trenches and buttress pits, carefully locating cut sections in order to see and record the nature of the load-bearing timbers, the scantling (cross-section) of planks that left their imprint at the base of the foundation trenches. The thickness of planks and posts implied the load they were designed to bear, and thus the likely height of the building. The intersect or spacing between timbers implied the way they were most likely joined, and Hope-Taylor inferred the use of mortice and tenon and or tongue and groove joints. The soil sections in the trenches show where timbers had succeeded each other or been extracted to make way for replacement buildings. The angle of the wood stain in sections across the pits alongside a building showed that they housed buttresses supporting high timber walls. In a rare use of nails, planks of doors 'carvel built' edge to edge were found to be secured with iron rivets.

Although nothing remained above ground level, and few surviving timbers below, he was able to use these investigative techniques to argue for vertical

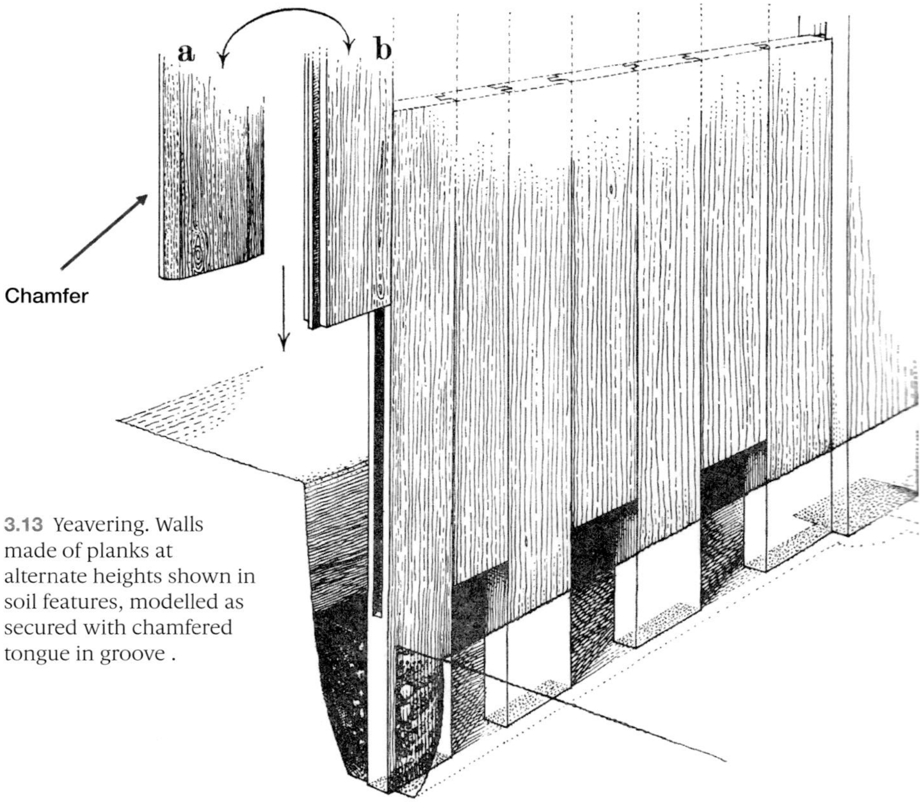

3.13 Yeavering. Walls made of planks at alternate heights shown in soil features, modelled as secured with chamfered tongue in groove .

squared and trimmed timbers standing side by side in carefully cut trenches, interlocked with vertical planking using tongue and groove (FIG 3.13). The soil patterns in the sections showed where vertical timbers had been extracted for reuse. The ingenuity of the builders was also reflected in the curved timber walls that formed the back of the assembly place, or "grandstand", replicating a section of Roman amphitheatre realised in timber (FIG 3.14). The roofs of buildings were missing of course, but Hope-Taylor was able to detect crucks or propose lofty walls bridged by beams on wall-plates supporting rafters. Furthermore, he showed how the halls were designed and laid out using a standard measure, the *Yeavering foot*. As a revelation of artisan sophistication, Yeavering was as startling as Sutton Hoo.

Perhaps the most important source of information was provided by sequences of halls replacing each other in the same place, showing both the importance of a hall as a long-lived monumental structure and offering a stratified account of the evolving carpentry.[48] The archaeological sequence, defined in *phases*, had very little absolute dating, so Hope-Taylor assigned

a)

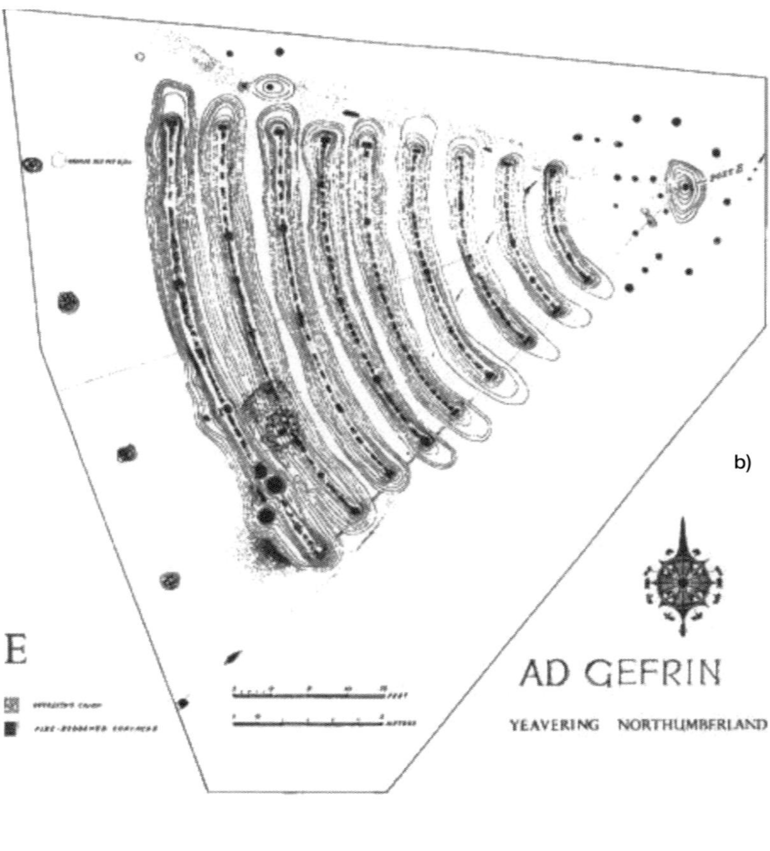

b)

c)

3.14 Yeavering – (a) the curved grandstand under excavation; (b) as planned and (c) as imagined by Hope-Taylor in 1977.

buildings to kings and events given in Bede's history (Chapter 1). These were an approximation, a model, an enlivened story of the site to assist the imagination of the reader.

The first halls were constructed using lines of posts in separate postholes, the gaps between filled with wattle and daub panels known as A6. Later (Phase II) successor buildings were constructed with heavy squared (7.5in scantling) vertical timbers resting edge to edge on the base of shallow wall trenches and there were pairs of opposed roof supports. Sometime in the late sixth to early seventh century (Phase IIIAB), Yeavering had a makeover by a new owner who built a grand hall (A2) on an east-west alignment. It was laid out in two squares of 40×40 *Yeavering feet* with a gap of eight *Yeavering feet* between them to accommodate opposed doorways, giving a ground plan of 40×88 Yeavering-feet. The walls were constructed using heavy 7.5 in vertical squared timbers but set now at intervals with vertical timbers between them, interlocked with tongue and groove and rising from ground level. As well as continuous interlocked wooden walls faced, internally at least, with fine white plaster, Building A2 had continuous external buttress posts, pairs of deeply founded roof support posts, massive doorposts, raised platforms and upper galleries.

In the next phase (IIIC) the site was redeveloped again and 'reached the zenith of its importance.' A2 was superseded by the larger A4 and accompanied by a series of minor halls adjacent to the west, beginning with A1a;

a)

c)

b)

3.15 Excavation at Chalton showing (a) a post-in-hole building (A20), (b) a post-in-trench building (AZ1) with a sunken featured building adjacent and (c) post shadows in the trench of AZ1.

between them, a fenced yard. The “grandstand” was enlarged to seat 320 people (by the measured length of the curving tiers). There was a variation in building technique, in that the new grand hall (A4) employed 5.5 in squared timbers and very large external posts, presumably to meet the lateral thrust of a heavier, higher roof. This phase was assigned to Edwin (616–633) who, as related in Chapter 1 was at Yeavering with Tata and the children, and with Tata’s chaplain Paulinus after the change to Christianity had been decided. Mass baptisms in the River Glen were conducted at Yeavering by Paulinus. However, the new palace complex was put to the torch and many were killed, and subsequently buried in lines of graves, dated by their backfill containing charred wood from the fire. Hope-Taylor thought such an all-embracing fire was most likely the result of just one catastrophic event, a raid by Penda, but it is possible that the temple had already been demolished, just as Coifi did at Goodmanham. In this case it would have happened just as deliberately, but in the conversion year. Penda is known to have killed Edwin and routed his army at the Battle of Hatfield in 633, probably having missed him at Yeavering, which he then burnt down.

The township was immediately rebuilt (Phase IV). A1b and A3a were double annex halls either side of the yard, their wall trenches black with the charred

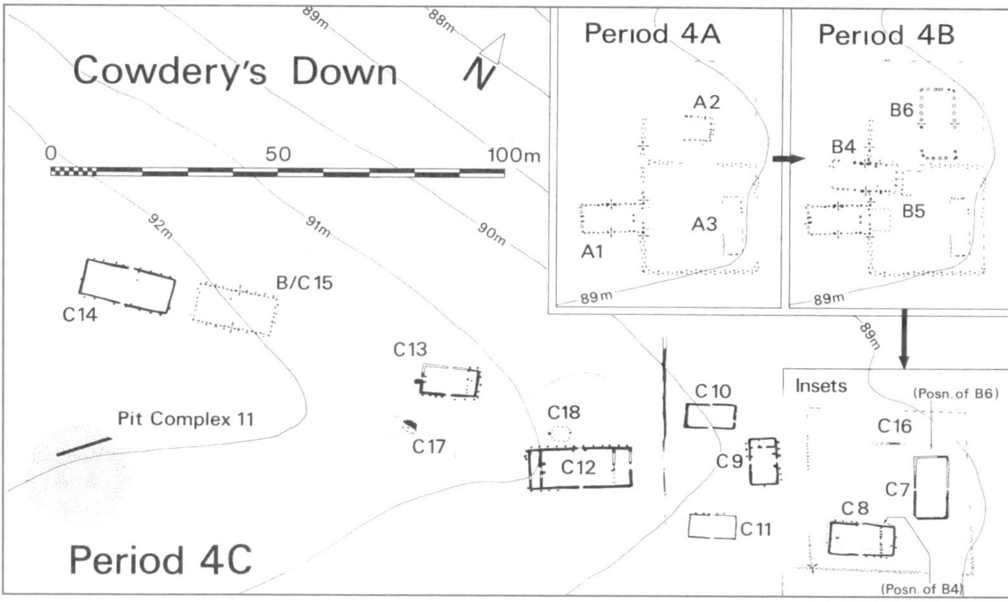

3.16 Cowdery's Down plan of excavations.

remains of their burnt down predecessors. New hall A3a used yet smaller timbers (average width 4.25 in). Buildings C1–C4 to the north have the look of barracks and their planks were still narrower at 3¾ inches average. Building B has appeared - a possible church and its cemetery. This phase is assigned to Oswald 634–642, but Penda killed him at Oswestry. Penda was again on the rampage and at the gates of Bamburgh in 651 so could have been responsible for the next fire that burnt Phase IV to the ground.

Oswiu (612–670) was king of Bernicia from 642 and, after killing Penda at the Winwaed in 654, of all Northumbria. He was Aethelfrith's son, and would have likely known Yeavering as a child. All the same, his Phase V rebuild was a minor one. The two halls with annexes A3b and A1c were cobbled together with portmanteau clinker-built walls. A1c was built with vertical timbers at 5 ft intervals fitted with clinker-built plank panels using iron rivets and caulked with daub. A3b also had rivets joining overlapping 1 inch-thick planks. Both were erected on previous buildings destroyed by fire. These resembled parts of a boat and may have been recycled from one. At least one rivet was from a door in C3a. The annexed C4b and the rebuilt chapel Bb imply a religious use. Was this perhaps a monastery? Oswiu was fond of founding them.[49]

As can be seen, while the sequencing at Yeavering was archaeological, the

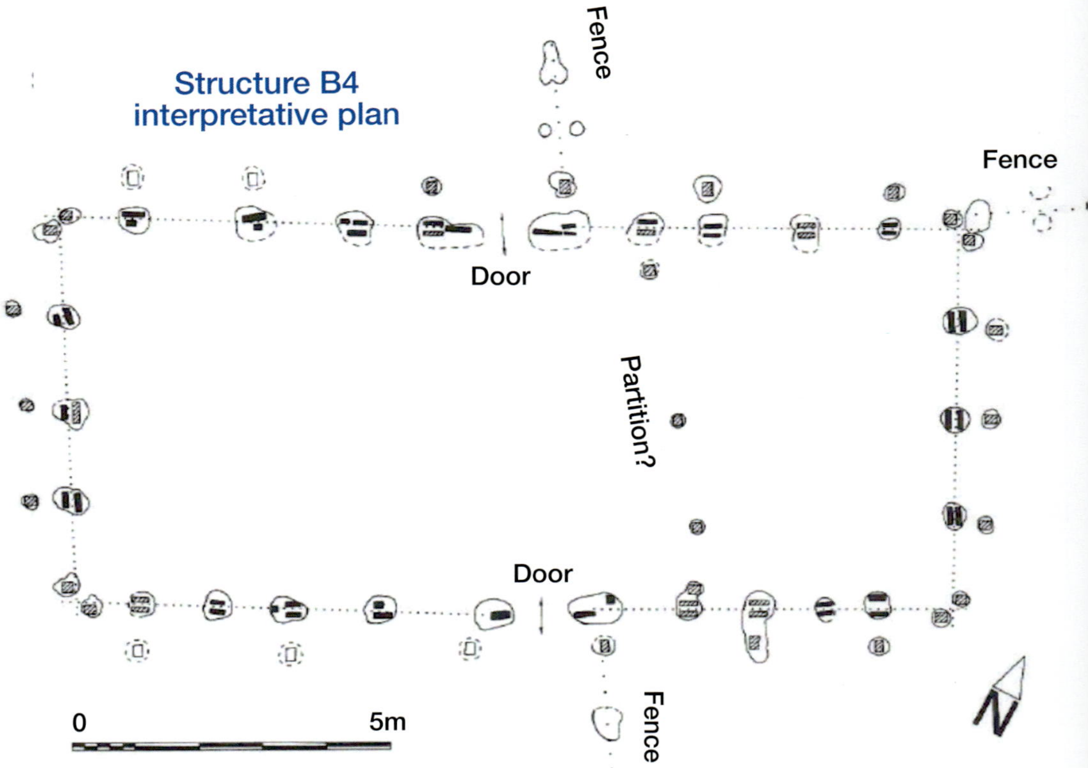

3.17 Cowdery's Down Building B4.

calendar dating was assigned by associating the sequence of buildings with the historical record as provided by Bede's history. There were very few datable finds, and radiocarbon dating had only just been invented and had yet to be recalibrated. The strength of the sequence as an exhibition of evolving carpentry, is the fact that the stratigraphic sequence of buildings, one on top of another and occupying the same footprint, is not accidental and provides a sound framework; and it has since been echoed in better dated sites. Its apparent weakness is the alignment of phases, structures and fires with the reigns of kings, but this is irrelevant to the sequence modelled on archaeological observations. This naturally has its own uncertainties, but all archaeology - all science - makes progress by addressing bold hypotheses or there would be very few advances. Investigations at Yeavering have recently started again, with intensive surface surveys and excavation of geophysical targets. Radiocarbon dating of new finds and samples in Hope-Taylor's archive have so far corroborated the placing of the sequence in the mid sixth to mid seventh century.[50] While this will no doubt be adjusted by future work, the message

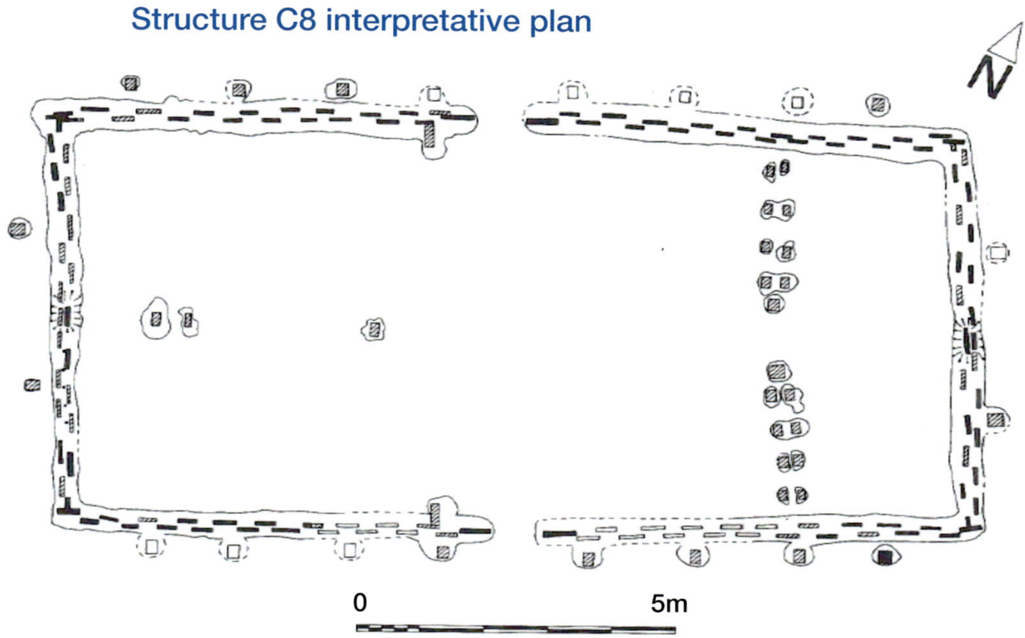

3.18 Cowdery's Down Building C8.

for our purpose is that Hope-Taylor's method of defining timber sequences - widely practised since - showed how closely the developments in timber architecture detected at Yeavering are reflected in the date and construction of the Sutton Hoo ship.

SEVENTH-CENTURY ADVANCES IN THE SOUTH

The same advances in carpentry have also been discovered nearer the ship's home. At Chalton (Hants) a sixth century village of post-in-hole rectangular buildings with sunken floored huts came to its seventh-century climax with Proto-hall AZ1, shown to have post-in-trench walls as well as opposed doors, stair lobes and a central wattle and daub oven **(FIG 3.15)**. More demonstrative still was the carpentry sequence in the buildings excavated at Cowdery's Down in Sussex; here too there was a rise of sophistication towards the early seventh century.[51] Building began in the late sixth century with a simple post-in-trench building like Chalton's AZ1 (Farmstead 1, A1-3) and developed rapidly **(FIG 3.16)**. Farmstead 2 (B4-6) (early seventh century) featured opposed pairs of planks set in the pits, rather than posts, and the doorposts in deep pits were carpentered timbers of rectangular section (10 cm (4 ins) thick); one example at least was radially split. The walls were fashioned with vertical planks erected in pairs, a 10 cm gap between them (FIG 3.17). These were chunky planks or baulks of timber always 10 cm thick and varying in width between 15-50 cms, average 30 cm - say 4 x 12 inches. They may have clasped horizontal timbers (probably pegged) and/or wattle fence panels (heavily daubed with clay). Farmstead 3 and 4 (the C buildings) belong to the seventh-eighth century. Building C8 featured large pits for plank clusters mid-way along each short wall implying gable posts (Fig 3.18). The walls were made of vertical planks averaging 25 x 10 cm set side by side in trenches but staggered either side of a centre line, like fence posts. Straight horizontal planks or wattle panels could have been clasped between them. The doors were 80 cm wide with doorpost timbers 10 x 50 cm in cross-section. Pits along the outside of the walls suggested buttresses or raking supports.

Farmstead 4 dating to the late seventh / early eighth century featured a grander building still, exemplified by the magnificently carpentered timber-frame hall, C12 (FIG 3.19). The excavators deduced a roof supported by pairs of crucks, stairs to upper galleries, a suspended floor 22.1 m long and measuring 8.8 m wide at the opposing doors and 8.5 m at the ends, so slightly bowed. Marks of vertical timbers on the wall-trench floors were staggered and had a scantling of 25 cm x 8 cm. Likely horizontal 'stringers' were pegged to the uprights at vertical intervals. A continuous line of stake holes ran between them, suggesting that at the lowest level at least, the staggered timbers embraced wattle panels or continuous wattle fencing woven on uprights (daubed). At higher levels wattle panels may have been inserted mid upright to mid upright. The excavators interpreted most of their buildings as having gable roofs with "rafters running on to wall-plates below head height. Internally the floor area was kept free of posts, roof supports being pushed back to the walls. Across the middle of most of the buildings were crucks which perhaps helped to tie the walls but were mainly designed to support a ridge-piece and perhaps purlins. These provided longitudinal stability and prevented rafter sag. The greater part of the roof load was transmitted to the wall plates and the walls."

Chris Scull's recent investigations at Rendlesham have shown that the new grand timber buildings of the seventh century were also present just a few miles upriver from Sutton Hoo. The excavated hall had few diagnostic soil patterns in its wall trenches but paralleled Cowdery's Down C12 in plan and was associated with pieces of window glass and limewashed daub. A smaller building has also been excavated, with features in common with the ceremonial building at Uppåkra (Sweden) in having deep trenches and a central group of post pits, implying a special structure of some height, perhaps a temple. These represent an imposing pair of buildings at a site that most likely had many structures, as well as its extensive metalworking activity.[52] Chris

3.19 Cowdery's Down Building C12.

Scull can now justly describe Rendlesham, rather than Sutton Hoo, as the real social and economic focus for the people of south-east Suffolk during the late sixth to eighth century.[53] However, I would suggest that in the early, pre-Christian part of that period, up to the mid seventh-century Sutton Hoo and Rendlesham, the past and the present, formed twin poles of allegiance. After that the spotlight no doubt shifted solely to Rendlesham and its church, and the Sutton Hoo cemetery lost its royalty and gained a reputation as the kingdom's Golgotha.

From Yeavering, Chalton and Cowdery's Down we learn that there was a dramatic progression in carpentry from the late sixth century to the late seventh century. As it can be tracked in both Northumbria and Wessex this suggests that seventh-century carpenters were in touch with each other and were innovators, making framed buildings using squared timbers and squared planks. Naturally in all these examples, where wood did not survive, it was hard to record mortice and tenon, tongue in groove and scarf joints directly, although all these were implied with increasing confidence. Very few fastenings had survived, making the routine use of wooden treenails (as opposed to iron nails) very likely. Of especial interest to that branch of carpenters at work on boats and ships were the raking timbers used to prop structures, curved timbers selected for crucks, wattle panels - an ubiquitous commodity for fencing and wall fillers - and designs that include the use of standard lengths, so that dimensions and ideal length/breadth ratios can be transferred from one builder to another - within a structure, from generation to generation, and probably within a region, if not wider.

THE NEW ARTISANS AND THE SHIP

What had changed? The social structure for sure. Kings may have invented lines of descent for themselves starting from Woden or Caesar (or both), but royal power with external recognition was exercised only now. Closely bound up with this was the rediscovery of the European continent, the Mediterranean, the concept of empire, the armies in which one's father or grandfather had served. And Europe meant coming to terms with Christianity, however intrusive its regulations. Rædwald's queen was right - old loyalties were important and you didn't throw them away lightly. But the matter of the day was political and geographical: Northumbria faced the North Sea and the Mercians, Wessex faced the Channel and the Mercians, Kent and East Anglia faced the North Sea and the Channel. No wonder they had varied foreign policies. But the continental option was the only one that promised treasure and powerful allies.

Rædwald's burial chamber showed the rewards of close relations with the continent, the Mediterranean and the Byzantine empire. But burial chambers would soon be a thing of the past. This was a moment to be seized by the East Angles as surely as by the men of Kent and Northumbria. Great halls of the late sixth and early seventh century have now been defined in Sutton Courtenay, Lyminge, and Rendlesham - all of them, especially the last, with a clear regional role.[54] Founded in places of previous assembly, with a wide outreach, and focused on monumental buildings frequently refreshed on the same footprint, they stamped the landscape with a message of ownership and secular permanence.[55] Their monumentality matched that of the burial mounds and like them can be seen as response to the rising investment in Church infrastructure. The south-east coast of England showed an increasing interest in sea travel, noted in subtle archaeological indications: from the late sixth century an increase in imported goods, and the practice of boat burial and graves that included rivets, and in the later seventh century the deposition of English silver *sceattas*. These all signalled a maritime familiarity with the southern North Sea and the Channel.[56] Hall, Mound and Ship: this triad could be claimed to define early English kingship.

In this brief account we have seen a late sixth-century upsurge in craft ambition, technique and expression, in metalworking and textiles and carpentry. The shipwrights who built the Sutton Hoo ships were also part of this innovative craft community. All the crafts would have had access to stable royal leadership, affected by the visiting experts, the enterprising mood, the determination to excel. It coincides with a strong interest in Byzantium as a model of enriched secular and spiritual power, indicated in imports of silver, fashion, ornaments, souvenirs, imitations of technique, and precocious contact with the east Mediterranean. The form and finish given to the jackets and cloaks and gold and garnet regalia would be applied on a larger stage by the shipwrights ready to share the new symbolic language and proclaim its message on the water. The pride in clothing and its use as a signal of identity and status suggest that halls and ships would be similarly decked out, one device in use being the tall 'flagpole,' the focus of the Yeavering assembly, its maritime role served by a mast. The textiles can be imagined as worked into flags, streamers and buntings without too much strain on credulity, and the patterns we have seen in the clothing of the Mound 1 king and the Mound 14 lady give us a starting point for their design. In carpentry we see the rise of the great hall with large numbers of finished and joined timbers enclosing wide spaces, with plank floors, staircases and galleries. The timber ghosts signal smooth flat squared-off surfaces of oak, their positioning implying scarf joints, tongue and groove, mortice and tenon, and the use of treenails. Some walls finished with fine plaster make the use of coloured staining also believable. The use of standard measurement suggests architectural planning of some precision.

At this point we can observe the convergence between hall carpentry and ship carpentry. The great hall evidently relied on large beams of wood and straight planks, the lower ends anchored by being set deep in the ground to make the four vertical walls of a rectangular building supporting a roof of rafters. In some cases, the walls were braced by buttresses; the wall-posts and rafters at a gable could be rendered by a naturally formed pair of crucks. The great ship was an upside-down hall, also using large straight or naturally curved timber and long straight planks of green oak, bent into a curve and secured with iron rivets to create the lines of the hull - but founded only on water. Both operations required large square timbers to be raised and secured with joinery, and most likely given a smart finish.

The later and well-preserved Viking ships were decorated with carved figure heads and ribbons of interlaced animals from the water line to the top of the stem and stern posts. Their art is later and different to that of the East Angles, but for our ship we have contemporary models in the stand-alone animals on the shield and the helmet and chains of red and gold interlace on the jewellery. We hope the ship we are building, and the way we present it, will add even more lustre to Sutton Hoo.

ENVOI

Through this book runs a theme of archaeological discovery that helps to pick out the seventh century as a pivotal moment in the history of England. In his magisterial *Building Anglo-Saxon England*, John Blair credits seventh-century change, exemplified by the monumental timber halls and mounds, to the "milieu of princely magnificence", emulating neighbouring cultures and especially by "trying to look Roman".[57] In *Formative Britain*, I saw additional drifts of power, from community to the individual, from localised to institutionalised spirituality and from women to men.[58] In this book, I credit the material changes of the period not so much to the kings and holy men we find in texts, or the noble warriors revealed in their graves, but rather to the network of artisans whose achievements survive mainly in their works. In an outward-looking interconnected world, the agency of artisans, it can be argued, is of more significance than that of princes - perhaps especially in the realm of ships and seafaring.

4 SEVENTH-CENTURY SHIPS
Forerunners and legacies

SEASCAPE

In archaeology and history, we read that the Irish, Scots, Picts, Welsh and of course the English all went to sea in the centuries before Sutton Hoo. Traffic along the Atlantic seaboard from Iberia to Orkney was active from the Neolithic period onwards marking their territories with megalithic monuments.[1] The Romans circumnavigated Britain and colonised its most fertile regions (the east and south). In early Christian times the route using the Gulf Stream brought pottery to Britons in the west, and the continental river system brought missionaries across the Channel. The Irish crossed the sea from the west and colonised Cornwall, west Wales, north west Britain and eventually Pictland; Germanic peoples crossed the sea from the east and north east, colonised eastern Britain and made it England.[2] So Britain is an island that has hosted at least four maritime nations, Roman, Britons, Irish and English, linked with neighbours and ancestors across seaways with many points of entry, estuaries, firths and bays. They will have encountered the same local conditions of weather, winds and tides as we do, the same sea areas and seasonal hazards **(FIG 4.1)**.

Modern studies suggest that the North Sea has a home-blowing system of seasonal winds, towards England in the spring and towards Scandinavia in the autumn, favouring the Germanic peoples of northwest Europe with journeys westward **(FIG 4.2)**. In the North Sea, the fjords, firths and estuaries were recognised destinations, learned and taught by generations of seafarers up to today. From later Viking records it seems that navigation in the North Sea was assisted by a bundle of techniques: gauging the maximum height of the sun, spotting the northern edge of the continental shelf marked by the congregation of fish and sea birds, observing the tides, noting the direction of the swell, feeling the winds on the skin (north - cold and dry, east - cold and wet, west - warm and wet and south - warm and dry), and, near the shore, guided by the profile of cliffs and the characteristic sound made by the breakers, which could apparently be identified by putting one's ear to the gunnel. Navigators in the Irish Sea made use of flying geese, in skein by day, by their honking at night bound for distant shores and islands where they must land to feed and breed **(FIG 4.3)**.[3] So, it is fair to begin by recognising that we have encountered only a tiny fraction of the evidence for boats and seafaring before

4.1 The island of Britain with its sea areas and points of entry.

the Sutton Hoo Ship and must never assume that nothing was happening. The default position is that British waters were alive with boats and voyages and only politics could alter this.

BEFORE SUTTON HOO

There was a rich inheritance. Travel by water is at least as old as the Mesolithic, when the melting of the ice raised the world's sea levels and created numerous islands. Apart from the cold, travel in the ice ages using sledges and skis to follow the herds had been relatively safe. Water crossing was a new challenge, and we can guess how the methods emerged, perhaps by imitating nature during a long period of invention: fallen trees led to floating logs,

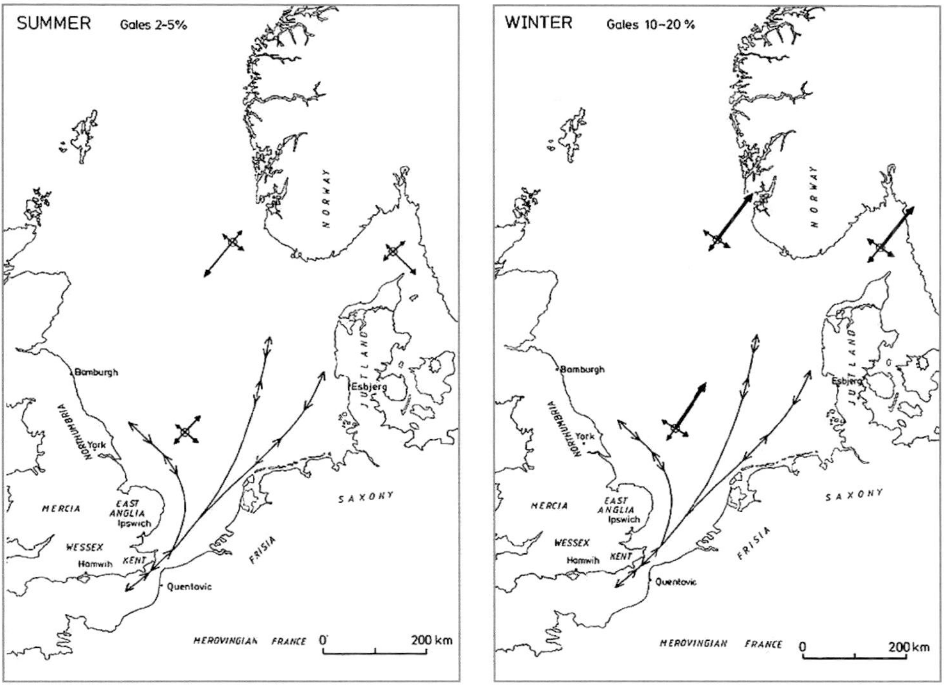

4.2 Tides and seasonal winds on the east coast of Britain.

these being dug out and fitted with raised freeboards to prevent swamping; animal hides stretched over a wooden frame imitated a swimming seal or dolphin. Paddled hide boats were in use in the Scandinavian Bronze Age and were still being built frame-first by those living around the Irish Sea and the Atlantic coast, as leather currachs and coracles. Probably of this kind was the legendary boat, later depicted with a mast and sail, in which St Brendan made his trip to islands, maybe including St Kilda and Iceland, driven by religious fervour to worship in the wild.[4] The Romans arrived in ships, fought in ships and traded in ships that were both rowed and sailed. The Angles and Saxons arrived in boats that were rowed like Nydam, but according to the linguist Katrin Thier, the word for sail (*segh**), and by implication the technology of sailing, existed in Celtic and West German languages before the Angles and Saxons arrived in Britain in the fifth century. That does not necessarily mean that they sailed there.[5] But by the seventh century the English will have known the ships that plied the waters round Britain, the Scandinavian ships travelling in the North Sea and Baltic, the Roman models, in the memory, on the Rhine or in the eastern Mediterranean, where the mercenary warriors of Sutton Hoo have now been seen to go.

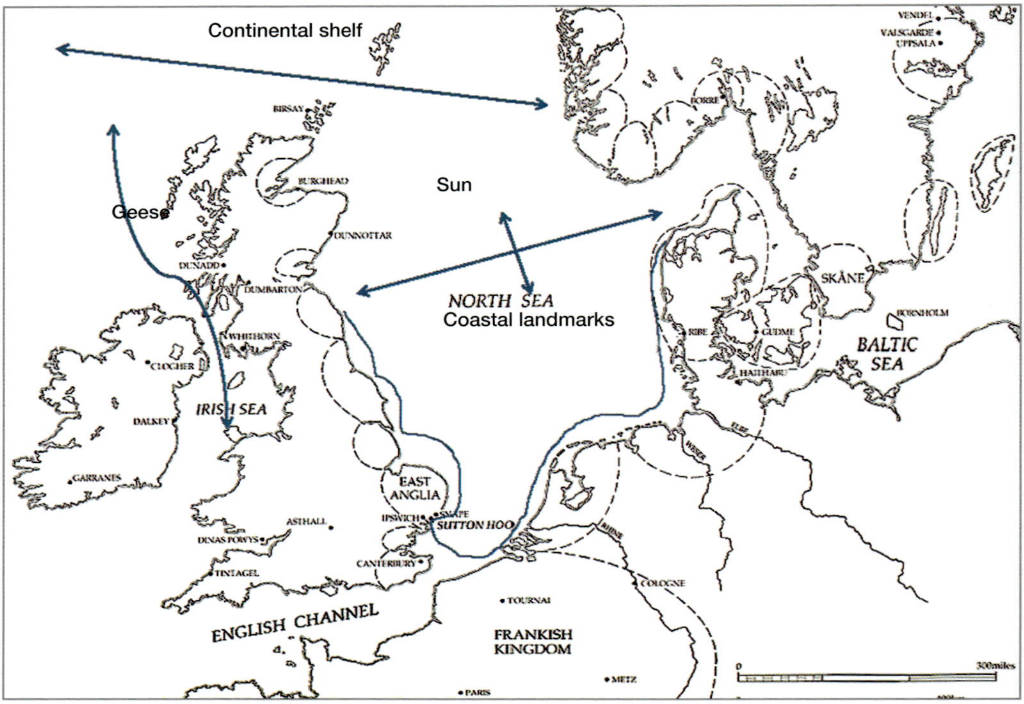

4.3 Early medieval navigation in the North Sea.

Numerous log-boats have survived in Britain (for example in bogs) across a long time-frame.[6] Nine well-preserved log-boats, dating from the Middle Bronze age to the Iron Age were excavated by the Cambridge Archaeological Unit at Must Farm, Flag Fen, Cambridgeshire, in association with a settlement. The boats were all made of oak, to a variety of designs. The oldest log-boat (no.3, at 1200–1250 BCE) was 4.34 m long and 0.70 m wide, with a transom stern and rounded prow incorporating a thick wooden lug, perhaps for fixing a towrope **(FIG 4.4a and b)**.[7] A dug-out log-boat was retrieved from the sea at Covehithe in Suffolk, and radiocarbon-dated to the eighth–ninth century CE **(FIG 4.4c)**.[8] The simple log-boat was developed into the more boat-shaped form of the expanded longboat. The procedure was recorded in Finland in 1935 **(FIG 4.5)**. It involved cutting into the log and undercutting it to give extra thin walls. These were expanded by heating and held open by struts. Then the struts were replaced by a permanent frame to which the wash strakes could be fastened, providing additional freeboard.[9] In the early medieval north, the prime assemblage of expanded dug-outs was excavated by Ole Klindt Jensen at Slusegård on the Baltic island of Bornholm. Among *c.* 1400 graves, 45 were burials in boats, surviving as thin-walled dark stains – about 4.5 m long and

4.4 (a) Bronze Age log boat (Boat 3) from Must Farm village at Flag Fen, showing (b) transom groove in the stern and integral lug at the bow (Courtesy Cambridge Archaeological Unit). (c) The eighth century CE Covehithe logboat (now lost). A photograph labelled "18.6.98 Dug out canoe (at Dunwich Beach) brought in by Rodney Collett from off Covehithe. Overall length 16'5"; width 2'2" tapering to 1'6"".

pointed at both ends - and determined by Ole Crumlin-Pedersen as originating as expanded dug-outs. The positive identifications of the wood used were of oak, that is freshly cut oak - or "butter-oak". "The trunks must have been perfectly straight and unblemished oak trees from Bornholm's own forests".[10] Two of the recently excavated boats at sixth-seventh century Snape have been interpreted as expanded dug-outs, comparable with those defined at Slusegård **(FIG 4.6)**. Organic preservation was good at Snape and the boats were also determined as being made of oak, also likely to be freshly cut oak.[11] These boats could be punted in shallow waters and paddled in deeper. The expanded dug-out had a very long usage and a wide geographical distribution from Scandinavia to South-East Asia. In Scandinavia and Britain finds continue to turn up into the medieval period.[12] Possibly they never became completely redundant until the invention of plastic.

The river Humber was crossed in the Bronze Age by a wooden boat *c.* 11 m long made from planks caulked with moss, stitched together with yew thongs rising from a base *c.* 2 m wide made of three planks joined together with bars rammed through upstanding cleats. It was found at North Ferriby and was presumably paddled across the tidal Humber to South Ferriby, and was large

4.5 The process of making an expanded wall dug-out (a *haapio*) recorded in Finland, in Ahlainen, Satakunda, Finland in 1935.

enough to carry cows.[13] The Dover boat, of a similar date and build, has been reconstructed and taken nine people for a trip around Dover harbour. It has also been to sea and taken part in the great river race on the Thames[14] (FIG 4.7). An Iron Age ship was found in many pieces of limewood (*Tilia*) with weapons in a peat bog at Hjortspring on the island of Als in Denmark – it was 19 m long and dated to the fourth century BCE. The experimental reconstruction of this 'war canoe', *Tilia Alsie*, was achieved by the Hjortspring Boat Guild with careful crafting and measurement assisted by personnel from the Marinarkæologisk Forskningscenter (NMF), Roskilde (FIG 4.8). It was found to be hard to steer but fast and seaworthy: 18 paddlers achieved 6.7 knots at 57 strokes a minute[15] (FIG 4.9). This project was a model of maritime experimental archaeology and we will revisit it in Chapter 5.

4.6 One of the Snape thin-walled dugouts being defined in excavations directed by William Filmer Sankey and Tim Pestell.

Britannia was a Roman colony for four centuries (*c.*43 to *c.*410 CE), and they left behind a considerable infrastructure of roads, farmland and monumental buildings. There were surviving harbours and ports, but remains of ships are, as yet, a rarity. Leaving aside the degree to which seafarers of all backgrounds can relay information from generation to generation (which might be more significant than we think), there are plenty of indications

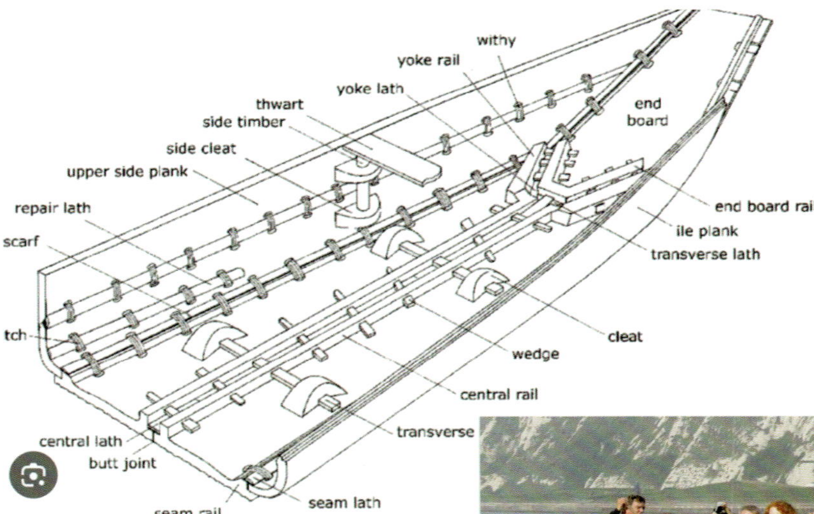

4.7 Axonometric projection of the excavated section of the Dover boat and the half-size reconstruction on an excursion.

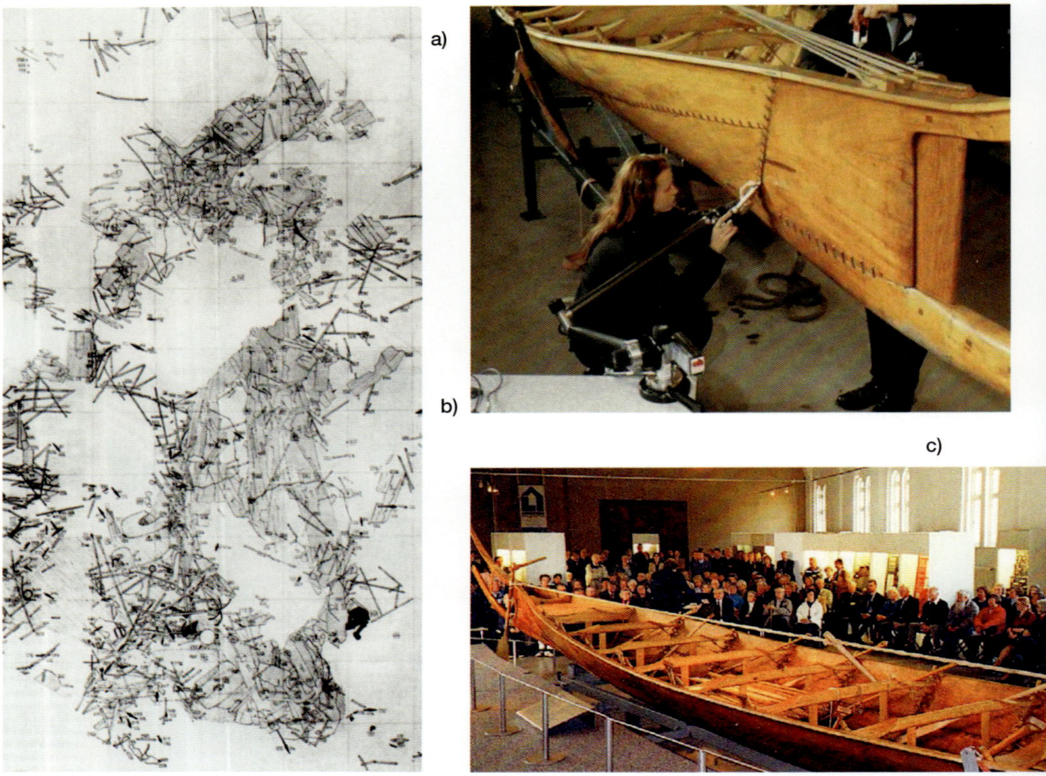

4.8 The Hjortspring Iron Age paddled warship *Tilia Ailse* (a) Plan of the remains as discovered in 1921 over a 1-metre grid, showing holes made through it by peat diggers (Rosenberg 1937, Planche III); (b) the reconstruction built of spars and panels of linden (*tilia*), sewn together with linden bast. It was surveyed in three dimensions by Marinarkæologisk Forskningscenter (NMF) Roskilde (Photo W.Karrasch); (c) *Tilia* on display at Schloss Gottorf. Note the (hypothetical) hogging truss and seats for the paddlers.

of Roman rowing boats from emperors Trajan to Allectus **(FIG 4.10)**. The fast Roman patrol boats that operated on the Rhine are likely to have left some kind of legacy. They were both rowed and sailed **(FIG 4.11)**. There have been a few excavations of Roman ships in Britain - notably Blackfriars I, a cargo boat carrying building stone that sank in the Thames, apparently after hitting another boat.[16] It was constructed with a carvel-built plank hull fastened to floor beams and side beams that constituted its frame, using massive iron hooked nails with the end hammered over the beam. It was flat bottomed without a keel, and had an upcurving carvel-built hull and a mast resting on the floor and supported by a cross beam **(FIG 4.12)**. It was dated by pottery, and a coin of Domitian found in the mast step, to the second century CE.[17] The build was thought to be untypical of the Romans, and the idea was

4.9 The Hjortspring Iron Age paddled warship *Tilia Ailse* (a) The boat in harbour; (b) the reconstructed vessel at sea, the wind at force 6 on the Beaufort scale, waves c. 1 metre high (from a video taken by Nadia Haupt).

4.10 Roman rowing ships depicted on Trajan's column and a coin of Allectus.

4.11 Reconstruction of a Roman military patrol vessel found at Mainz on the Rhine, dated to the fourth century CE.

floated that it was conceived in Britain or in Brittany, land of the Veneti, since its frame-first build and massive cross-beams seem to match Julius Caesar's description of the Veneti ships.[18] Caesar had some experience of the Veneti: before he invaded Britain (in 55 BCE) he had to deal with them since they were controlling traffic in the Channel. His rowed galleys were no match for their tall sailing ships, that is until the Romans equipped themselves with long poles with hooks on the end to cut the shrouds supporting their masts. A drop in the wind then made them easy prey for the Roman galleys: a useful lesson in how fighting ships may be more reliable and effective rowed rather than sailed - a rowing ship is not necessarily inferior in effect. There is a logic in proposing, as a generality, that load-carrying ships, or ships on long distance diplomatic and trading missions, or ships on the way to meet an adversary, do so under sail. But they fight under oars.

Given the likely exchange of information between shipbuilders, even across political borders, the Blackfriars 1 ship may have been built for the Roman fleet.[19] Paul Johnstone also explored the origins of Atlantic craft still in operation, such as the Portuguese *saveiro* and *meia luas*, with their prominent rising prows and powerful oars pivoting on iron spikes for operating off the Atlantic beaches **(FIG 4.13)**. If we do not want to label these Atlantic craft as "Celtic" it is certain that they are built for action in their particular western seas. The prominent rising prow might put prestige in the minds of those who

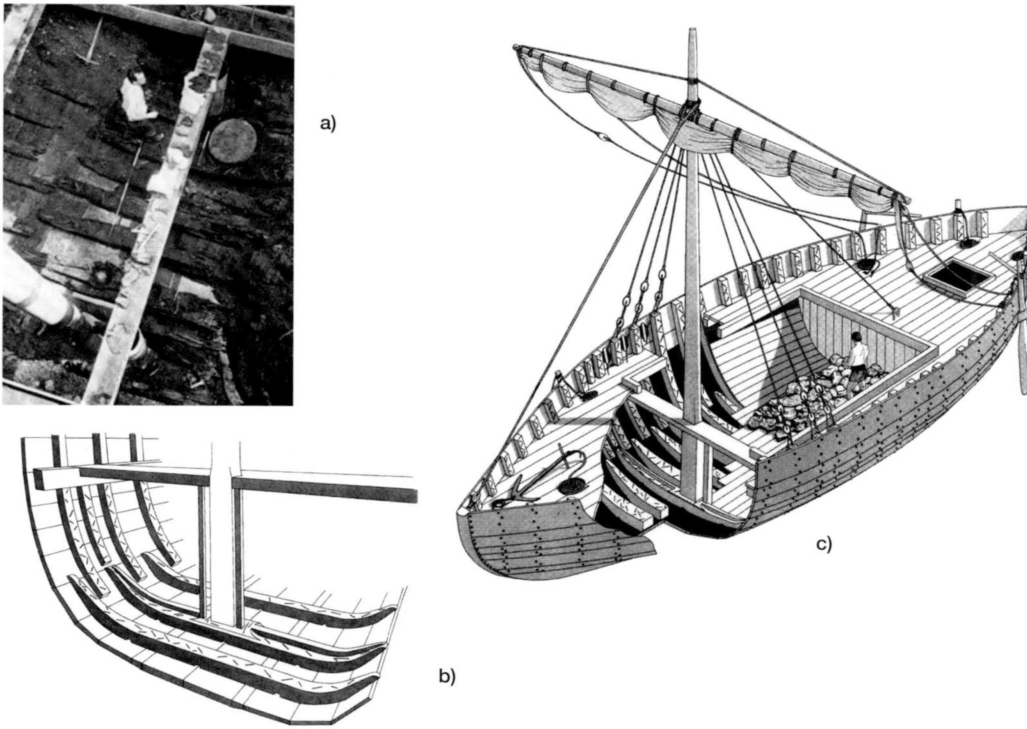

4.12 The Blackfriars I Roman ship: (a) Peter Marsden on site (b) construction and (c) reconstruction.

4.13 A Portuguese *saveiro* entering the Atlantic, pushed through the breaking waves by oxen bearing on a timber fork at the stern.

built *Sutton Hoo 1*; or it might ease entry and exit procedure at the entrance to tidal estuaries, or it might be coincidental. However, even if there is a Roman or Romano-Celtic type of ship-build, it does not seem that it was transferred seamlessly to the English.

INLAND AND COASTAL BRITAIN

In early medieval Britain travel by river was supplemented by travel along Roman roads (or vice versa). The savage encounters between the emerging kingdoms of East Anglia, Northumbria and Mercia recounted above took place on a Roman road from Lincoln to York where it crossed the Rivers Trent, Thorne and Winwaed, leaving open the question of how much of the journey was by water and how much by road. The two modes were most probably used in combination, depending on the purpose of the journey and its load, as recounted in Chapter 1. A modern-day yachtsman-archaeologist, John Makepeace, studied a range of east coast summer voyages under sail connecting the landfalls between the Humber and the Firth of Forth. He wanted to investigate the coastal connectivity between Northumbria and Pictland. Here are the times he recorded under sail:

Sailing times on the Northumbrian coast

Assuming steady wind on the starboard quarter (easterly) and a speed of 5 knots.

Humber- Scarborough	9.5 hours
Scarborough - Whitby	2.5 hours
Whitby- Wearmouth	7 hours
Wearmouth to Jarrow	2 hours
Wearmouth to Budle Bay	10 hours
Budle Bay to St Abbs	4 hours
St Abbs to The Forth	3 hours
Total: Humber to the Forth	**c.36 hours** [20]

Suitably rigged and cannily steered, a shallow-keeled boat of Viking type could be sailed into estuaries and up rivers to reach the major settlements on their banks (especially monasteries). Such boats could be beached in tidal waters (and kept upright on hard standing where necessary) or moored afloat on the river bank for a rapid getaway. A mooring near an old Roman bridge or a new Saxon one would allow a quick transfer of troops or cargo. In the seventh century, combination journeys like that supposed for the battle of the River Idle, or Utta's journey from Gateshead to fetch King Oswiu's new queen from Kent, would seem to be the norm (Chapter 1). It is not impossible to imagine horses as well as warriors on board – they were to cross the channel at the

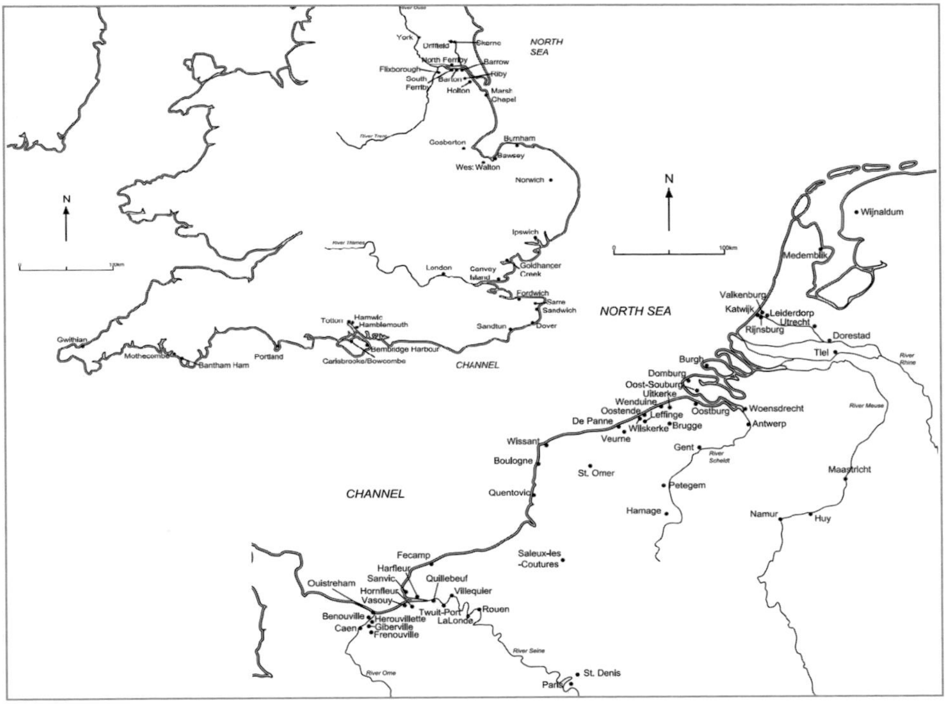

4.14 Britain's busy coasts: harbours, beachmarkets and landfalls in the Channel and North Sea, sixth to eighth century.

time of the Norman Conquest. After the Roman imperial regime collapsed, the regulations for land and water traffic may have collapsed with it, introducing a brief era of unsupervised travel. If this is credible, the tidal beaches, estuaries, rivers, Roman roads and ancient trackways would have made the island of Britain in its formative period a place with a diversity of free movement, its waterways alive with boats of all sizes. By the eighth century, however, new key destinations were planted on coasts and estuaries, monasteries in the north and west and *wics* in the south and east. The royal connections and exotic assemblages suggest that *wics* (beach markets) may have revived a toll of some kind. This shift may reflect an increase in overseas traffic and of journeys under sail. When that happened is unknown, but, for East Anglia at least, a case is building for the seventh century.

Britain's southern and eastern waters were getting increasingly busy during the sixth, seventh and into the eighth century, and we have already taken stock of the development of sea traffic implied by finds along the south-eastern seaboards.[21] Finds are the silent signals of this connectivity, whether due to trade or people moving between communities they know on either shore

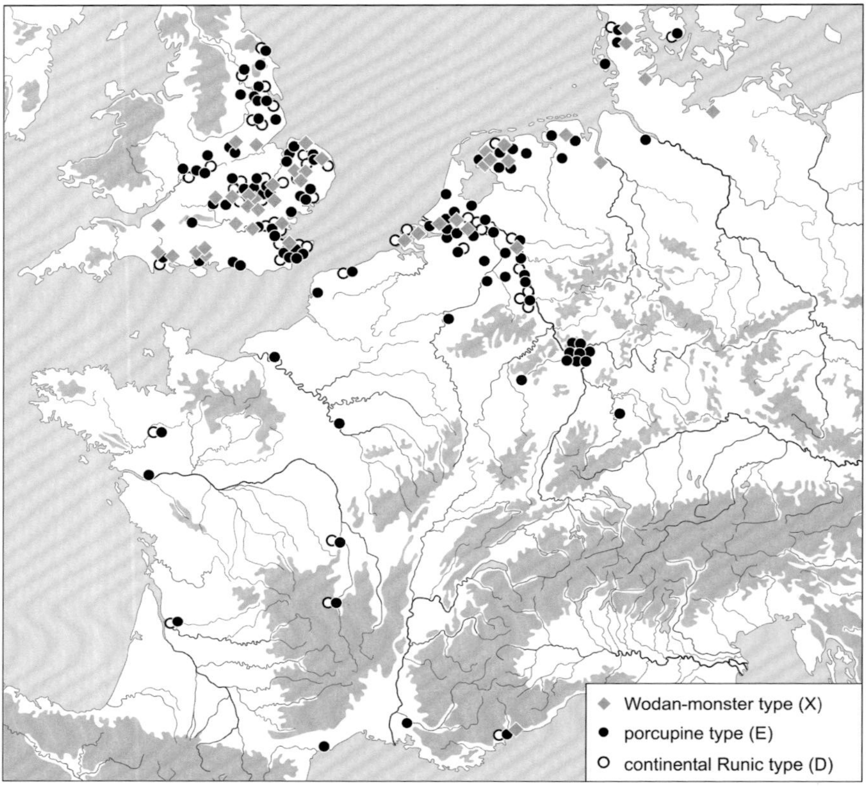

4.15 A new trade axis: eighth-century trade networks implied by the distribution of silver sceattas.

(FIG 4.14). We have already noted a host of exotic imports including bag rings of African ivory, and raw glass (and objects made of it) originating in the east Mediterranean from the fifth century onwards, coins, used or recycled from the Rhineland or the Aegean, beads of glass and amber, and in the late sixth century, drop handled bowls, buckets and flagons from the Byzantine empire. Sutton Hoo and Rendlesham exercised magnetic attraction to these later imports, but they are not alone. Objects made in England are also going the other way, from the island to the continent, activating a large maritime zone. But as the seventh century progresses there is an increased emphasis in the axis of exchange from Britain towards the Rhine mouth and the continent **(FIG 4.15)**. No doubt religious, economic and political forces were encouraging this move. Previous links were not eradicated; evidence of continuing exchange with Scandinavia has been detected in the eighth and ninth centuries as we shall see.

4.16 The Nydam boat built *c.* 320 CE, in the Museum at Schloss Gorttorf, Schleswig, with detail of an oarlock and the rudder.

THE NORTHERN SEAS: PAST AND FUTURE

The Germanic immigrants came across the sea from Saxony, Jutland and probably Norway, so it makes sense to seek the rise of English seafaring in the North Sea and the Baltic. Unfortunately, rather few boats have been found so far in the northern seas, and we only have suggestive images provided by documentary hints and images carved on rocks until the Nydam finds dating to the fourth century **(FIG 4.16)**. Since we are looking at traditions as well as innovations, it seems legitimate to look also at the better documented Viking periods, for signs of what might have been practised already, but not yet rediscovered. Thus, in the case of the northern seas we shall look forwards as well as backwards in the search for ship-building inspiration.

The Nydam boats were clinker built and equipped only for rowing, while

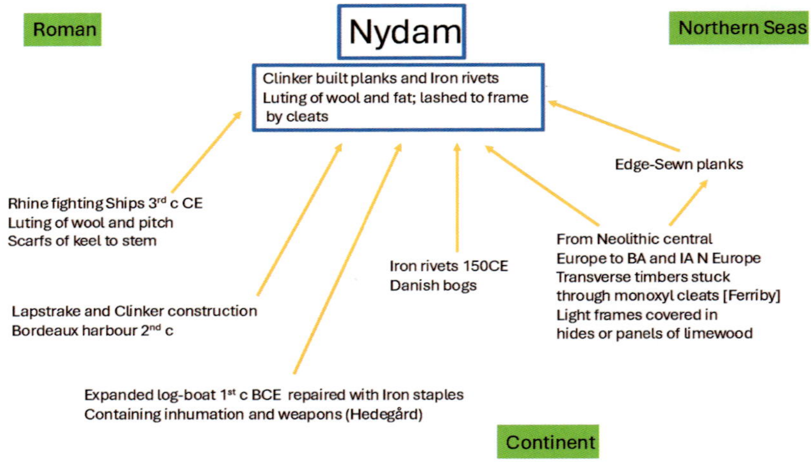

4.17 Contributions to Nydam's ancestry: hypothetical sources of elements of construction in a Nydam ship (Bockius 2013).

Logboats and expanded logboats

Clinker construction

'Nordic' rowlocks

Iron staples

4.18 Geographical sources of Nydam's ancestry (Bockius 2017).

Nydam: early fourth century

Kvalsund: late eighth century (reconstruction)

Oseberg: early ninth century

4.19 Nautical evolution in the Baltic: Nydam - Kvalsund - Oseberg.

the first undoubted sailing vessel of the Vikings is still that found intact under a mound at Oseberg, made in *c.* 820 and buried in 834.[22] It is interesting to note the research that reveals that Nydam itself had deep origins, with fittings and building techniques being drawn from sources as far back as the Neolithic (FIG 4.17). The geographical distribution of these attributes is also interesting. Although rare, evidence of clinker building and rowlocks has been found in central Scandinavia. The Nydam boat's essential ancestry has been seen as rooted in the expanded log boat, while the change from paddling to rowing, the introduction of iron fastenings and (less certainly) clinker building itself has been credited to Scandinavians serving in the Roman army and bringing ideas back home (FIG 4.18).[23] The Nydam analyses suggest a wide and deep range for the boat-builders' discourse which is unlikely to have narrowed in the following two centuries.

After Nydam, a rowing boat, the search has continued for the first signs of sail, which was to flourish in Viking times with well-preserved ships excavated at Oseberg and Gokstad (FIG 4.19). The fragmentary remains found at Gredstedbro belonged to a clinker-built rowing ship 20–25 m long, dated to the seventh century by dendrochronology. Large enough to carry people or cargo, it had a well-worn flat keel enabling it to penetrate creeks or the river where it was found.[24] A new stepping stone towards sail is claimed for two

4.20 Oseberg reconstruction *Edda*, on trials in 1988.

boats found and excavated under rescue conditions at Salme in Estonia in 2008-2012.[25] The boats were discovered during the laying of a pipeline and were badly damaged. Clinker-built construction of planks with iron fastenings was clear, and both had a final use for mass burial supposedly of their crews. *Salme 1*, was 11.5m long and deemed to be a rowing boat well-suited to travel round the Estonian islands. It contained 8 bodies. *Salme II* was 17-17.5 m long and contained the remains of 34 individuals, all men, and determined by stable isotopes to have emanated from Sweden and by DNA to include several brothers.[26] Various dates have appeared in the media, but for *Salme II* the excavator Jüri Peets is quoted as saying "our ship dates from the year 750".[27] The radiocarbon dates of the skeletons and other finds suggest that the men, who bore the scars of battle, died and were buried around 750, so the boats themselves will have been built earlier, although presumably still later than *Sutton Hoo 1*. Under *Salme II* there was a vertical soil shadow suggesting the stub of a keel, and "remains of coarse fabric of linen weave may belong to the sail draped over the bodies". On this basis *Salme II* has been hailed as "the oldest archaeologically excavated sailing ship in the Baltic region." Details of a rigging, if there was any, await publication. *Kvalsund II*, was discovered dismantled in a bog in Herøy, near Ålesund in 1920. It was clinker built, about 18 m (59 ft) long with a detachable steering oar, and was discovered together with a smaller, 9.5 m (31 ft) long rowing boat (*Kvalsund I*). Once thought to be close in date to Sutton Hoo, and to have been designed to sail, *Kvalsund II*, has been redated by dendrochronology to 780-800 and its sailing credentials are doubted. It is regarded as 'transitional' between the pre-Viking rowing boat and the Oseberg ship.[28]

Oseberg's keel, its mast, the fixtures for rigging, the steering oar and the so-called 'tacking spar' all point to a ship intended to sail. All the same, the performance of the reconstructed ship (*Dronningen*, later named *Edda*)

a) b) c) d)

4.21 Postcards from a capsizing. (a) Attemping to tack. (b) Capsized, author clinging on. (c) Flotsam. (d) Aftermath.

emphasised the skills required to sail close to the wind. One of the research questions for the sea-trial of this ship was whether it could tack, this implying how dependent it was on oars and a crew to handle them, as opposed to space for weapons, cargo or warriors who must arrive fresh **(FIG 4.20)**. The answer was, yes it could make a few points to windward, but it was risky; it made only a few runs before capsizing and sinking to the bottom of the Herøy fjord **(FIG 4.21)**.[29] This experiment, which was carried out in 1988, was not conclusive since, naturally enough, instructions on how to sail such a fast moving shallow-keeled ship were not buried with her. The build may have been at fault, leading to a weakened prow, or the sail too large (based on the angle of the shrouds). The crew were expert sailors, but there may not have been enough of them: the Viking ships seen on Gotland picture stones show the full sail controlled by eight or more crew manning sheets, giving, in theory, more chance of rapid adjustment to gusts of wind **(FIG 4.22)**.

Experimental archaeology can rarely be decisive, especially in performance: its limits have to be approached by trial and error, with the long inheritance of the original crew in mind. The first sailors must have had something

4.22 Gotland picture stones of the eighth century, showing sail handling with multiple sheets.

in common with the first hang-gliders, a high level of courage combined with an instinctive reaction to the anarchy of the winds. *Edda* was resurrected as the *Saga Oseberg*, following new studies at Roskilde of the archaeological (rather than the exhibited) ship, giving it greater keel rocker. It was found to perform badly, something at first attributed to the new design. Persevering with the trials, it was found that a good balance between hull and sail was achieved by moving the ballast to the centre of the ship and repositioning the off-duty crew. The ship could then successfully beat to windward and tack.[30] Similarly, while all the oars from the Oseberg ship were found complete, some had been interpreted as being too short for the ship, compared to more recent oars for open boats. The length of the Oseberg oars varies up to half a metre, so the shorter oars could have been used amidships and the longer oars in the bow and stern, which rise higher above the water. When the replica oars for *Saga Oseberg* were made equivalent to the originals, their individual lengths proved to match the longitudinal curved shape of *Saga Oseberg*, and trials showed that it was possible to row the ship at a speed of 5.0 knots.

Following the successful second sailing test of *Saga Oseberg*, Vibeke Bischoff remarked: "All ships have a personality that will reveal itself with use. If the ship does not manoeuvre effectively, the test sailor must keep asking questions and try to understand the deeper relationships between the ship's

4.23 (a) Gokstad ship in the Viking Ship Museum, Oslo. (b) detail of hull and oar-ports. (c) Photo of *Viking* leaving Bergen, with a jib set. (d) The *Viking* at Chicago in 1892.

parts and details. Doing this means that one must be willing to change one's preconceptions in order to let reconstructions 'speak' for themselves." The implication is that the crew is on trial as well as the ship. Bischoff's 2021 article includes a 19-point plan for trials that trust the design (and the archaeology) which is not without its utility for our reconstruction of *Sutton Hoo I*.[31]

The ocean-going ship (length 23.8 m) built around 890 CE and recovered intact from a blue clay burial mound at Gokstad was altogether more robust: its 'replica', named *Viking*, sailed the Atlantic from Bergen to Newfoundland, then to New York and via the Hudson river and the Erie canal to Lake Michigan and to Chicago, where the historic arrival of Columbus was being celebrated. **(FIG 4.23)**. This was in 1892-3, still in touch with the great days of sea-going sail. The hull was clinker-built with 16 planks a side, guided in position by temporary moulds, and fastened along their lower edges. As in the original, the lowest nine planks on each side, those below the water-line, were double

a)

b)

4.24 Humber Keel (a) making way against the wind, and (b) being bow-hauled by a crew of two.

thickness with small cleats left upstanding with a hole so they could be lashed to the frames at this level, while the upper seven planks were thinner and fastened to the frame with iron nails. The captain, Magnus Andersen, reported that the flexible join to the lower hull allowed it to weather heavy seas without leaking. Sixteen oar-ports per side were situated on strake 3 from the top, allowing for two planks of freeboard above the oars. These design factors seem to have allowed for greater stability under sail. Captain Andersen was proud of his (starboard) steering oar and reported no great difficulty in tacking; on the other hand he had equipped the vessel with a triangular foresail, claiming that the Vikings probably used one, although Arne-Emil Christensen was not convinced.[32] The five Skuldelev ships, celebrated in the museum built for them at Roskilde, Denmark, are the best studied first millennium ships of the northern seas. Their reconstructions include *Ottar*, *Roar Ege*, *Helge Ask*, *Kraka Fyr* and the largest, the *Sea Stallion from Glendalough*, a reconstruction of the Skuldelev 2 warship built in Ireland in 1042, and at 30m the longest of the early clinker-built ships so far encountered. Its slim shape, propelled by 60 oars or an enormous sail, also make it one of the fastest.[33]

Where would the Sutton Hoo ship fit in? The development of the sailing ship in the northern seas, as we have it so far, is placed in order by the dates obtained by radiocarbon, or better, by dendrochronology. The earliest claimed is *Salme II* at *c.*750 with its stubby keel, and perhaps *Kvalsund II* with an associated mast, but the consensus still lies with Oseberg as the first actually built to sail.[34] After the Vikings, the story continues through into the second millennium with heavy broad flat-bottomed hulks and cogs. These became floating castles in the Middle Ages, and sailed into the nineteenth century with ever broader, heavier hulls, carrying larger cargoes or companies of fighting men. They could still capsize, as shown by the fate of the Mary Rose which came to grief and sank while going about with the lower gun ports open.[35] But the square sail on these more stable hulls could allow a ship to make to windward. The *Humber Keel*, equipped with a square mainsail, and often a topsail, could gather a head wind that propelled it along the line of a canal, fending off the bank as necessary with a long pole (a 'stower'). When the wind dropped, the two-person crew could don a canvas harness and bow-haul it along the tow path **(FIG 4.24)**. The Humber keels sailed up the Hull river to Beverley, up the Trent to Nottingham or along the canal network to Sheffield.[36]

In the northern seas it would appear that all the ships so far discovered were propelled by oars alone, both before Sutton Hoo and for a century after. The Sutton Hoo ship is, however, part of another story that concerns the subset of monumental ship-burials defined by Jan Bill.[37] This definition leaves aside the ships of lesser rank or different context, such as mass burial or as offerings (which includes Salme and Kvalsund), or small (which includes Slusegård on Bornholm, Vendel and Valsgärde). On this basis, the rise of monumental ship burial in Norway begins at present with the two well-preserved rowing ships in mounds on Karmøy, the Storhaug ship built *c.*770, buried 779; and Grønhaug ship built *c.*780 buried 790–5, while the earliest ships in the series of the monumental mounds of north-west Europe are the two at Sutton Hoo (early seventh) and one at Snape (perhaps later sixth century). It has therefore been argued that monumental or royal ship burial, as we have it, began in East Anglia in the late sixth/early seventh century and was taken up in western Norway in the early eighth.[38] But by that time the Norwegian polities were forming and the context of monumentality was firmly within the Scandinavian social and belief system of the time, to be manifested further in the full Viking age.[39]

Even if East Anglia had provided some kind of prompt for high status ship-burial in Scandinavia, it does not follow that Sutton Hoo provided a model for the Viking ship: there is a gap between the one and the other of 150 years. But evidence for continued pre-Viking connections between Scandinavia and the British Isles in this period has been creeping up over the years, in part due to metal detectorists. Evidence for exchange in the fifth to seventh century is strong in the form of personal brooches and glass, after which it tails off.[40] The hiatus in the contact across the North Sea can be explained as this period (mid-seventh to late eighth) was the time of the conversion in England, and while there may not have been much enthusiasm for it in East Anglia, England as a whole switched its interests to the Rhineland and the Continent. Nevertheless, new evidence from Ribe in Denmark (whetstones and reindeer combs) suggests that long sea journeys from Norway to the southern North Sea were being made in the eighth century. These, it has been argued, allowed a new generation of pre-Viking sailors to get to know the English east coast.[41] In general, it would not be surprising if contact between Norway and East Anglia continued through the eighth century, so to speak, under the radar. It is at least certain that East Anglia, and Sutton Hoo in particular, constitute a frontier zone in the seventh-eighth century between the Germanic, British and Roman worlds, a hot spot where amazing things can happen. Clearly the picture will be modified by discoveries of more monumental ship-burials, but, since Sutton Hoo has been nominated the instigator of the ritual, it could play a pivotal role in the development of the ship – so all eyes are on us. The grave goods in Mound 1 are an amalgam between British, Roman, continental, Byzantine, Scandinavian and early English cultures; and as with these artefacts, so with the ship. For this reason, if no other, we need to consider the potential influence of Christian Europe, Rome's successor.

IN THE MEDITERRANEAN

Some kind of interchange between East Anglia and the Mediterranean was intimated by the large number of finds from Byzantium and the east reaching England in the sixth and seventh centuries (FIG 4.25). The link between Sutton Hoo and the Mediterranean lit up following the Christianisation of the English that took root in the late seventh century, at which time Rome and the Holy Land became key destinations. But, as already noted, a connection between East Anglia and Byzantium was already active a century earlier. In addition to the tally of imports and exports, the most striking links with late sixth-century Byzantium are provided by the drop handled bowl and flagon from Prittlewell, the officer's bucket and silverware from Sutton Hoo, the warrior's jacket from Taplow (also depicted on the Sutton Hoo helmet) and the items of imitation Byzantine jewellery worn by elegant East Anglian women noted by Helen Geake.[42] The idea that these finds, especially the copper alloy vessels, were souvenirs taken back to England by mercenaries and buried with them in the homeland was advanced by Marlia Mundell Mango, notably in the case of Prittlewell and Sutton Hoo, as we saw in Chapter 2. In a recent article Helen Gittos has taken the hypothesis further by identifying the military action that the East Anglian warriors might actually have been involved in. She draws attention to the efforts made by Tiberius II (578–82) to recruit fighting men

4.25 Sutton Hoo in the Mediterranean. Provenance of objects found in Mound 1 and sites of early monasteries.

on both sides of the Alps, in order to reinforce the Byzantine army in its war with the Sasanians. The Prittlewell prince who died between 575 and 605, and whose grave goods closely resemble those of a warrior burial at Sardis, may have been one of those recruits, and a comrade in arms with the future occupant of Sutton Hoo's Mound 1.[43] She concludes "I am arguing that it is likely that the men buried in the princely burials at Prittlewell and Sutton Hoo Mound 1 served, with a group of their contemporaries, as cavalry soldiers in the *Foederati* recruited by Tiberius in 575 in the wars with the Sasanians on the eastern front."[44]

In the likely supposition that this idea has substance, it can be deduced that East Anglian warriors knew the Mediterranean ships of the late sixth century and indeed spent long voyages on them. Our travellers would have been exposed to the ships and boats of the Mediterranean in all their variety, from fishing boats to patrol boats to cargo boats to galleys and fighting ships, together with variations in regional building traditions.[45] The Mediterranean maritime tradition of wide-bodied cargo vessels under sail would seem to extend back to the Bronze age in the fourteenth century BCE, with the Ulu Burun ship. The Kyrenia ship (fourth century BCE) had a broad sail on a spar. The Phoenician second-century ship depicted on a bas relief had a foresail (*artemon*) to help the ship turn. A Mediterranean contemporary to Sutton Hoo is the Yassi Ada ship that sank off Turkey in *c.* 626 CE.[46] All these had deep sides and a space below deck for cargo – or passengers.[47] *Yenikapı 16*, one of 37 shipwrecks in the Theodosian harbour outside Constantinople, dated 720–890 CE by radiocarbon, was an imperial naval galley with 25 oars each side.[48] *Yenikapı 11* is a ship from the same find spot, its timbers dated within the first half of the early seventh century. It was 11.2 m long and 3.8 m in the beam built of Turkish pine with a keel of oak. The build was a combination of shell first and frame first, mortice and tenon joints below, nailed to the frame above. *Yenikapı 11* was defined as a 'round ship', that is, a ship propelled primarily or entirely by sail. This structure could imply that the shift from a shell-based to a skeleton-based building philosophy was already well underway by the early seventh century.[49]

All six of the round ships documented by the international team, with the possible exception of *Yenikapı 24*, were sailed with a single mast fitted with a lateen or settee (quadrilateral lateen) sail, and they would have been steered with a pair of quarter rudders. Another near contemporary to *Sutton Hoo 1* is the Ma'agan Mikhael B ship discovered in shallow water off the coast of Israel (**FIG 4.26**). It was 23 m long, with a hull constructed of softwood planks nailed to a hardwood frame and dated between 650 and 750 CE. A mast step and masthead, blocks, ropes and textiles had survived in striking detail. Comparison of the hooked masthead with illustrations showed that the boat had a lateen (triangular) sail. The ship was carrying a cargo of early Islamic period glass.[50]

EARLY ENGLISH JOURNEYS

Viking ships crossed the North Sea, the Irish Sea and the Channel, and also travelled by rivers, extending their range up the Baltic into Russia and via the Dnepro and Black Sea to Byzantium where some served in the imperial guard. In earlier chapters, we have met adventurous East Anglian warriors of two centuries earlier, seeking their fortune in the Byzantine army. They may have travelled by road but must have made sea crossings, and perhaps also travelled by river, in the process encountering different kinds of watercraft. The plausibility of such journeys to the continent and the Mediterranean, is markedly improved in the later seventh century when the travels of the newly converted English Christians began to be documented. A glimpse of the possible routes reaches us via the documented journeys of the clerics of the first generation of English Christians to Italy, Sicily, Syria, the Levant and the Bosphorus,

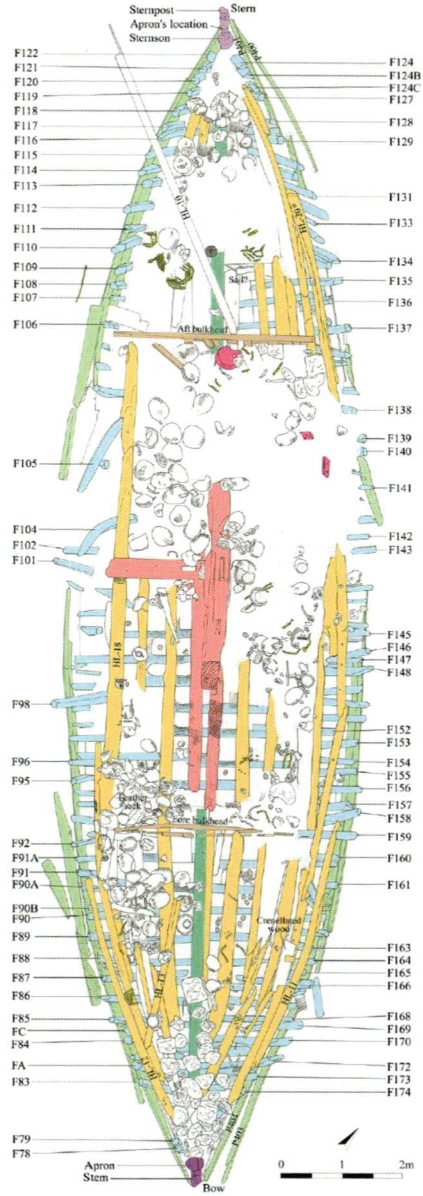

a)

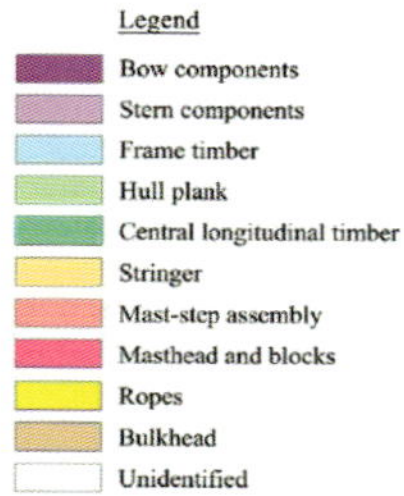

4.26 The well-preserved shipwreck Ma'agan Mikhael B excavated off the Mediterranean coast of Israel and dated mid-seventh to mid-eighth centuries (a) Plan of the ship measuring 19.6 x 4.9 m. (b) The hook-shaped mast head showing the sheaves. (c) Turning blocks (d) Rope as restored in the laboratory.

b)

c)

d)

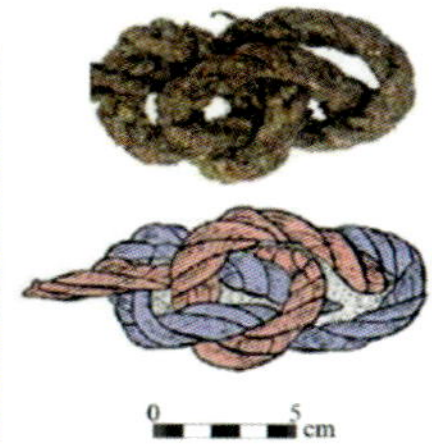

e)

4.27 Willibald's trip from Southampton to Syria via Sicily and back to Naples via Constantinople.

gateway to the Black Sea. Benedict Biscop, founder of Wearmouth (628-690), and Wilfred, Bishop of Ripon (633-*c.*709) made many journeys to the continent and to Rome, in one case at least travelling via Lyon. The numbers of books brought back to Northumbria implies some serious transport. Ceolfrid (*c.*642-716) abbot of Wearmouth-Jarrow, undertook a journey to Rome in the summer of 716, conveying a massive Bible weighing 34 kg as a present for the Pope from the distant north. He travelled by land from Jarrow to the Humber via Wearmouth (and probably other monasteries) to show off the Bible and say goodbye. On the fourth of July he embarked at the mouth of the Humber and crossed the Channel into France, but on the subsequent journey he fell ill and was carried on a horse-drawn litter as far as Langres where he died.[51] Across France he could have been following the river route via the Seine and the Marne (the longest river route in France) as far as Pont de Marne, a few kilometres north west of Langres. The journey may have been intended to continue by the River Saône, joining the Rhône at Lyon, arriving at Marseille, and thence by a Mediterranean passenger vessel to Ostia, the port of Rome.

The travels of the monk Willibald (*c.*700 - *c.*787), a native of Hampshire, are known thanks to the travelogue written by his literate and alert companion, a nun, Sister Hygeburg.[52] They left the Hamble in 721, crossed the Channel, thence to Rouen via the Seine, and probably the river route via the Langres

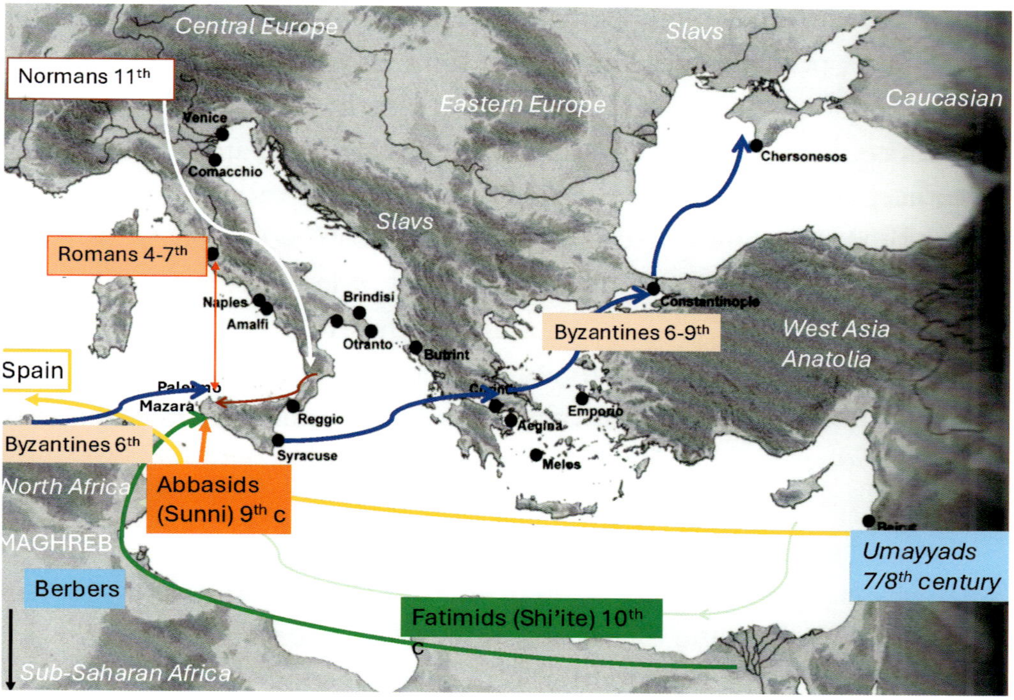

4.28 The unresting Mediterranean, sixth to eleventh century CE.

plateau and the river Saône and Rhône to Marseille, by sea to Lucca, then down the Italian peninsula to Rome, Naples and thence to Sicily's eastern ports, Catania and Syracuse. From there they crossed via Ephesus to the Levant. All these journeys were made by sea, port to port and no doubt depended on local crews with a wealth of inherited know-how **(FIG 4.27)**. In 725 Willibald and Hygeburg were touring Bethlehem and Jerusalem.

The party returned to Sicily by way of Tyre, Paphos in Cyprus, Ephesus and Constantinople. The sainted Willibald evaded the customs on departure from Syria, by sealing a consignment of precious balsam secreted in his calabash, with a layer of petroleum.[53] Off Sicily he collected pumice for smoothing vellum from deposits on the volcanic Lipari islands.[54] From Sicily they returned to Naples, reaching Benedict's monastery at Monte Cassino in 729 where Willibald would stay ten years. In 739 he was in Rome sent by the Pope to join his brother in Bavaria where he would found the Abbey of Eichstätt, dying there at the age of 87. He set a standard for visiting holy places rarely to be matched, but his journey is probably most singular in being recorded. The seventh- and eighth-century Mediterranean experienced a surge in traffic thanks partly to Christian pilgrimage, to the spread of Islam and the increased trade in slaves. Less than 100 years after the Sutton Hoo ship was buried, the English seemed to be well at home in the Mediterranean.

The emergence of Islam after the Hijrah (Muhammad's iconic journey from Mecca to Medina in 622CE) was redrawing the map of the Mediterranean as well as in seas to the east of Muhammad's Arabia[55] **(FIG 4.28)**. The Muslim army arrived at the Mediterranean coast in the early seventh century using the familiar camel route from Yemen to Syria run by the *Qureshi*, and were initially without ships. Caliph Uthman was persuaded by the governor of Ash-Sham (Mu'aawiya) to build a Mediterranean fleet in order to invade Cyprus. Having refurbished the port of Acre, Mu'aawiya assembled a variety of Byzantine boats from the Levantine coast, repaired them and invaded Cyprus in 649, forcing the surrender of the Cypriots at Qustantina (Salamis). He returned in 653, this time with a navy built by the Copts in Alexandria, with whom they had good relations. Al Muqawqis (the Head of the Copts) presented Muhammad with two slave girls one of whom became the mother of his son Ibrahim. The Copts also provided the first crews. The ships were built of planks of cedar from Lebanon either nailed or stitched together with coconut fibre, a technique known from Oman. The same fibre was used to make ropes and shrouds. The ships seemed to have resembled the Byzantine galleys (*dromons*) and used square sails for travelling with one or two banks of oars, without sails, for fighting battles. The Muslim navy also adopted the triangular *lateen* sail, which gave additional speed by lifting the bow. Naval weapons of the time were limited, but ship-to-ship combat mainly consisted of catapults for throwing rocks and fire, along with rows of archers firing ordinary and flaming arrows. Ropes with iron hooks were also used to bring down an enemy ship's mast and sails. In an engagement of 654CE, where the Muslim ships were outnumbered 3:1, they nevertheless manoeuvred their vessels in amongst the Byzantine ships, so the Muslim marines could slip overboard and tie the ships together. This created a platform for a land battle which the Muslims won. After this *Battle of the Masts*, Islam conquered the larger islands and were able to dominate traffic in the Mediterranean Sea.

These earliest engagements of Islam took place when Rædwald, Edwin, Penda and Oswiu were fighting to establish their kingdoms and vacillating between alignment to native Britain, ancestral Scandinavia, or the Christian empires of Rome or Byzantium. In the year that saw the Battle of the Masts, Oswiu king of Northumbria defeated Penda at the Battle of Winwaed and determined a Roman Christian future for Northumbria. Once the horizons of the English leaders had been raised above battles with each other, and beyond Scandinavia and the North Sea, there could be no retreat into insularity. There were too many attractive prospects in the new lands, new commodities, new ideas and technologies to confront. Potentially these included how to build, adapt, handle and navigate ships in new ways. To illuminate the inventive and ambitious mood of seventh-century East Anglia, if for no other reason, it is good to take these exotic happenings into account.

THE SUTTON HOO SHIP BUILDERS

This chapter has tried to evoke the world of Rædwald's shipwrights, the traditions they encountered on the island of Britain, the local memories of the Roman occupation and its fleets, their increasing knowledge of the neighbouring seas, west and south as well as east, and the new ideas encountered on the continent via its rivers and the Mediterranean via its ships. To this end, we explored the possible inheritance from their past and their likely understanding of the present, taking a tour in pursuit of contemporary fleets. Maritime knowledge can live long in ship's timbers, so it was legitimate to explore also the ships of the later Vikings, brought to light by Scandinavian archaeology, out of burials and from the seabed. At one further remove we can draw on the experiments these archaeologists have made, and the procedures they created for designing their reconstructions and recording their performance. Reconstructing an ancient ship is a collegiate affair, where the virtual college extends widely in time and space.

The creation of the Sutton Hoo Mound 1 ship was undertaken by the craft community in the Deben valley at the turn of the sixth to seventh century, at a time of increasing connectivity and innovation. New knowledge of travel in the continent and the Mediterranean has widened the potential exemplars available to the Sutton Hoo ship-builders, and the maritime world that the design, build and performance of our own reconstruction has to take into account. New ships continue to be discovered in the continental rivers and in the Mediterranean, and it is essential to keep a weather eye on them. However, it has to be said that the examples of such ships garnered from the Byzantine seas - built frame first, decked, with a cargo below, and carrying lateen sails - have provided few hints that nautical know-how was taken back home along with wrap-round jackets, drop-handle basins and folding camp stools. That is not to say that such rare items as the rigging of Ma'agan Mikheal B might not inspire ideas for rigging the Sutton Hoo ship. However, the archaeology of ships and shipping seen to date suggests strongly that the immediate technical ancestry of the Sutton Hoo ship has few contacts with imperial antecedents in Britannia or further afield and must lie in the surrounding seas, as many have long supposed. This is in keeping with the Germanic origin of the English and the likelihood that a ship would be designed to match its home waters and coasts. It would be good to have additional hard evidence for rowing and sailing boats nearer the date of Sutton Hoo, evidence which must still lie in the estuaries or coastal waters of south-east England or in the wider area of the southern North Sea and eastern Channel, the maritime zone in which the coastal and estuary areas of East Anglia, Kent, and the north west continent operated.

The natural geography suggested five kinds of boat for the English region, rafts, paddled log-boats and expanded log-boats for use in the lakes and calmer waters; more elusively, sharp-prowed rowing skiffs on the coasts and in the rivers - to cope with current - and, eventually, wider-bodied boats that could carry a sail for use in tidal waters and sea crossings. The handling of these watercraft demanded an intimate knowledge of the local waters. The monks mentioned in Chapter 2 being swept away by the currents on Tyne-side were using rafts to deliver building stone to a new monastery. The log-boats, like the rafts, were no doubt making numerous journeys by paddling or poling, perhaps too routine to mention. The clinker-built technique using hull-first overlapping planks fastened with rivets to a keel plank and to each other is the one used at Sutton Hoo and was seemingly developed in the north. It was possibly a local development from the Bronze Age plank boat or the expanded log boat, bringing the hull to a point fore and aft. This greatly increased the beam and carrying capacity and the control of steering. Other elements such as the keel with stem and stern posts, the use of iron rivets rather than stitching and the change from paddling to rowing, which took place at some time between Tilia Alsie and Nydam, may have been brought back by an earlier generation of mercenaries into Scandinavia, as concluded by Ole Crumlin-Pedersen.[56]

On the other hand, I believe that there is compelling evidence that the late sixth century in England was a time of outstanding innovation over a range of crafts (Chapter 3). The Sutton Hoo shipwrights were part of a creative community, engaged in an innovative project at a key moment in history. Between old allies in the east and north, new political interest in the south and west and the revival of Rome, they were creating a convincing English kingdom. While the smiths of the Deben community might have imitated some ideas from the battlefields of Syria, the shops in Sardis or the streets of Byzantium, they were nothing if not inventive, as shown by the animal menagerie exhibited in the Mound 1 metalwork, the variety of sword pommels in the Staffordshire hoard and the range of objects cast from Roman coins in the buckles using their own piece-moulds at Rendlesham.

The weavers were moved to develop luxury textiles as a combination of the new with the old. Preceding the builders of Northumbrian monasteries 'in the Roman manner', the Southumbrian carpenters designed and built halls that were "more ambitious than any other timber structures known from pre-Viking England" (or indeed Britain).[57]

These observations converge towards a conclusion that the Sutton Hoo ship, whatever its genesis, was an original invention - and why not? For the ship-builders at Sutton Hoo, Nydam would lie in the distant past, and only in that distant sense is it a model for *Sutton Hoo 1*. Even on an island where many kingdoms were being fashioned or refashioned from Roman or Iron Age models, the burials and crafts visited in Chapters 2 and 3 suggest that it is legitimate to see what has survived on the Deben as a sign of something original. From the many influences around it, it created a complex realpolitik designed to retain the friendship of the pagan ancestors and equip itself to interact with the Roman neo-Christian empire, while still retaining its independence. This is clearly what geography demands. I would not go so far as to suggest that the Sutton Hoo ship burials inspired similar practice in Scandinavia, let alone pre-ordained the idea of the Viking ship; these things belong to a zeitgeist rather than a brain wave; and their rediscovery is too sparse as yet to serve a generalisation - too much still lies buried. Considering, and discounting, a wide range of possible sources is a duty of research, which, granted, is never complete. But then working with what we have to create a reconstruction and a programme of experiment is itself bound to open new avenues of discovery - which is one sure reason for doing it. Then (as now) the ship was an ambassador for the kingdom. What inspired its design? What was its purpose? What was the message that it signalled? How would a reconstruction help to rediscover these things? To learn how all these challenges were met we will need to return to Suffolk, and fast-forward our readers into the twenty-first century.

5 | CONCEIVING THE PROJECT

Genesis of the reconstruction: purposes, principles and design

How the reconstructed Sutton Hoo (Mound 1) ship came to be proposed, initiated and funded is a somewhat entangled tale. The principal players of the early days were the Sutton Hoo Research Trust, the National Trust at Sutton Hoo and the Woodbridge Riverside Trust, all fiercely independent local organisations. They were also particular in their aims: some saw the reconstruction as an international research project, aligned with comparable ventures by other maritime nations, notably Denmark, Norway and Greece; while others saw it as an addition to the Sutton Hoo story designed to serve a wider public, and others again as a local initiative celebrating Woodbridge and its maritime heritage. Ideally these aims should be combined, and it was this that would become the mission of the Sutton Hoo Ship's Company.

The reconstruction of the ship from Mound 1 was certainly an enterprise with multiple objectives: to boost the cultural identity of the locality, to relive the earliest days of English seafaring, to promote an adventure that could be shared by the nation and to provide a fulfilling experience for a host of dedicated volunteers. But underpinning all these were the research objectives, the search for new knowledge which would last longest and have the greatest net impact for people of all ages in the future.

To ensure their long term value, research projects have a particular structure: defining the research questions (what we would like to know), evaluating the evidence (what's available), isolating the objectives (what we want to do), designing a programme to deliver them, carrying it out and publishing the results for the public, the participants, the sponsors and the academic community, custodians of the long-term memory of what was done and why. Applying this procedure to an experimental ship would be an aim in itself.

The Sutton Hoo Ship project began with an organisational phase 2015-2018, deciding where the ship should be built and who should do it; and a planning, design and procurement phase 2018-2021, at which point the keel was laid and the build began. At the time of writing, the build is expected to be complete in 2026 or 2027, to be followed by trials and voyages and eventual retirement to a place where it can be cared for and seen by visitors. This chapter focuses on the events and progress up to 2025, including ideas for the future as then perceived - these will undoubtedly change, but an important part of the research result is recording what was said and done. Here we

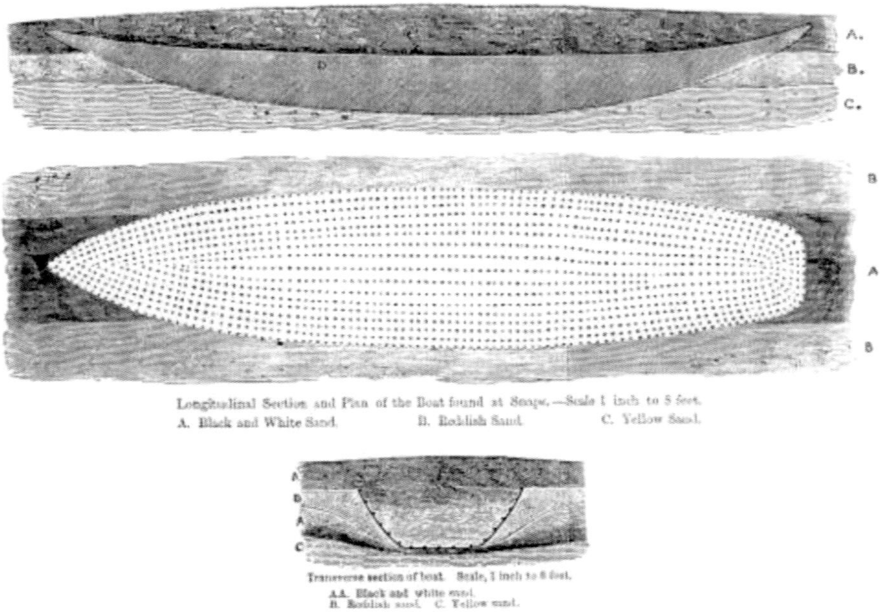

5.1 The somewhat schematic plan of the Snape ship; an engraving published in the *Proceedings of the Society of Antiquaries* in 1863.

take the story from evaluating the evidence available - what remained of the ship, to defining the motives for its reconstruction, designing the research programme for the build, socialising the project inside and out, and floating ideas for the future trials and voyages.

WHAT REMAINED

Buried ships of the Anglo-Saxon period were scarcely known before 1938 and 1939, when Mrs Pretty and Basil Brown unearthed two of them and recalled the one found at nearby Snape in 1862 **(FIG 5.1)**. As a result of Brown's discoveries, Anglo-Saxon ship burial became synonymous with Sutton Hoo and not only in Britain, but all over northern Europe and in the United States of America. While it hit the headlines in 1939, appearing in the *Illustrated London News*, the fame of the discovery has never waned, and its academic and historical interest has generated many hundreds of publications, and recently a film that well portrayed the social context in which the pre-war investigation took place.[1] The first Sutton Hoo ship was encountered in an excavation of Mound 2 in 1860. It took the form of a large number of dispersed ship-rivets, not recognised at the time (termed "screw bolts"), so carted away to a blacksmith to be made into horseshoes.[2] Mound 2 was revisited by Basil Brown in 1938 when boat-like traces were brought to light, accompanied by iron rivets that he

a)

b)

5.2 (a) The Sutton Hoo ship looking towards the stern with the rows of roves in situ. Left to right: Crossley, a workman, Commander Hutchison, Basil Brown and (on the baulk) Barbara Wagstaff. (b) Basil Brown (right) with Commander Hutchison (left) inside the hull, amidships.

recognised from those found with the Snape ship and curated at Aldeburgh.[3] Fifty years later in 1988, the mound was shown to have originally contained a clinker-built ship about 20 m long, held together with iron fastenings and placed over the top of a burial chamber, where it had been much disturbed.[4]

The larger and better-preserved example of a Sutton Hoo Ship was brought to light in 1939 under Mound 1. It lay in a trench with a burial chamber amidships, its clinker-built hull deprived of wood but represented by thousands of corroded iron rivets that remained *in situ* **(FIG 5.2a, b)**. It was recognised for what it was by Basil Brown from the moment that his assistant John Jacobs

a)

b)

5.3 (a) Hutchison revealing the gunwale on the port side, with a thole (oarlock) showing (right) between frames 21 and 22.
(b) Thole pin between frames 19 and 20 on the port side.

called out 'Here's a bit of iron' on day 2 of their excavation. This led Basil to expose each rivet, one at a time, pre-empting its presence as a reddish stain and bringing it into focus by dusting off the rove with a pastry brush. This is a well-known incident in an oft-told story, but its significance here is considerable. The main objection to the reconstruction of the ship encountered in the 1930s was that it lacked sufficient evidence; but in practice the lines of this vessel - preserved on land with its remarkable burial chamber - were in many ways more secure than that of a wreck scattered with its cargo on the seabed. In the Sutton Hoo Ship, structural wood did not survive, but the rivets left *in situ* were significant signs to its shape. Archaeologist Angela Care Evans, who studied the ship for the British Museum, wrote that, thanks to the lines of rivets, the plank runs were as recognisable in 1939 as they were to the men who had built and buried the great ship in the seventh century.[5] After the excavation of the chamber had finished and on the eve of war, Commander J.K.D. Hutchison brought a team from the Science Museum to make a record of every alignment and anomaly that could be seen. Hutchison

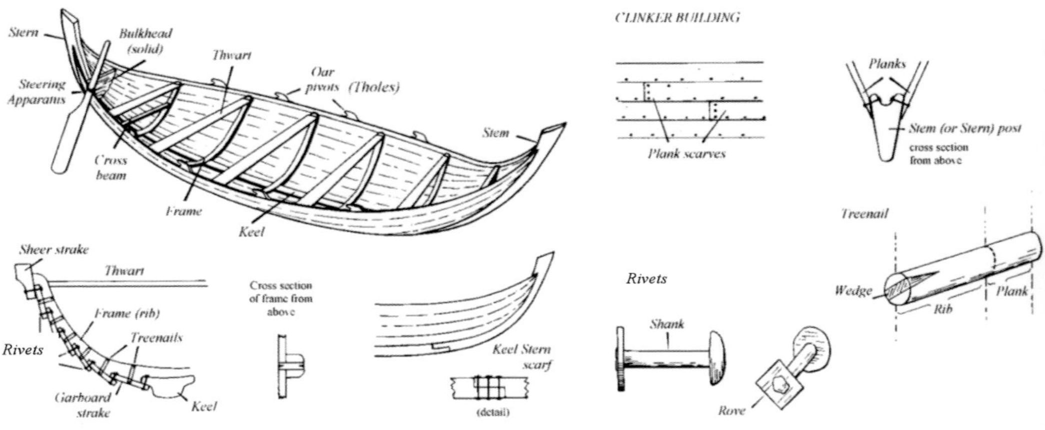

5.4 A diagram of a clinker-built vessel indicating parts often referred to the in text.

cut sections across the line of the keel, detected as a dark shadow at various points, to determine its cross-section. This varied from a squared keel amidships to deeper cutwaters at the stem and stern. He located an apparent scarf joint connecting the keel to the rising stern, as indicated by a line of rivets, and he searched unsuccessfully for signs of a similar join that must have attached the keel to the stem section.[6] At the starboard side of the stern, where a cluster of rivets suggested a steering oar, he hunted outside the hull for signs of an expected large boss on which the oar would be pivoted. He found the base of the ship, with the rivets in place, and along the top of the gunwale defined the soil shadows of several thorn-shaped oar-locks or tholes, indicating the positions of rowers **(FIG 5.3a, b)**. Two teachers on holiday, the photographers Mercie Lack and Barbara Wagstaff, joined the team and took more than 1000 black and white plates, plus coloured slides and an 8 mm movie.[7]

The miniature drawing in **FIG 5.4** is intended as a guide to the parts of a clinker-built ship, some of which have more than one name. To fit on the page and still remain legible it is not to scale, but indicates the nature of some of the more often cited pieces. The *keel* is the backbone, made of five pieces held together with *scarf joints* secured by *treenails*, and curving up at each end via an *underloute* to form the *stem* and *stern* posts. The first *planks* (strakes) are fastened with *rivets* to the wings of the keel and then overlap from the *garboard strake* (lowest) to the *sheer strake* (highest). Each plank is fastened to the one below with *rivets*, each consisting of a *nail* and a *rove.* The *frames* are inserted into the hull and secured with treenails or bolts. The ends of the frames support *thwarts* (benches) for the rowers to sit on. They pull the oars against thorn-shaped *tholes* (oar pivots, oarlocks) which are fastened to the

5.5 An original ship rivet (nail and rove) held in the hand (above) and a replicated nail and rove compared with an original (below).

sheer strake. The ship comes to a point at each end and the *steering oar* is attached at the stern on the starboard (steerboard) side.

Still largely in place, the rivets showed that the hull of the Sutton Hoo ship had been constructed of nine ascending overlapping planks one inch thick; they were of different widths from 14 inches wide amidships, narrowing to 4 inches or less where they rose and converged to a point at the stem and stern posts. The rivets consisted of iron nails with domed heads and round shafts, reduced in most cases to rust, but retaining their form **(FIG 5.5)**. The overlapping 1-inch planks were fastened with rivets measuring 2 inches from head to rove, the wood leaving its metallic ghost at each end. A thin hard line in the centre of the shank showed where the planks had lain together, a line of caulking originally between them. In the centre of the ship, the lowest rivets were vertical, showing that the lowest (garboard) planks had been joined horizontally to the thin 'wings' of the keel (the lands). By contrast, the rivets high up at the ends of the ship reflected the way the narrowing plank ends ran into the stem and stern posts. Half-length rivets with a sloping centre line also showed where two 1-inch planks had been scarf-joined, end to end.

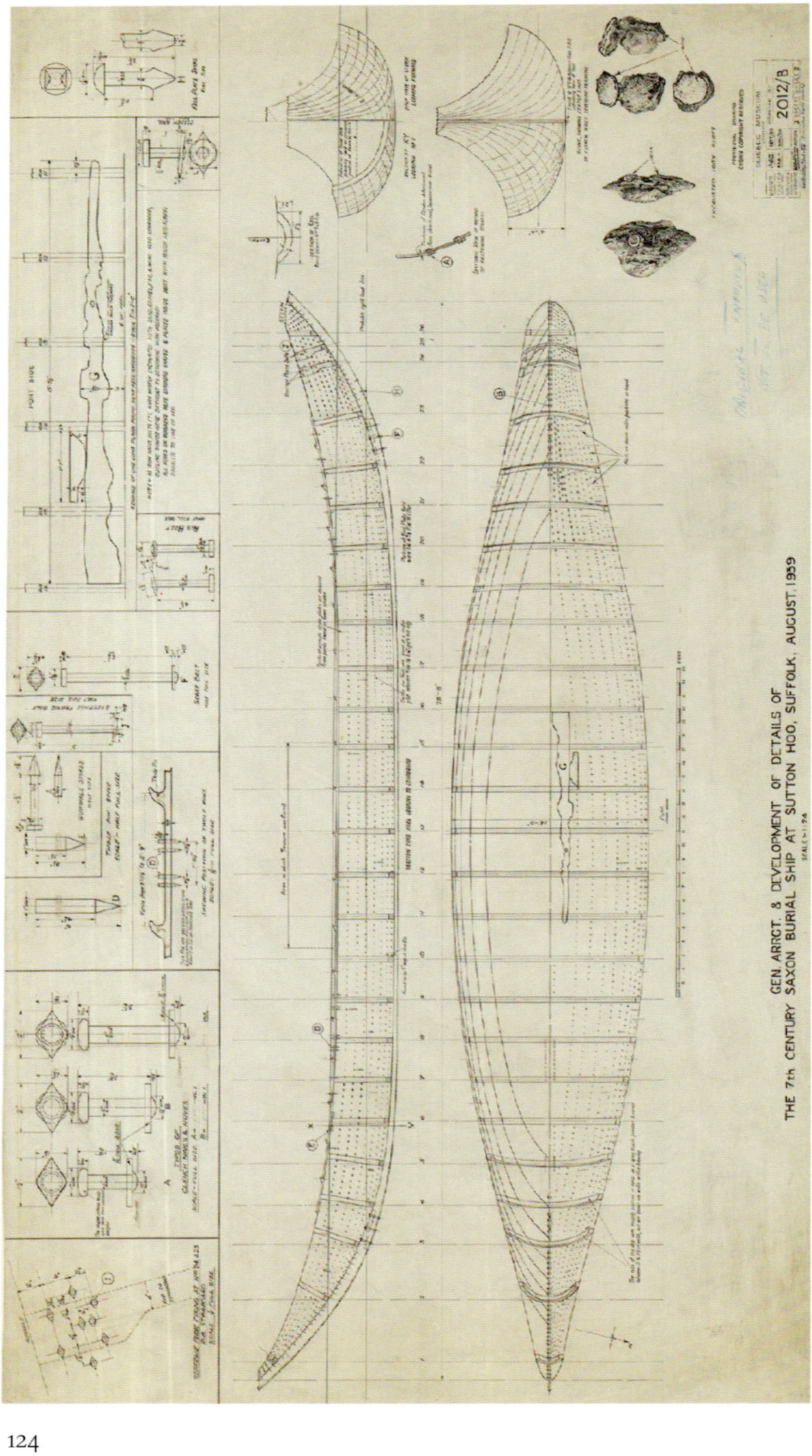

5.6 Plan and elevation of the ship made by the Science Museum in 1939.

Twenty-six heavy frames of squared timber had survived as parallel sand casts running across the inside of the hull.[8] The grain of the timber frames was also captured in ferrified wood where their underside had rested on the iron roves of rivets fastening the hull. This showed that the frames had been cut to fit snuggly over the profile of the overlapping planks of the hull. Tree-nails were used to secure the frames to the planking below the top strake or sheer strake, integral with the gunnel that carried the tholes secured with iron spikes. Frames 24 and 25 lay close together and had enlarged heads secured on the starboard side with five and three rivets - the reinforcement suggesting the support of a large steering oar. The upper part of the stem and stern posts, and the very ends of the upper planking were missing - perhaps they had originally projected outside the surface of the mound, perhaps as much as 4 m above the keel. The hull fitted well into its trench; sand filled the gaps before the turfy mound was piled on top.

By the time the recording reached its end, World War II was a reality, and the remaining sand-form of the ship was hastily covered with bracken before the team departed, to deter disturbance. Disturbance there was, since the wartime use of Sutton Hoo included the training of infantry, who dug slit trenches and practiced driving bren-gun carriers over the mounds, before being warned off by archaeologist Ted Wright, by then in uniform.[9] Even so in 1939 the Science Museum produced a plan and elevation of the ship, based on the measurements made on site in that year **(FIG 5.6)**. The finds retrieved from the chamber spent the war in the London Underground and study began in the British Museum as soon as the war ended. In 1966 archaeologists re-engaged with the site: the British Museum team who were writing up the finds returned to cull every scrap of evidence in aid of a meticulous study of the burial. The tasks of this expedition included all possible measures to examine and record what was left of the ship, data that were added to the 1939 records and used, together with the notes and photographs amassed in 1939 to create a new and definitive plan.[10] What we know of this ship is thus owed to Basil Brown, Charles Phillips, Commander Hutchison, A.S. Crossley, Mercie Lack and Barbara Wagstaff, who all saw it exposed on site, to Rupert Bruce-Mitford who was entrusted with its publication and to his British Museum team, Susan Youngs, Valerie Fenwick and most of all to Angela Care Evans who wrote the definitive account published in 1975.

NAUTICAL STIRRINGS

A reconstruction of the ship was already an ambition nursed by Angela when the new campaign of research at Sutton Hoo began in 1983. After I was appointed to lead this campaign, I took up the reconstruction challenge in

5.7 BBC film and radio crews recording in the 1980s, with Ray Sutcliffe and Malcolm Billings.

turn, first consulting Neil Cossons and Gillian Hutchinson (no relation) at the National Maritime Museum, and then Sean McGrail at Oxford. I had a meeting with Woodbridge Town Council in 1983 and in 1984 with Ken Spence chairman of the Maritime 1982 committee, Proctor Mailer of Suffolk Coastal and Tony Travis, tourism expert, who was a colleague at Birmingham University, meetings where the possibility of an Anglo-Saxon Heritage Centre with a ship replica was also aired. At the Seckford Hall hotel in 1984 the Sutton Hoo Society was formed with Mac Miles as Chair, and Mike Weaver and John Aldridge as organisers of tours for the visiting public. The Society supported the investigations of the site between 1984-1992 and have remained champions and effective publicists of Sutton Hoo - and its experimental ship - ever since. The new campaign was the subject of a series of BBC 2 programmes under the *Chronicle* label, promoted by David Attenborough and directed by Ray Sutcliffe **(FIG 5.7)**.

At this point there was a strong interest in helping to generate the right sort of publicity for the project and the ship was in the conversation. The project's *Bulletin* no 2 published in April 1984 carried a statement from Sean McGrail on behalf of the National Maritime Museum, who were to contribute a grant to the project over five years. They were promoting research on the River Deben, and "a full-size replica based on the excavated evidence is being

5.8 Visit of the Duke of Edinburgh as president of the Sutton Hoo Society in 1984, with Martin Carver and Angela Evans.

investigated."[11] Sean McGrail visited on 2nd August and agreed to push forward the reconstruction, approving of an initiative by Mike Wade to build it at Kyson Point, down river from Woodbridge.

However, it was evident that the Sutton Hoo Research Trust, which was funding the new research project, thought that a reconstructed ship should stay firmly docked in the imagination for the time being - that is until the fieldwork was complete. As their director of research, I was inclined to agree with them. Public interest was very clear from the numbers of visitors hosted by the Sutton Hoo Society and from the number of viewers of the TV programmes made by BBC *Chronicle*. The site needed to exert its identity amid busy and productive farmland, and we took our project forward by negotiating, with the help of the landowners, a route of access and a right of way for visitors. The TV programmes and the agreement of the Duke of Edinburgh to act as president of the Sutton Hoo Society were also influential in bringing about a more secure workplace **(FIG 5.8)**. As a long-term priority, I set about finding a way of moving the Sutton Hoo site into the public domain, in discussion with Annie Tranmer, owner of Sutton Hoo and resident at Sutton Hoo house, and with her legal advisor John Miller, advancing the National Trust as a potential owner with the help of Elizabeth Walters and Merlin Waterson, its regional director.

5.9 The bronze ship sculpture at Sutton Hoo on the stance originally prepared for the ship.

The friendship and support of these colleagues were to bear fruit in Mrs Tranmer's bequest of the whole estate to the National Trust in 1993. As was its practice, the Trust began by assessing the different values of their new property, among them its potential for conservation, for public engagement and for research. A committee was formed which consulted experts and designed a visitor centre and a visitor itinerary. The proposed development was costed and submitted to the National Heritage Lottery Fund. At this stage, the bid also included the research, reconstruction, trials and publication of an authentic full scale Sutton Hoo Mound 1 ship.

It was not to be. The bid to NHLF was successful apart from the reconstruction of the ship that was dropped by the assessors. The fund's archaeological advisor was David Wilson, former director of the British Museum and member of the Sutton Hoo Research Trust. If he was against it, which seemed entirely probable, then the ship would stay unbuilt, at least with help of the NHLF. This left us with the problem of how to use the large space prepared to display the ship next to the visitor centre. In discussion with Merlin, we came up with a large constructivist sculpture, inspired by the skeleton of metal ribs used to display incomplete ships at the Viking Ship Museum at Roskilde **(FIG 5.9)**. The visitor centre was built and formerly opened in 2001 by Seamus Heaney, the distinguished Irish poet, and in its first ten years welcomed over a million visitors.

RESTARTING THE SHIP PROJECT

Undeterred by the disappointing loss of a part of its bid, the new National Trust team at Sutton Hoo set about using its own resources to develop the research basis, the ways and means and the funding to reconstruct the Mound 1 ship whatever the obstacles might be. On 1 Oct 1998 I proposed a project to the National Trust whereby the ship was to be built on the Sutton Hoo estate and copied the plan to a potential consortium including Ole Crum-

5.10 *Sæ Wylfing* built by Edwin Gifford in 1993 and here trialled on the River Deben.

lin-Pedersen, Edwin Gifford, Robert Simper and Angela Care Evans. A National Trust in-house committee was formed to take the venture forward that would take advice from experimental ship builders, notably those at the Viking Ship museum in Roskilde. Interestingly, within this committee there appeared the first cracks between those who wanted to design a research project for the reconstruction and those who wanted to just get on and do it. Edwin Gifford, a modern yacht-builder, was an enthusiastic member of the committee, who together with his wife Joyce designed and built a half-length replica ship, named *Sæ Wylfing,* which has successfully rowed and sailed the Deben ever since **(FIG 5.10)**.[12] Edwin was a little dismissive about my wish to consult the Scandinavians, whom I regarded as leaders in the field of experimental boats: "I'll remind you" he commented in one of these ding-dong to-dos, "that Alfred beat the Danes". He no doubt felt we should do the same. The legacy he left us in *Sæ Wylfing* is that research comes in many guises: study of past examples is part of it, so is accurate measurement, and debate and discussion, but the determination to realise a vision is often the crucial driver.

A SECOND SHIP

In 2013 word reached the National Trust committee of a parallel initiative to build a Sutton Hoo ship on the Woodbridge waterfront, by a pressure group WAMAG (Woodbridge and Melton Action Group), led by John Gibbins and including Malcolm Hodd, Pete Clay, Annie Leech, Andrew Fitzgerald and Paul Constantine. They were much engaged in the fate of Whisstocks, a famous boatyard founded in 1926 and responsible for Francis Chichester's *Gipsy Moth*, Alastair McLean's *Mary Deare* and many other yachts besides. The demise of Whisstocks in 1991 left a big hole on the waterfront and a major problem of how to fill it. Naturally, developers were interested in such a prime site, but

5.11 Members of the Woodbridge Riverside Trust outside Whisstocks premises: left to right Pete Clay, Malcolm Hodd, Paul Constantine, Annie Leech.

WAMAG raised a petition with 1500 signatures and began to press for the inclusion of a community space as a condition of planning permission. In pride of place was their proposal to build a replica of the ship found under Mound 1 at Sutton Hoo. The plan was to deliver the freehold of the Whisstocks boat shed - the 'Longshed' - and an adjacent building housing the museum, into the care of Woodbridge Town Council. For the better management of the community site, WAMAG morphed into the Woodbridge Riverside Trust (WRT) a registered charity with the same objects: "To protect, preserve and enhance the character of the natural and built environment of the Deben riverside for the benefit of the public; and to advance the education of the public in the maritime heritage of Woodbridge" **(FIG 5.11)**. As the group's council representative, Charles Notcutt was instrumental in procuring for the WRT the lease of the Longshed for 35 years at a peppercorn rent.

On hearing of their proposed project, I made overtures to the WRT much in the spirit of Rædwald visiting Kent: should we join their project, or they join ours? or should we compromise by each erecting altars to our different missions in the temple of the *Sutton Hoo Ship*? As the director of the Sutton Hoo Research Trust my own interest in building the ship was neither to erect a local monument or even to create a national icon, but to find out more about the way the earliest English used their watercraft. On the other hand, 'community archaeology' was the coming thing, partly as a result of the thirty-year transformation of archaeological investigation into a profession. In June 2014, I produced a Feasibility Study for building a full-scale reconstruction of the Sutton Hoo Mound 1 Ship, validated by maritime notables Anton Englert, Søren Nielsen, Vibeke Bischoff and Julian Whitewright. It included 40 illustrations and a bibliography and urged that the ship should be delivered by a research partnership. In the interests of collaboration (one ship was enough), I drafted a proposal for an 'Experimental Ship Committee' and sent it to the WRT Chairman Malcom Hodd. He replied on 6 September 2014, suggesting I chair a separate "expert reference group" to advise WRT. The WRT Project Board would manage the project, and the funding would be provided "by or on behalf of Woodbridge Riverside Trust" which would take overall control. They were upbeat about raising the money, but a closer partnership was not envisaged, then or in the future: "Your suggested long-term objective of creating a homegrown centre for experimental ship research in England takes the project beyond what WRT was set up for. However, we have always thought that Whisstocks might well become the home of related Anglo-Saxon ship construction expertise in the UK, so there is no reason why it shouldn't in the longer term be affiliated with a national experimental ship research centre to be based at Southampton or elsewhere".[13]

Continuing to press for a partnership with a research institution, I explored possible links with my own university at York, the Viking Ship Museum at Roskilde and with Southampton University, in the latter case seeing Julian Whitewright as a likely research director. The Royal Naval Dockyard at Portsmouth, closely linked with Southampton, would be a splendid place for the construction and, eventually, for the display of the seventh-century royal ship in the company of the *Victory*. In June 2015 I circulated an enlarged version of the Feasibility Study as a *Scope of Work*, now with details of management including shipwrights, a yardmaster, volunteers, academic researchers, and a committee of prominent patrons for fundraising.

In the following month I had a turn of good fortune in meeting Andrew FitzGerald, senior WRT member, who was considering the terms of reference of a separate body to build the ship. Its stated objectives were: (a) to reconstruct the seventh-century ship found in Mound 1 at Sutton Hoo; (b) to carry out trials of the reconstructed ship on lake, river and sea waters and over land; (c) to enact and monitor the activities of (a) and (b) in accordance with the best modern practice of modern research and nautical archaeology; (d) to promulgate the build, the trials and the results of research to the academic community and the wider world of public interest; (e) to plan for all possible volunteer participation as is compatible with safety and liability; (f) to promote interest and investment in the study and reconstruction of historic ships in England. One could hardly ask for more. Although it did not lead to a formal partnership, this was a breakthrough-moment in many ways. It had been accepted that the ship was a major undertaking that would not only need to satisfy its academic and community clients but would need to raise its own funds and pay its own expenses. On the other hand, it could also design

5.12 The Longshed completed and in occupation; *Sæ Wylfing* on a trailer in the foreground.

its own programmes. This was the basis for the organisation that would be named *The Sutton Hoo Ship's Company* (SHSC).

In 2016 the site was cleared for development and work began on preparing the newly conceived Whisstocks Place with its waterfront, and of course its Longshed, measured up and tailored for the building of the Sutton Hoo Ship. WRT raised £130,000 to provide the Longshed with a mezzanine floor to host lectures and exhibitions, and a community workshop in the space not already reserved to build the ship. The proposed governance of the operation took a further step the following year. The Ship's Company held its first informal meeting on 19 July 2017 in The Crown Hotel. Later in the same year WRT met with IBTC (The International Boatbuilding Training College), represented by Mike Tupper, to devise a joint IBTC, WRT and Ships Company management of the Longshed, waterfront and ship build, with WRT in charge. They proposed a waterside management team with a Longshed Manager, workshop Manager and a 'lead shipwright'. WRT would also co-ordinate volunteers including IBTC students. In the event, this did not come about, but IBTC skills lived on in the many Ship's Company shipwrights and volunteers who were previous graduates of the College. In 2018 WRT signed their tenancy agreement with the Town Council and were handed the Longshed keys, while the Ship's Company, undertaking the task of building the ship, were designated its 'Associated Party' **(FIG 5.12)**.

The project began with modest funds and little expertise, but thanks in no small part to Andrew FitzGerald, its treasurer, and to its first appointees, Jacq Barnard as Project Manager and Tim Kirk as shipwright, the company took shape, was tooled up, and resourced. Donors supported the project in cash and in kind and by 2021, native oaks had been donated and procured, and the keel fashioned and laid – forming the backbone of our leviathan. In addition, a trawl of small subsidies in reach of all was created by Jacq, opportunities to sponsor a rivet or a plank, buy souvenirs made out of waste oak and above all to offer labour as a volunteer. Consultation with Roskilde and the archaeological wood expert Damian Goodburn allowed volunteer trainees under Tim's supervision to become adept with axes and address the immense challenge of the ship's carpentry. The number of dedicated volunteers rose, covering every aspect of the company's activity. In numerous meetings and presentations, the programmes for research and for public engagement grew with the ship. Thanks to the energy and ingenuity of the Shipwright and Project Manager, the reconstructing of the Mound 1 ship became a major community project – one of the largest single focus archaeological projects so far seen in Britain. It can be said that, while there may sometimes be friction, the community aims of the Woodbridge Riverside Trust and the research aims of the Sutton Hoo Research Trust are converging in the Sutton Hoo Ship's Company.

DESIGNING THE RESEARCH: WHY? HOW? AND TO WHAT END?

It was clear that the agenda for the newly formed Company should be underpinned by a project design addressing three fundamental questions of importance to the crew, to funders and to our clients both academic and public. These were: why are you building this ship? how will it be done? and with what anticipated outcome? To aid debate, draft Project Designs were circulated for comment in 2015, 2016, 2017, and 2018.[14] In 2018 a Symposium was held in the Longshed with a number of prominent shipbuilders, archaeologists and digital modellers to agree the design and the method of build.[15] In 2020, the digital model of the Sutton Hoo Ship prepared by Pat Tanner, Julian Whitewright and Joe Startin, was published, the first announcement to the professional and academic community.[16]

In order to move the whole project nearer to the front line of archaeological and historical research, in 2021 we created an advisory body, appropriately named the *Witan* (an Anglo-Saxon Council), to which a number of Anglo-Saxon and maritime researchers, together with teachers, marine professionals and councillors were invited.[17] Revised research programmes were put before the *Witan* in 2021, 2022 and 2023, which, if nothing else, hoped to serve as preliminary road maps for the project and provoke debate.[18] Many of these debates were concerned with decisions on the build, integral to the experimental process. As well as determining the form of the ship, such decisions marked key moments in its conception, the success of which will be apparent when the ship takes to the water.

There are some useful generalities in designing such programmes: the agenda needs to address archaeological, historical and social interests, the scope needs to be local, national and international; and the procedure needs to imitate the course of scientific experiment. We did not need to stress that the Sutton Hoo Mound 1 was an exceptional discovery, enlarged by the British Museum in the 1960s through re-excavation of the ship, rediscovering Mound 5 and exploring the prehistoric presence on the site; and then published by them in ground-breaking detail.[19] Nevertheless, the Museum, as recipient of the finds, and the Society of Antiquaries, as a purveyor of archaeological opinion, decided there was more to do to put Mound 1 in its temporal and spatial context: addressing the questions why that? Why there? Why then? This was the task that had been assigned to the campaign that took place from 1983 to 2005. This showed that the Mound 1 burial was a prominent event in a series of three successive Anglo-Saxon cemeteries dating from the fifth to the eleventh centuries, highlighting the changing social and political emphases exemplified by six different kinds of burial rites linking it to wider Europe.[20] It also chronicled a 5000-year prehistoric prelude at Sutton Hoo, the remains of which provided a platform for the royal cemetery to develop (Chapter 2). The search for context was expanded to include the neighbouring kingdoms that were forming at the same time, and how the people buried at Sutton Hoo had interacted with and reacted to their contemporaries in Scandinavia, on the Continent and the Mediterranean. And this is where the ship came in.

In 2021, Historic England published its maritime archaeological research agenda, of which the Early Medieval was one part. As in other periods, it looked to understand coastal change, coastal settlement, the context of seafaring, and the degrees of connectivity as well as the technology of boats. It noted the lack of live study and regretted that "unlike Scandinavia, the coasts of Britain have not been subjected to intensive experimental voyages".[21] Such reconstruction projects being relatively rare in England and negligible for the Anglo-Saxon period, we have been glad to study the best of experimental research in Europe, at the Danish centre of Roskilde in particular. We have combined this with the procedure for doing archaeology on land, well developed in Britain, and produced what we hope will be an exemplary formula: beginning with the study of the historical, archaeological and maritime background, to which Chapters 1-4 here offer an introduction and summary. This chapter is concerned with the rationale of the project, its aims and objectives, viability and management, following the basic itinerary: design, build, trials and publication.

There were more specific reasons for undertaking reconstruction. The British Museum had spent 36 years reconstructing the 237 artefacts in the burial chamber, in most cases with arresting and influential results. The helmet, for example, was reassembled from numerous fragments of iron of various sizes, producing a first version in 1947 which was dismantled and reassembled in 1971 to give the helmet we know today.[22] This took time, and trial and error, and it was not clear from the outset what the helmet should look like. That had to be deduced by finding which pieces fitted together, and further informed by the shape of other helmets in existence at the time. By contrast, the ship, the largest artefact of them all, had yet to be reconstructed. The reconstructed helmet, known all over the world, had steered history; the reconstructed ship, much bigger, self-propelled, fashioned, like the original, by dedicated hands and minds, and its creation observed in three dimensions by a multitude of admirers, had an even better chance of similarly evoking a new view of the European past.

The research drivers of such a reconstruction project should be local, national and international, since that is the ultimate constituency that judges its success. In more than 80 years of study, the historical value of Sutton Hoo had grown, from explanations focused on identifying Rædwald, to an understanding of the creation of one of England's first kingdoms and its struggles with new alliances and ideologies. In these, the tensions between the inheritance of pagan Scandinavia and the Roman-Christian continent had proved revealing, not only for the seventh but for all subsequent centuries. Of the many factors, large and small, that power history, one of the most significant is communication, the ease with which armies, diplomats, preachers, friends, families, commodities and news can travel. The summary narrative revisited in previous chapters hints at new kinds of immersion in Europe, and a new outward-looking political attitude: what should they know of England, that only England know? The structure and performance of a full-size Sutton Hoo Ship should make real this wider maritime context.

The procedure of this experiment, as others, should be scientific in form, namely, given X (the excavation records), if we do Y (build and trial the ship), then we should learn about Z (the roles and capabilities of the ship in its day and the inland and overseas reach of its people). Accordingly we needed to go beyond the surviving evidence for the form and material of the ship, in order to construct and test hypotheses for the tools used, the methods of finding and preparing oak and iron, the nature of the propulsion by rowing (the length of the oars) or by sail (the form of the rigging), navigating the waterways appropriate to the ship, inland, coastal and at sea, the possibilities of portage, the finished appearance, all leading to an evocation of the ship's intended purposes and actual use.[23] The data collected in the trials and voyages will enable maps to be drawn of the feasible and likely journeys undertaken, the payloads, weather resistance, adaptability and their implications for society, commerce, communication and war. Above all, it would allow us to map connectivity between south-east England and the numerous coastal communities that could primarily be reached by water.

In experimental ship construction, as in archaeological excavation, teamwork is fundamental and leadership by consensus essential. In the light of this project's birth, the risks of domination by native instinct as opposed to scientific procedure were high. On the other hand, it was equally important to recognize that this kind of project is not led by science alone. The interpretation of much archaeological work relies on searching for parallels in previous discoveries - but interpretation also relies on analogies from the present day. In the case of a nautical experiment, the latter have a special status, since the experience and common sense of those involved in modern sailing and ship-building can be influential and even determinant. A balance has to be struck between expertise and enthusiasm, between nautical know-how and *nous*, in what is essentially a social and creative way of winning new knowledge. The formation of a group of volunteers provides free labour and well-being for themselves, but it is more valuable than that: if effectively mobilised, the members, individually and as a group, contribute directly to the research programme.

Few have managed this better than Ole Crumlin-Pedersen who began his career as a naval architect and ended it as founder of the Viking Ship Museum at Roskilde and first Director of the Centre for Maritime Archaeology of Denmark. He was a seaman, an archaeologist, museum director, scholar, lecturer, supervisor and mentor to numerous colleagues. His discovery of the Viking ships originally sunk to block the harbour at Skuldelev gave the Viking Ship Museum its basic asset, ships being discovered, excavated and exhibited and often reconstructed, one after another. The study of the ships following the first discoveries in 1956 continued beyond his death in 2011, and the way the project was developed has become a model for ship and boat excavations: *Reconnaissance*: preliminary investigations - *Excavation*: followed by post-excavation recording; conservation and analysis - *Interpretation:* using science and comparative evidence - *Experiment:* building a full-scale model of each vessel and undertaking trials of this "floating hypothesis" - *Display*, to the public - *Publishing* in books, monographs, and articles, and by lectures and informal talks.[24] The reconstruction of the ships was accordingly baked into the research of any discovery from the start. He commented: "In order to exploit the full potential of a ship-find, a multidisciplinary approach is needed, archaeologists, historians, wood specialists, environmentalists, naval architects, boatbuilders and mariners ... The strength of [these] projects rests on the fact that a ship is a self-contained and functional unit which we must study in its complexity and context - and here experimental archaeology is a splendid tool."[25]

An example of the Danish initiative can be found in the story of the experimental Iron Age ship from Hjortspring, *Tilia Alsie*, which we met in the last chapter, fully published by the Centre for Maritime Archaeology in 2003 **(FIG 4.5)**.[26] The build, led by Knut Valbjørn, was based in the island of Als near the original find spot and began with the formation of a legally constituted *guild* of around 50 members, aged between 40 and 75, with diverse experience and professions, including that of farmer, teacher, computer specialist, engineer, physician, lorry driver and ship's cook. The members signed up to principles of authenticity, honesty, quality, and the practice of thorough documentation, and were organised in nine research groups, dealing, among other topics, with design, wood-procurement, toolmaking, boat-building, history and testing. A total of 10,000 manhours was logged from the splitting of the first lime-tree to the launch of the boat - of which an estimated 25% were spent in discussions among the boat builders. The governance was flat and even, dependent on a group of about 30 persons, meeting monthly.[27]

Procurement for the *Tilia Alsie (Linden of Als)* was more complex than ours, since three kinds of wood were employed, lime for the panels, floor boards and thwarts, with lime bast for sewing, hazel for the ribs and ash for the deck beam. There was also no model to work from, other than images depicted in rock art. The boat was conceived, constructed and recorded in the round, using a theodolite and a three-dimensional digitising arm, in order to provide data for hydrostatics, including the theoretical stability of the ship on the water. The sea trials, led by Max Vinner, aimed to subject the ship to practical experiments relating to its suggested original use, so that previous assumptions could be endorsed or rejected.[28] Everything was systematically measured: the crew members were weighed before each trial, and the physical strength and technical skill of the paddlers assessed. The power produced by the crew was also measured by four *sphygometers* (sphygmomanometers, for recording blood pressure). The average speeds were calculated by stopwatch against distance between two points determined by GPS. The hydrodynamics - resistance of the hull to the water - was measured by a spring balance on a towrope attached to *Tilia Alsie* and towed by a motor yacht. The science of paddling was studied with the help of crews of the 'dragon boats' - shallow sporting craft, racing competitively with crews of 20, "who knew each other's paddling rhythm". The trials were spread over three years, during

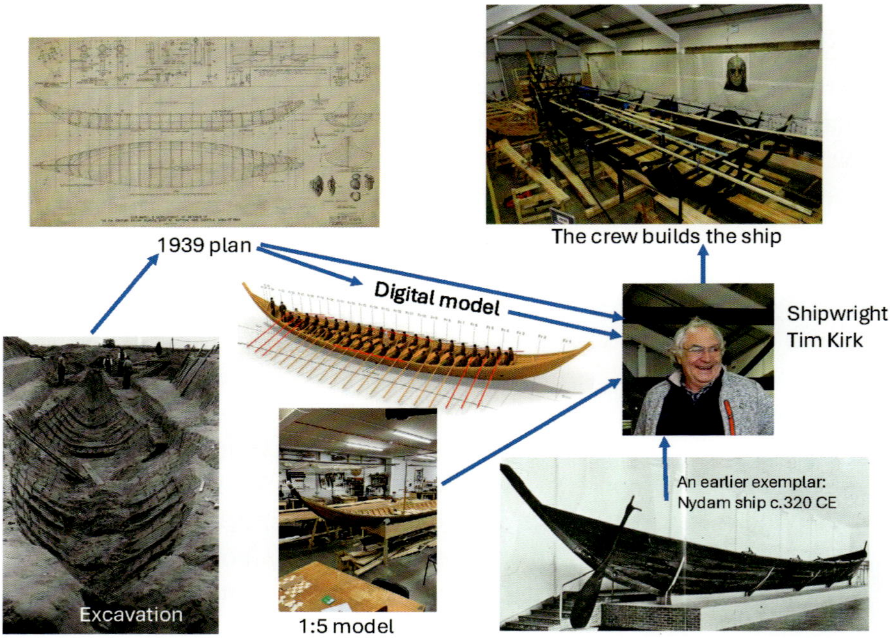

5.13 The shipwright's mind-map.

which effective paddling, and speed, increased with the experience of crews. Although the actual periods on the water were inevitably short, data was systematically collected and assessed. The result was an experimental boat, successfully paddled by an experimental crew that may not have exactly replicated the originals but opened eyes to the possibilities of Iron Age travel in the northern seas.[29]

THE SHIP'S COMPANY UNDER WAY

Our ship's company can be closely paralleled in these matters of mission, principle and organisation, but has navigated its own route to the desired reconstruction. Tim Kirk, our Master Shipwright, worked from measured drawings of the Sutton Hoo Ship in the ground, originating in the detailed 1939 drawing made by the Science Museum, enhanced by the numerous photographs taken at the time by Mercie Lack and Barbara Wagstaff, moderated by the digital analysis, informed by advice directly from Angela Care Evans, and tuned, corrected and moderated again by building a 1:5 scale model to deduce how the planks had lain together and were secured to the stem and stern posts. Study of similar and broadly contemporary craft, notably the earlier Nydam ships and the later ships of the Viking period, provided help over missing or puzzling parts. The shipwright directing the reconstruction has to combine all

5.14 Volunteer members of the build team with the master shipwright, Tim Kirk: (left to right) Norman Macritchie, Simon Lamb, Tim Kirk, David MacDonald, Alec Newland (seated).

these factors with the know-how of an experienced seaman into an integrated concept **(FIG 5.13)**. In this sense, he is not so far from the situation of the seventh-century shipwright, who, although that person had an advantage in the inherited know-how of previous generations, he was most likely being asked to do something quite new. Given this, our ship had an evidence-base at least as good, and arguably better, than *Tilia Alsie* or the Sutton Hoo helmet.

A volunteer force, now around 170 persons with diverse professional backgrounds, was gradually recruited by our Project Manager Jacq Barnard, as they came forward to offer their help. Master Shipwright Tim Kirk was joined in 2021 by Laurie Walker, a graduate of the IBTC, as assistant and (from 2025) succeeding Tim. Carl Moore joined as assistant shipwright in 2023. A core team was formed under the shipwrights, dedicated to procuring oak, making tools, and using them to shape and finish timbers to precise specifications, following the agreed blueprint **(FIG 5.14)**. These volunteers contributed to the final form of the ship in subtle ways. All learnt much from the acts of axing and finishing the timbers, and joining the planks with rivets **(FIG 5.15)**; and from the assembly of the five parts of the keel, their scarf joints secured with treenails (wooden pegs). The different angles of joints between keel and planks implied by the rivets, had to be reconciled to real pieces of wood, as opposed to dark stains in the sand. Alec Newland (*treewright*) showed that this meant that the

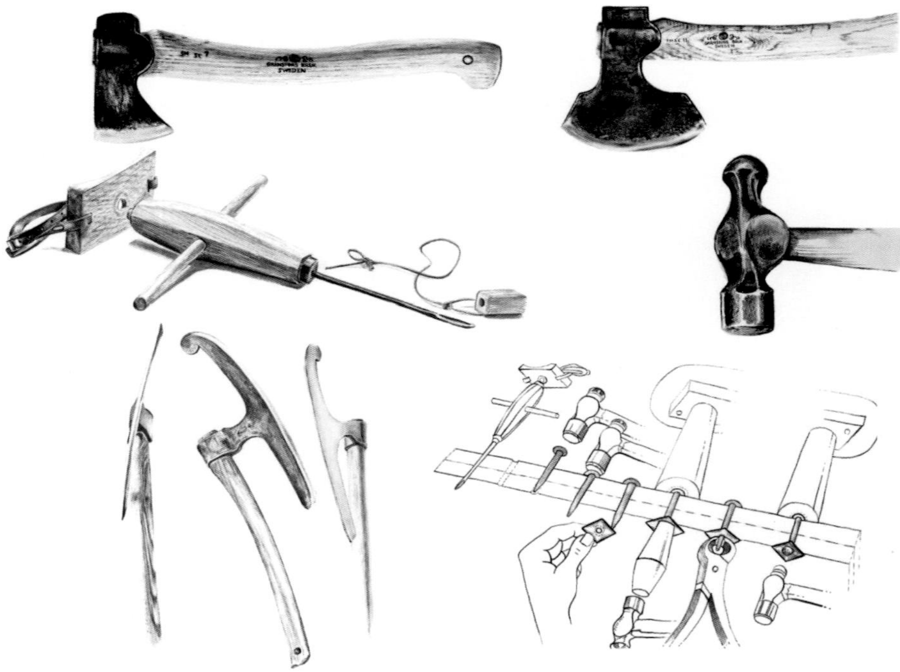

5.15 Woodworking tools appropriate to the seventh century recreated by the Ship's Company. Top: axes for chopping and trimming. Centre: spoon drill and peen hammers. Bottom left: a finishing axe with left-handed and right-handed versions to left and right. Bottom right: procedure for fixing a rivet (from left): drilling the hole, inserting a nail, driving a nail, adding the rove, punching the rove home against a dolly, nipping the nail point, burring the nail point over the rove with a peen hammer. Drawn by Catherine Hoy.

top surface of each end of the keel needed to be scooped out to provide wings to which the planks could fastened - an effect accentuated more as the keel rose towards the stem and stern posts.

Experimental archaeology, which goes forwards like building, and not backwards like digging, also has a particular procedure: study of all the available evidence, study of possible parallels, modelling the two, and (like the helmet) deciding when the 'best fit' has been achieved. It is not strictly a matter of seeking 'authenticity' but rather of matching evidence to a model, ring-fenced by historical probability. In a large-scale construction like ours, there are three other controlling factors, one negative, two positive: negatively, there are few chances of reconstructing the reconstruction, as was done with the helmet. But secondly, unlike the helmet, there is a modern international community of contemporary users, on rivers and the sea; and third, the construction is undertaken by a team: every decision is strengthened at the time by the responses of a large group of participants. It is the membership of the company acting together, that puts a break on excessive guesswork, and supports or rejects a model. Their number, and their diversity, compensate, to some extent, for the fact that none of us has ever been to the seventh century (and come back). The crew building the ship resemble a permanently assembled jury, mitigating evidence with their intuition.

As an example, consider two debates requiring decisions. The first, on the choice of materials needed to make the ship, was quickly resolved as being oak and iron since this could be verified by the original evidence.[30] The idea of using copper nails had some support, since the fastenings would last longer, but because the iron rivets actually used were fact, not hypothesis, the choice was clear. We were reconstructing a particular ship not designing a look-alike. The second, more difficult, was its mode of propulsion. We had good evidence that the ship was rowed (the tholes or oarlocks), but little that it sailed: a shallow keel, no step for a mast, no fixing points for shrouds. On the other hand, the British Museum study had pronounced the hull as "sufficiently developed for sailing".[31] The question therefore depended on inference, a philosophical marsh with which archaeology is quite familiar. The limits of inference were fairly clear: the mast and rigging could have been removed before the ship was prepared for burial and hauling up the hill. This, and the poor survival of wood, cloth and ropes, could account for its absence. Given that the early seventh century in England was a time of technical experiment (Chapter 3), it was not impossible that Sutton Hoo was a rowing ship that experimented with a "jury rig", a temporary arrangement that would leave little trace. To these limits of inference can be added a fact: the ship was a working ship and had not sunk.[32]

The Sutton Hoo Ship was built for northern waters at time when the use of sails was apparently not documented but was about to happen (Chapter 4). Inference was in favour: sailing was exercised freely by the Romans who had conquered Britannia and left many a cultural bequest behind them when they departed. As related in earlier chapters, sailing was well known in the Mediterranean, and East Angles had gone there in Rædwald's day. But the 9-strake hull suggested a lower freeboard and was consequently more liable to take on water under sail, than the slightly shorter but 16-strake hull of the Gokstad sailing ship, with its flexibly attached lower frame (see Chapter 4). On the other hand, a boat as large as Sutton Hoo's would have very limited use or reputation if confined to the Deben. It must have gone to sea, but the prospect of managing tides and wind without a sail invited scepticism: the winds and tides would affect the rowing boat without necessarily propelling it in the desired direction.

So, while the use of oak and iron were justified by evidence, the use of sail

5.16 The decoration on the stem-post of *Edda* 1988, and (right) the decoration on the 2012 *Saga Oseberg*, showing that when the ship is correctly trimmed the decoration terminates at the water line both fore and aft.

was driven mainly by reasoned judgement and could only be given credence through experiment. This left open the form of the sail and the rigging, which could be drawn from contemporary ships, and with more relevance by the ships to come, starting with Oseberg. Here the argument is still equivocal. Given the nature of the surrounding seas, and the numerous artefacts and people travelling to and from the island at the time of Sutton Hoo, it would not be surprising to encounter, one day, examples of northern sailing boats earlier than Sutton Hoo. The main burden of the experiment will rest with performance. The sail would be neither the first nor the last component to go beyond the evidence at hand, while staying within the probability of the context. All archaeology is a combination of science and imagination, record and inference, parallel and analogy. Never entirely scientific nor entirely imaginary, its results and models occupy the messy territory in between – the joined-up synthesis. All such reasoning is duly recorded, providing a paper trail to the newly defined 'reality'. In maritime experiment, there is of course one more external principle in play that trumps all the others: the need to ensure stability on the water, not only for the protection of participants, but because we can be quite sure that the people we are studying knew what it meant to be seaworthy. The Sutton Hoo Mound 1 ship was not a shipwreck.

A third example, not yet resolved, is the matter of the ship's final appearance. Following the evidence of the earliest Viking ship, that from Oseberg dating a century later than Sutton Hoo, the carving of artistic patterns in the wood was an integral feature of the design.[34] The patterns moreover are descendants of the animal ornament so prolific among the early Germanic peoples **(FIG 5.16)**. Although anachronistic, an artistic retrofitting is permissible, based on the Sutton Hoo repertoire. Such details as we have from the ship's structure show an expert awareness of symmetry and shape; the rivets were fitted in perfect lines with the long axis of the roves aligned with the strakes. The reconstructed wooden parts were crafted to fit their original purpose and emerged as smooth geometric forms that Barbara Hepworth would have admired. There is good reason to believe that the builders of the original ship would have aimed at their own versions of the same meticulous artistry, seen in the early seventh-century community of crafts argued for in Chapter 3, whether metalworkers, textile workers or carpenters of halls. In this spirit, the artists of our day may legitimately carve linked animals on the stem and stern posts, interlace on the tholes and contrive three-dimensional effigies on the figure heads.

SOCIALISING, NATURALISING AND FUNDING THE RESEARCH PROGRAMME

The building of the ship has certainly excited public interest, and this could be greeted favourably; but inevitably there will be doubts about our project's contributions to the modern world. All research shares this hazard, in that much of it is led by curiosity and has no obvious or immediate benefit to society. You could say something similar about astronomy, a science that attracted Basil Brown. Research does bring social dividends, in that research ultimately benefits everyone. But at ground level there are anxieties about wasting natural resources in a stressed planet, and we initially incurred some criticism for felling oaks. In practice, our oaks were mainly felled by their owners in the course of their management: many were dead or dying or needed clearing for environmental or commercial concerns. These oaks were often subsequently donated to the project. Our Project Manager also drove an imaginative scheme of conservation whereby acorns were collected from an oak about to be felled and nurtured into seedlings before being planted in a piece of dedicated land near Woodbridge. Twenty descendent oaks for every oak felled was the goal. Every scrap of unused wood is recycled, not burnt, much of it fashioned into souvenirs, such as bowls and spoons for visitors. The oak chippings have also reinstated many woodland floors, oak bark has been incorporated into school project bird houses, and oak shavings flavour our Saxon Ship Gin.[35] We planned to be a green project in other ways too, notably our championing of rowing and rivers. And our project is embedded in the local and the wider community.

Since the 1980s, and arguably earlier, social engagement has become its own prominent driver in all high-profile archaeological projects. Ole Crumlin Pedersen showed how chance discoveries can be socialised by gently steering local loyalists into the waters of international fame through continuous inspiration, encouragement, dialogue, engagement, participation and empowerment. Business-orientated trustees can be oblivious to the rewards of research dividends. But equally, social benefits can be somewhat taken for granted by academic archaeologists used to working with seasonal volunteers, and sometimes opposed altogether by professional excavators who object to unpaid, untrained people participating in their operations against the clock. But the ability to recruit and credit public engagement is now an essential aid to fund-raising. Thanks to its Project Manager and Shipwrights, the building of the Sutton Hoo Ship was extensively socialised from the outset, both in its intense cultivation of a public following and in its recruitment of volunteer helpers not only to assist the build, but to serve in every domain of the company's activity.

Funding is also affected by the way a project situates itself within national and international values. In this case, the design, archaeological, historical and social, was in favour of raising the ship from a local venture to a higher level, increasing the number of potential donors and stressing the wider impact. There is a marked difference between three common strategies of fund raising: (1) pitching to fiercely competitive research councils and charitable institutions, (2) relying on individual wealthy donors, who may have their own agenda, or (3) appealing to the many supporters who buy souvenirs, put coins in a box or contribute to crowd funding, but who may not succeed in meeting the project's total expenses. My own experience of funding archaeological projects has been diverse: a consortium of institutions (Sutton Hoo), the National Lottery Heritage Fund (Tarbat) and an international central fund, the European Research Council (Sicily). These were all competitive in their different ways, involving close scrutiny of the applicant, but more finely focused on the submitted design. The NL Heritage Fund also requires a dedication to the local community, while the goal of the other two projects was the pursuit of "blue skies" discovery. The funding of the ship seemed to demand something different from all these. Experimental archaeology was, and still is, considered only marginally fruitful to the big questions, and often only occurs as an afterthought. Faith in the methodology is weak, and the outcomes not seen as determinant: how we built our ship and what happened to it in trials need not replicate the experience of the past. In brief, the humanities may see the venture as recreational, and the sciences may regard its results as untestable. However, research councils are slowly beginning to realise that research is given a separate value and credibility by the endorsement of the public at large (they call it impact, or citizen science).

Our goals require us to combine research and impact, to devise funding packages in which both the experts and the public are potential allies, and which serve local, national and international communities. These goals were delivered by creating a wide following of volunteers inside, and stakeholders outside, the Longshed: in this way donors, sponsors and those contributing to crowd funding or offering their own labour provide a solid foundation. As well as building the ship, the volunteers form a cadre of guides and assist the Project Manager in administering a project of ever increasing size and public attraction, in particular via a massive social media network. The Ship's Company has found a moving picture partner in *Time Team*, the crowd-funded archaeology broadcaster, so greatly increasing its outreach to the general public. We have remained in formal partnership with the National Trust team at Sutton Hoo, the Sutton Hoo Society, and in friendly association with experimental shipbuilders in Roskilde. These partnerships and alliances will be fully appreciated only when the job is complete and the ship is launched, two or three years away at the time of writing. Museums were built at Sutton Hoo and Tarbat on the back of research excavations and both have remained active for 24 and 26 years respectively. The ship too will hopefully continue to enchant its public when its trials are complete.

LOOKING TO THE FUTURE: THE TRIALS AND THEIR REWARDS

Before any trials start, the ship has the potential to make a lasting research impact. You only have to think of the size of the vessel as it looms in the Longshed, surprising even to those who saw its impression in the sand; it is astonishing to those in the know that have only seen photographs; and to those that knew little or nothing about it, the effect is stunning. Just encountering a ship the size of a whale elevates the Anglo-Saxons to the status of the imperial Romans - which was no doubt the intent of its builders. The ship came with no instruction manual, and the techniques that our Master Shipwright and his crew have been obliged to devise, in order to create a robust sea-going vessel, has undoubtedly provided numerous pointers to seventh-century seafaring even while it is still on the stocks. Embedded in the complete reconstruction are signs of early English thinking: in metric units the ship was approximately 27 m long, the beam 4.5 m, and the height 1.5 m amidships, so that an attributable ratio of length to beam was 6:1 of beam to height, 3:1. Such ratios may be signs of wider learning, given the use of standard measures and ratios in contemporary hall carpentry, as was found at Yeavering (Chapter 3).[36] In brief, the research outcome anticipated from the build is likely to lead deep into early English society, which in turn is relevant to people living today.

The success of Roskilde's Vibeke Bischoff in sailing the *Saga Oseberg*, mentioned in Chapter 4, produced a nineteen-point plan which had some salutary advice for testing experimental ships. Once the design is fixed (based on the archaeological evidence), assemble a team with experience of an equivalent type of ship, ensure the ship lies in the water with the decoration on the stem and stern posts ending at the water line, make the oars of different lengths and vary the placing of the crew and ballast to achieve trim: "it is all about how the ship prefers it, not how the test sailor prefers it".[37] The Sutton Hoo Ship starts from a rather different place: the archaeology provides a good indication of the form of the hull and we can be sure she was rowed, but there was no evidence for oars, rigging, sails or decoration. Our programme requires an unusual amount of hypothesis-testing and lateral thinking, but we will not always have the luxury of repeating the tests with revised hypotheses.[38] After the launch will come the trials and voyages - and here I reflect briefly on the form these might take; only briefly, because although they form part of our research ambition, much can change between the time this book first appears and that special moment when the ship is launched.

Six *objectives* of the trials predominate: the first to remake a seaworthy ship, the second to learn to row it, the third to navigate in different waters under oars, the fourth to experiment with sails, the fifth to undertake voyages under sail and the sixth to move the ship over land. All six will have the ultimate goal of remaking history, and there is some logic in programming them in that order, for reasons both of handling and safety. Before the ship is launched there is much measuring to do, together with the creation of a data bank that can be used to monitor the performance of each part of the ship once it is on the water. Only then can the basic tests of stability and seaworthiness begin (*Objective 1*). While the overall shape of the hull cannot be altered during trials, there are many fixings that can: the steering gear, the length and shape of the oars, the tholes, the height of the thwarts and the ballast, can all be modified if necessary, following stability trials - which would be conducted in calm water.

Rowing, as an endemic early medieval activity, is much less well tested in experimental archaeology, which is odd since it was the major form of propulsion at the time (*Objective 2*). For fighting vessels, rowing was the reliable and flexible method of manoeuvre - for sprinting, charging, turning (or beating a retreat). Rowing takes you onto islands and far up estuaries and rivers, whatever the wind and current. The *Tilia* enterprise showed how much of the performance of a paddled ship is dependent on the crew, their training and monitoring over extended periods. The crew of a rowed ship presents this challenge tenfold: the working crew is the subject of the experiment, no less than the seaworthy ship. The crew is to be carefully chosen, matching their position in the ship - they must learn to row in time in spite of the differences in height above the water line, learn how to avoid the person in front, how to communicate when the wind is high, how to stop rapidly using oars and anchors, how to get on and off a beach, how to approach a landing place, how to get on board and how to disembark over a 2 m drop.[39] Loading the ship with crews and horses, rations and cargo, losing, breaking and replacing oars, coping with wind, tide and current, reversing, steering, racing to a destination, anchoring, mooring, beaching and relaunching are all activities associated with early English people and their settlements.

When we are planning *Objective 3*, testing voyages under oars, the natural starting point is the history we already have, briefly assembled in Chapter 1. Here we have seen that the age of Sutton Hoo was highly mobile; within the island, journeys by Roman road and prehistoric routes and voyages along the east coast and into estuaries were the norm. Broad estuaries like the Humber could be crossed by rowing boat, as they had been since the Bronze Age, and short sea passages, for example across the Channel, or from the Rhinemouth to the Wash, could be rowed as the ancestral Anglo-Saxons had done. The likelihood of river journeys is endorsed by the settlement pattern - much of it, whether of Roman origin or due to the immigrant Angles, focused on rivers. This is in some ways a new departure, since the majority of early experimental ships, especially the Viking ships, have been tasked to sail across the sea from one port to another. They were often out of sight of land, so that neither the public nor the crew could engage with the historic ship in its historic seascape. There are positive gains for our experiment in assuming a community of rowers. The rowing clubs associated with each river can be pilots and participants so that many people nationwide can experience what it is like to row the flagship of an early English kingdom. The voyages could take the crews to named places inland, where recorded events, such as battles, had occurred. Here the experimental ship could moor and the crew and guest-crews and the media could celebrate the occasion. This would provide a mobile theatre in which to promote a great form of exercise, healthy, peaceful and safe, not mention to fund-raise. Filming the ship on rivers will also help to draw attention to their poor condition, pollution and peremptory maintenance, which have climbed high in the public agenda since our project started.

The logistics for crewing these voyages will not be simple. A reserve crew is essential to maintain travel against adverse wind and tide. A sheltered rest area in the middle of the ship (where the chamber was and where no tholes were found) could be a solution. Storage of food and clothing will be needed, perhaps in a modified bilge under the deck. These crews will need to be weatherproof, tough, alert and cheerful - but a rare adventure awaits them.

One historical and two green benefits must also help win support from supporters and donors. The proposed voyages themselves could be designed

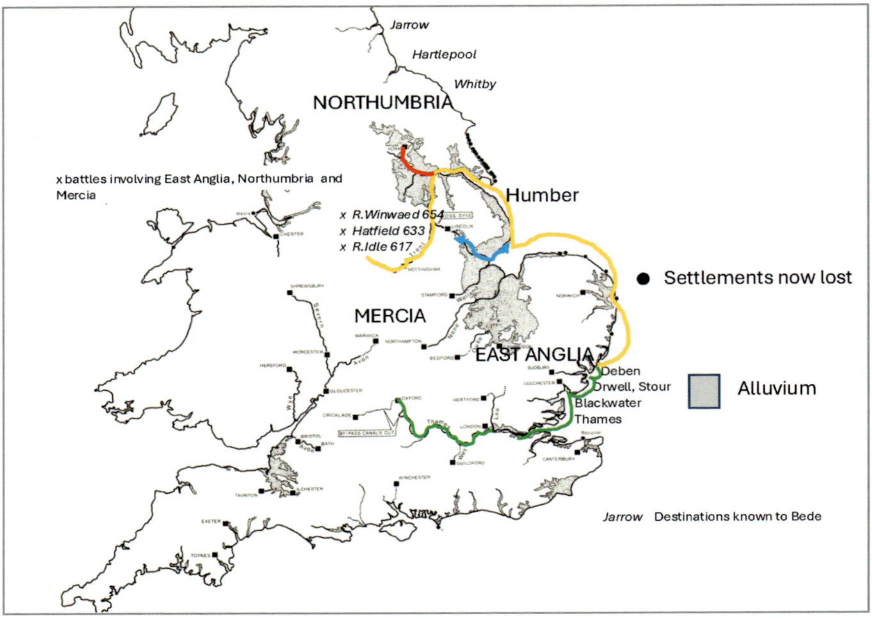

5.17 Hypothetical river journeys made from East Anglia to its seventh-century neighbours: *Green* - Kent, London, Wessex, Oxford. *Amber* - Wash, Humber, Trent, Mercia; *Blue* - Wash, Lincoln, Trent; *Red* - Humber, Ouse, York.

both to illuminate seventh century life and to promote the ship in its ultimate role as a national icon. There are benefits to be won from voyaging down the coast to Kent where Rædwald reviewed Christianity and both Edwin and Oswiu obtained queens, and into Wessex where Edwin quelled their churls. This would provide an opportunity to parade our ship along the Thames and through London, with evident research and funding benefits. A second journey might follow Rædwald and Edwin and their army northwards to the battlefields of the Northumbrian/Mercian border. A third, still further north, could take us up the Ouse to the Deiran capital of York **(FIG 5.17)**. Is this what our ship was used for? The three major battles of the wars of the seventh kingdoms took place on the frontier between Northumbria and Mercia, marked by the Humber and its tributaries. But there was a Roman road south of the Humber that ran from Lincoln round the Humber estuary via Tadcaster to York. All three battles lay on this road: in 617, when Æthelfrith was killed, where it crossed the river Idle; in 633, when Edwin was killed, where it crossed the River Thorn and in 654, when Penda was finally despatched, where it crossed the River Winwaed **(FIG 5.18)**. It was not a given that no ships were used, but it meant that - as suggested in Chapter 1 - journeys were planned with the combination of land and water best suited to the speed and payload of the

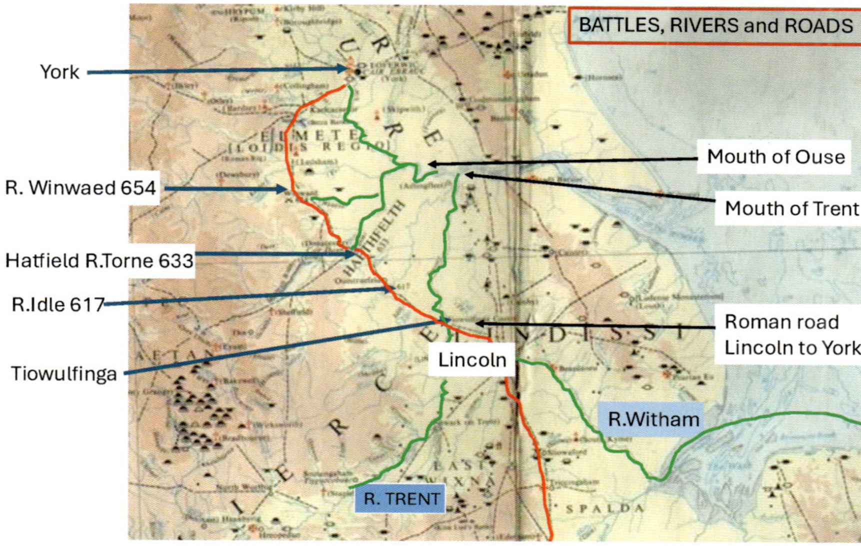

5.18 Map of the Mercia - Northumbria frontier with Roman roads and battle sites.

operation. This means that the river trials must be composed in partnership with more searching exercises in connectivity: tracking functioning roads, hill routes, navigable rivers, estuaries and coastal waters. There is an opportunity here to bring in recent research on Anglo-Saxon signalling systems that gave early warning of Viking intruders from beacons on hill tops.[40] Such hill tops were of course already there in the seventh century.

Other factors may broaden the agenda beyond "Can we do it?" to "Did they do it?" Testing whether our ship made such river journeys, will have to face up to the alterations to Britain's waterways since the seventh century. Initial reconnaissance has revealed a number of impediments: river channels have been narrowed by locks, canalisation and flood banks. Some bridges are too low for a mast and those that once welcomed a square-sailed Humber Keel no longer swing or lift **(FIG 5.19)**. These journeys (especially up the Trent and its tributaries) are not completely excluded, since a mast that could be readily lowered was also a feature of nineteenth century barges and could also be of our ship.

Once our ship has been built, and tested as a top-class rowing vessel, aligning with authenticity to the maximum, sailing experiments with dismountable rigs will come to the top of the agenda (*Objective 4*). Any model for early seventh-century travel certainly allows expeditions within the island by road, using horses and carts, and by rivers and coastal waters using rowing ships. Journeys further abroad, to and across the continent and into the Mediterranean, did not necessarily involve native mariners who sailed, since 'public

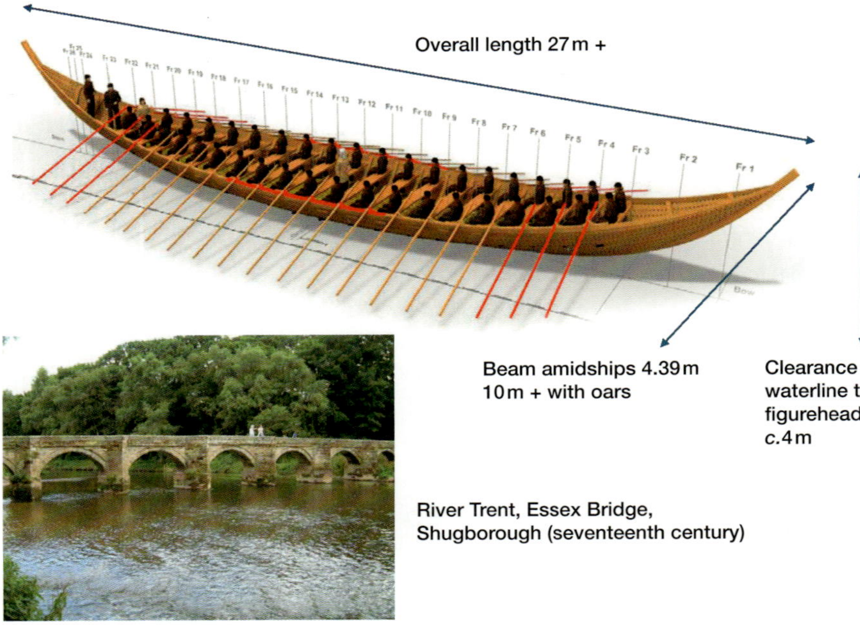

5.19 The reconstructed Sutton Hoo ship will have trouble with modern bridges and locks.

transport' could be provided by those that did, and who knew the way, and were available to take any party of warriors or pilgrims in relays from eastern England to Syria. But, as time went on, there were more documented journeys from Britain to the continent and into the Mediterranean, and many seem to involve sailing or waiting for favourable winds. If the Sutton Hoo Ships did not sail, the innovative artisan community we have visited make sailing experiments likely; they were on the threshold of sailing. Within a few generations of Rædwald's burial, sailing was the norm. By the later seventh-century and into the eighth, monasteries flourished on the banks of estuaries, connected by ships - and vulnerable to Vikings.

Assuming sailing in a variety of waters and winds proves viable, flexible and stable, further connectivity can be more easily investigated by planned voyages (*Objective 5*), with our ship visiting ports along the east and south coasts of Britain, crossing the North Sea to Ribe, Esbjerg, Roskilde and Gotland, crossing the Channel, travelling up the Rhine into Germany, up the Seine into France, down the Saône and the Rhône to the Mediterranean. The documented journeys, traced in earlier chapters, leave little doubt that East Angles of the early seventh to early eighth century knew something about the geography of the coastal waters of the Channel, the North Sea, the Baltic, the Mediterranean and its islands, and the continental rivers that led to it. It is right to include this larger area in our field of study and acknowledge the

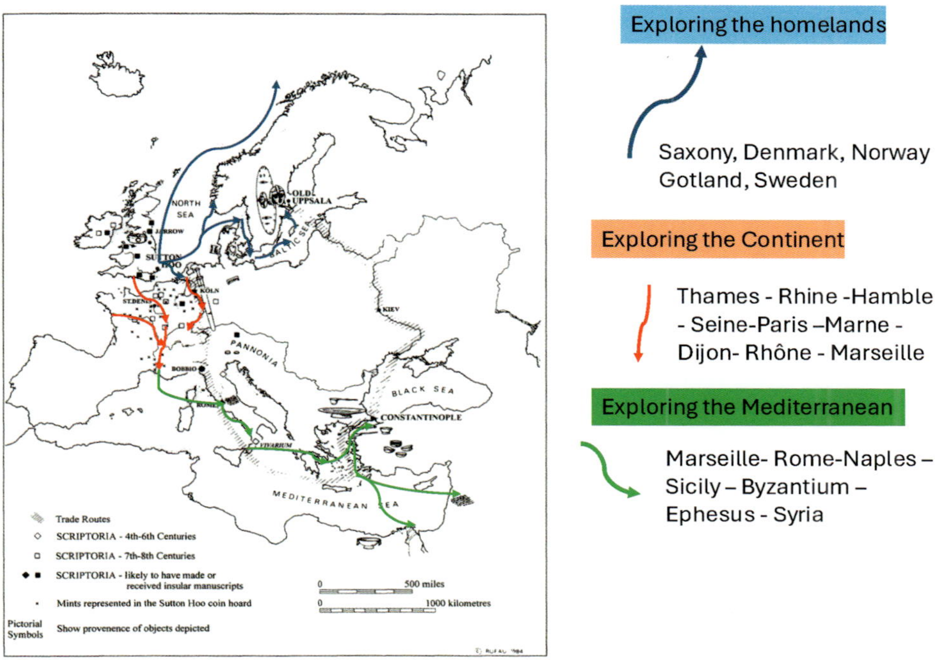

5.20 The potential range of seventh century English river and sea travel, Scandinavia, the Continent, the Mediterranean.

broad and varied context in which the building and the eventual trials take place. The homelands, the continent and the Mediterranean are three areas that concern our ship and invite us to bring these early medieval pioneers to life before they are entirely forgotten **(FIG 5.20)**. Maybe the passengers transshipped to more local vessels, but who knows? The world of the early English was opening up. Maybe only warriors, kings and prelates travelled. Maybe a prelate pulled an oar. But more likely the seafarers and merchants must have gone too. Their experience, intuitions, dangers and pleasures are unrecorded. But like the artisans, they are the real heroes of this research enterprise.

The trials and voyages will hopefully address some other fundamental matters such as the national attitude to the sea, from the people who find it fun or fearful to the people who depend upon it for their livelihood. From century to century, the North Sea in particular changes its role from a thoroughfare to a barrier and back. In Britain's formative period we have studied this from a technical point of view - the difficulties of relying on oars in ferocious tides, the perils of sailing in winter. But we have also seen how the traffic can switch direction and frequency due to changes in the economy or religion. The artisans can make everything possible: but politics and ideology can make the possible impossible.[41]

5.21 The River Deben and Sutton Hoo, showing a possible portage route from the river to the ship's place of burial.

The final experiment (*Objective 6*) is to discover how the ship was taken from the water and dragged up the hill to the 100ft (30m) contour. The route of least resistance from the Deben to the site of Mound 1 is probably the one that follows the valleys **(FIG 5.21)**. This one-way portage is hardly typical of the short cut across the neck of a peninsula commonly serving Irish Sea mariners in the fifth to seventh centuries, but we will be bound to learn something of its challenges and logistics. It cannot fail to be a splendid spectacle, a great mass of people, horses, ropes and rollers. It would be very pleasant and appropriate if the ship could then go into retirement on the Sutton Hoo site itself, to be exhibited and curated by the National Trust. But these are conversations that have scarcely begun and other long-term possibilities remain.

ENVOI

Our ship has the potential to be a national ambassador, creating a public following through Europe; each stage of the trials programme has the chance of publicising, and funding, the next. But its role as a research vessel is paramount, if less obvious. Its performance, the logistics of its voyages, the experiences of its crews in fair weather and foul, in all kinds of waters, can yield far more than admiration of a technical and artistic achievement of seventh-century Suffolk. Directly or indirectly, it will address many of the key issues of maritime history, past and present; the establishment of former groups of

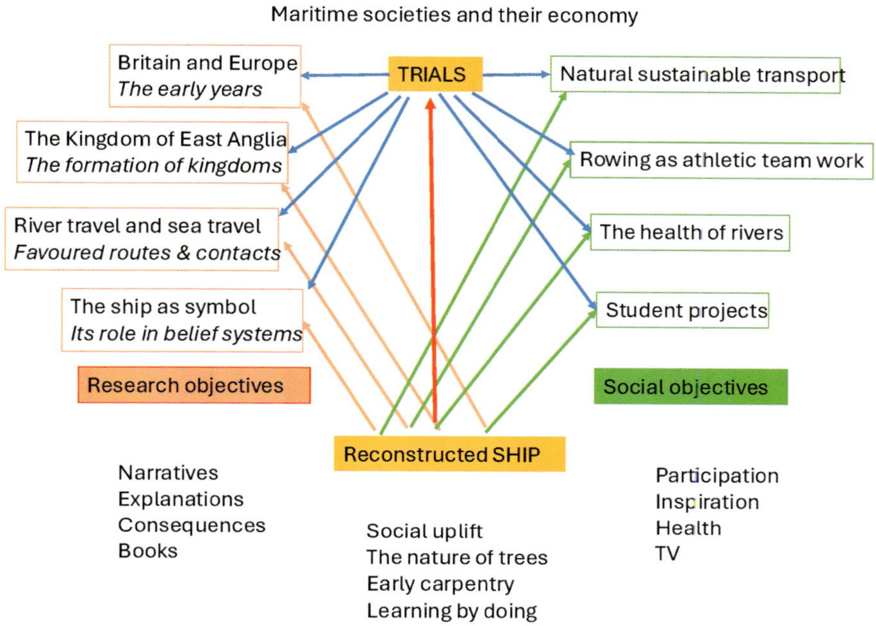

5.22 A mind map for the project, summarising research and social gains.

5.23 Members of the Ship's Company in 2023.

international coastal communities by the ease of the passage between them, exploring natural cultural and trade associations, and the flow of ideas and genes implied by artefacts, architecture and burial rites, exposing in this way a natural web of interconnections. The early English were real people rediscovering the potential of their geography. Ships, the most important machines in their lives, directly affected not only the connections, but the politics, economies and societies of early medieval Europe.

Ideally, the construction and trials of the Experimental Sutton Hoo Ship will prove to be the founder-vessel in a continuing initiative dedicated to historic shipbuilding. As can be seen from Chapter 4, there are many candidates for reconstruction and trials that would take the maritime story forward, from Bronze Age logboats, like those found in Must Farm, Roman cargo vessels like Blackfriars 1, expanded oak canoes like Snape, early medieval rafts, and rowing and sailing boats for traveling on the sea, royal barges, medieval merchantmen and traditional farming and fishing boats as in Orkney, known from photographs and fast disappearing from our shores. The construction of the Sutton Hoo ship will have created a college of historic ship-builders, equipped with the skills and discipline for reconstructing any historic vessel for which there is evidence, and to teach others to do it. In a world that likes their museums to be alive and their visitors to touch as well as see, building and paddling, rowing or sailing reconstructed historic and prehistoric boats is an attractive way to bring the past to life. England, belonging to an island nation, needs such a hub and nowhere is more suitable than its east coast.

That's for the future. Meanwhile, I end this introductory presentation with a *mindmap* illustrating the hoped-for outcomes of the present build and the trials, as contributions to research objectives and social benefits **(FIG 5.22)**. Each of these objectives and the benefits they deliver will need continual development - we are not even half-way through the project. The first step is to get the ship built, for which we need the shipwrights to lead us, and to understand how the business of the Ship's Company was developed and performed, for which the Project Manager is our guide. The gilt-edged capital of the Ship's Company is its crew, whose ever-increasing skills promise a long term future in historic ship construction **(FIG 5.23)**. Then we will sit in on the grand debate of the Trustees and crew on the future trials and journeys of the ship after the build and be at the waterside as the ship is launched. After the launch, still a few years away, the ship will undergo its trials prior to her maiden voyage. Then we will hope to learn at first hand the complex and influential relationship that early English islanders had with the sea. I leave you with the mixed feelings of an Anglo-Saxon *Seafarer*, as expressed in some tenth-century hostelry.

The River Deben winding to the sea. Low tide.

THE SEAFARER

I can tell you about life on the sea; it's grim. Many a long day I've suffered at the end of an oar, fearfully managing wind and wave; or at nightfall clenched in the bows peering at passing cliffs. With freezing feet and pangs of hunger, trapped in a boat, nothing to hear but hail and spray, no pals but gannets, no laughs but the screech of gulls, no helping hand. You'd do better on land, I tell you.

Sitting at table, pushing out the wine with fellow traders, you've no idea what we go through. Yet when the cuckoo calls we're off again, leaving the blossom, never seeing the fruit, missing the glint of rings, the love of women, the fellowship of the cup, all this, to brave the sea and its tricky ways. But then the swell takes us, raising us up in the water, onto our bearing, pulling, heaving and lurching towards the horizon, and my heart lifts.

Profit and admiration are earned though the perils of seafaring; it's not without honour. Sure, a boat can go to the bottom; but life on land ends too: in illness, in old age, in a fight. It ends for earls, for kings, for emperors no less than seafarers. None escapes life's end, white hair, pale face, bent body, muttering, all friends gone before. Tip gold into his grave - you won't bring him back. But at sea the whole ocean is there to mourn you.[42]

PRINCIPAL ACTORS

[spelling after Bede HE edited McClure and Collins]
æ is short a as in 'cat'

Ælfflæd, daughter of Oswiu
Ælle, K. of Deirans, father of Edwin
Æthelberht, K of Kent
Æthelburh (Tata), d. of Æthelberht, 2nd. w. of Edwin
Æthelfrith, K. of Bernicia
Æthelhun, son of Edwin and Tata
Æthelthryth, daughter of Edwin and Tata
Cædwalla, K. of Britons
Cwichelm, K. of Wessex
Cwenburh, 1st wife of Edwin
Eadbald, K. of Kent, brother of Tata
Eadfrith, son of Edwin and Cwenburh
Ealdwulf, K. of East Anglia in Bede's time
Eanflæd, d. of Edwin and Tata; wife of Oswiu
Eanfrith, son of Æthelfrith; K.of Bernicia
Ecgfrith, K of Northumbria
Edwin, K. of Northumbria
Eomer, attempted murderer of Edwin
Eorpwald, K. of East Angles
Osfrith, son of Edwin and Cwenburh
Oswald, son of Æthelfrith, K. of Northumbria
Oswiu, son of Æthelfrith, K of Northumbria
Penda, K. of Mercia
Rædwald, K. of East Angles
Regenhere, son of Rædwald,
Sæberht, K. of East Saxons
Sigeberht, K. of East Angles
Tytil, K. of East Angles
Uscfrea, son of Edwin and Tata
Wuffa, K. of East Angles

SEVENTH CENTURY TIMELINE

According to Bede, *History of the English Church and People*
[ ] = events not recorded in Bede]

563	Columba to Iona
565	Columba's mission to the Picts
571	*East Anglia*: Wuffa K. of East Anglia
578	*East Anglia*: Tytil K. of East Anglia
597	*Kent*: Augustine arrives in Britain; conversion of K. Æthelberht
599	*East Anglia*: accession of K. Rædwald
603	*Bernicia*: Battle of Degsastan. Æthelfrith of Bernicia drives Scots out of England
604	*Essex*: Conversion of Essex under K.Sæberht by Mellitus
613-617	*East Anglia* (on the Deben): Edwin at the court of King Rædwald.
616	*Kent*: Death of K. Æthelberht
616	*Essex and Kent*: Kings of Essex and Kent revert to paganism
616	Battle of Chester. Æthelfrith slaughters the monks of Bangor
617	Northern Border: Rædwald and Edwin defeat Æthelfrith at Battle of the Idle. Edwin marries Æthelburh daughter of Æthelberht of Kent, also known as Tata
625	Tata arrives in Northumbria
624/5	[*East Anglia*: Death of K. Rædwald. Burial of Rædwald at Sutton Hoo] Accession of K. Eorpwald
625	Paulinus appointed Bishop of Northumbrians
626	*Mercia*: accession of Penda of Mercia
626	*Deira*: April 20 Easter day. Attempted murder of Edwin at his royal palace on the Derwent
626	*Deira*: Same day: Eanflæd, daughter of Edwin and Tata, born
626-7	*Deira*: Edwin and Tata receive admonitory letters and gifts from Pope Boniface
627	*Deira*: Edwin baptised at York in the church of St Peter on Easter Day (April 11)
627/8	*East Anglia*: Eorpwald, Christian successor to Rædwald, killed by pagan Richberht
630/1	*East Anglia*: accession of Sigeberht, half brother of Eorpwald
633	*Bernicia*: Paulinus accompanies the royal family to Yeavering; baptises in the River Glen

633	*Bernicia*: Another letter from the Pope (Honorius)
633	*Deira*: Edwin killed at Battle of Hatfield Chase (near Doncaster) by Penda. Succeeded in Deira by Osric, cousin of Edwin and in Bernicia by Eanfrith son of Æthelfrith
633	Birth of Edwin's grandson Yffi, Osfrid's son. Tata takes flight with Paulinus back to Kent, with Eanflæd, Uscfrea, Yffi, escorted by Bassus
634	*West Border*. Death of Osric son of Æthelfrith, fighting Cædwalla, in Wales. Death of Eanfrith, son of Æthelfrith, killed by Cædwalla at a parley with 12 thegns. Succeeded by Oswald
634	*Northumbria*: Oswald sets up a wooden cross at Heavenfield
634	*Northumbria*: Oswald destroys Cædwalla, at Deniseburn. (Rowley Water, Northumberland)
635	*Bernicia*: Mission of Aidan to Lindisfarne
635	*Wessex*: Baptism of Cynegils of Wessex
636/7	*East Anglia*: K. Sigeberht and cousin Ecgric killed by Penda
638	*Northumbria*: Oswald at war with Mercia
641-3	*Wessex*: Old Minster at Winchester begun
642	*Mercia*: Oswald killed by Penda at Battle of Maserfelth (Oswestry = Oswald's tree) on his way to Wales
642	*Northumbria*: Marriage of Oswiu and Eanflæd
644	Paulinus dies
644	*Northumbria*: Accession of Oswine of Deira
644	*East Anglia*: Accession of K. Anna
651	*Northumbria*: Oswine murdered
651	*Northern Borders*: Cuthbert enters Melrose
651	Death of Aidan
651	Utta rides to Kent to fetch Edwin's daughter Eanflæd as a bride for Oswiu - and returns by sea
*c.*651	*Northumbria*: Penda invading and besieging Bamburgh and trying to burn it down
653	Conversion of Middle Angles under Peada
653	Reconversion of Essex
655	*Northumbria*: Oswiu tries to buy off Penda with an "incalculable and incredible treasure"
655	*Northern Border*: Penda killed at the Battle of the Winwæd by Oswiu; and Mercians became Christian
658	Mercia rebels against Oswiu
664	*Deira*: Synod of Whitby; Oswy rules for Roman Christinaity
670	Northumbria: Oswiu died aged 58

670 *Scotland*: Arculf on Iona
672 *Pictland*: Pictish army massacred by Ecgfrid. Bridei son of Bile, K. of Picts until 693
673 Synod of Hertford
674 *Northumbria*: Foundation of Wearmouth
675 *Kent*: Hadrian and Theodore arrived from Rome. Institutional Christianity applied.
675 *Mercia*: Wulfhere, king of Mercians died after a reign of 17 years [ie from 658]
680 *Northumbria*: Death of Hilda at 66
681 *Northumbria*: Building of Jarrow begun
681 *Pictland*: Bridei son of Bili attacks the Orkneys
685 *Pictland*: Ecgfrith of Northumbria killed by the Picts at Nechtansmere 21 May
685 *Northumbria*: Consecration of Cuthbert
685 *Northumbria*: Consecration of Jarrow 3 April
690 Willibrord in Frisia; 692 in Rome
697 *Mercia*: Queen Osthryth killed by her own people, the Mercian chiefs
698 *Pictland*: Bertred, Northumbrian general killed by the Picts
700 *Northumbria*: Lindisfarne Gospels composed
704 *Mercia*: Ethelred resigns and becomes a monk after a 30 year reign
705 *Northumbria*: Death of Aldfrid of Northumbria
709 *Mercia*: Coenred of Mercia resigned and goes to Rome
710 *Northumbria*: Ceolfrith of Jarrow writes to Nechtan K of Picts
711 *Pictland*: Earl Bertfrid fought the Picts
716 *Northumbria*: Osred of Northumbria killed,
716 *Northumbria*: Ceolfrith of Jarrow died at Langres on his way to Rome with the *Codex Amiatinus*
716 *Scotland*: Egbert converted the monks of Iona to Northumbrian Christianity
725 *Northumbria*: Osric of Northumbria died; Egbert died
731 *Northumbria*: King Ceolwulf was captured, tonsured and restored to his kingdom
731 *Kent*: Archbishop of Canterbury Berhtwald died
Tatwine consecrated in his place
735 *Northumbria*: Death of Bede

NOTES

CHAPTER 1

1. The text used is Bede *The Ecclesiastical History of the English People* trans. Bertram Colgrave, ed. Judith McClure and Roger Collins (OUP, 2008) abbreviated to HE, with the book and chapter: for example HE.II,12 for the plan to murder Edwin. A list of characters and a timeline is provided on pages 157-161.
2. HE I.34
3. Degsastan is perhaps Dawstan Ridge in Liddesdale.
4. HE II.12
5. HE II.5
6. HE II.9
7. HE II.15. A tall building of temple type has been found in the current investigations at Rendlesham. (Scull et al. 2024b, and see Chapter 3).
8. HE II.2
9. HE II.12
10. For the Roman roads and other aspects of early British geography, I have made use of the still excellent *Ordnance Survey Map of Britain in the Dark Ages* (HMSO, 1966).
11. In this summary account I accept the unproven assumption that Rædwald, cited as king of East Anglia, was active around the Deben in the late sixth and early seventh century. He had a palace at Rendlesham and was buried in Mound 1 at Sutton Hoo, both investigated archaeologically with results that have done nothing to diminish the association and great deal to support it (Bruce-Mitford 1975; Scull et al 2024a,b).
12. HE II.9
13. Where I happen to live.
14. HE.II.9; HE.II.12
15. HE.II.10, 11
16. HE II.13
17. HE II.16.
18. HE II.20
19. HE III.9
20. HE III.24
21. HE.III.24
22. HE III.25
23. HE III.24
24. HE III.18
25. *Anglo-Saxon Chronicle* under year 866 (Whitelock 1961, 45).
26. For example those posited on the invaluable *Ordnance Survey Map of Britain in the Dark Ages* (2nd edn 1966).
27. And more strongly asserted by archaeology as suggestive of a seventh-century equestrian class (Chapter 2).
28. See archaeological evidence from Rendlesham cited in Chapter 3.
29. See Spong Hill and Sutton Hoo in Chapters 2 and 3.
30. HE.III.15
31. HE.V.9
32. HE.V.15

CHAPTER 2

1. Bonde et al. 2016, and see below.
2. See Carver 2019, 634-7 for overview of changes. The 'Dark Ages' is there renamed Britain's *Formative Period*.
3. Blair 2018 for buildings; West 1985 for West Stow; Hope-Taylor 1977 for Yeavering; and see now Scull et al. 2024a,b for Rendlesham.

4. Carver 2019, 84-99 for overview.
5. Carver 2019, 63; Caruth and Hines 2024.
6. Hills and Lucy 2013, 24, 229.
7. Carver 2019, 390-409.
8. Carver et al, 2009.
9. Dickinson 1993.
10. Hines in Caruth and Hines 2024, 229-230. And See *Saxon*, 76, 7-8 for a report on the cemetery at Eriswell, RAF Lakenheath.
11. Dickinson 1993, 53.
12. For overview of women as spiritual specialists Price 2001 and 2002, 112- 122; as part of a pre-Christian circumpolar belief system, pp 279-328; for Fyrkat pp150-157; in England, Geake 2003 for the control of pagan burial procedures by female specialists.
13. Speake 1989.
14. Helena Hamerow (2016) portrayed bed burials as serving the interests of family land-holding, and perhaps spiritual authority of a kind that would pass to the Abbesses in the first Christian generations. I saw them as evidence for women continuing their own religious prescription in the face of a new authority that was placing spiritual welfare in the hands of a male god with an attendant male hierarchy (Carver 2019, 405, 645). Emma Brownlee (2022) defined a concentration of (non-Christian) bed burials in central Europe and Sam Leggett showed (via stable isotopes) that some of the English examples may have come from there. See *Saxon 78* (2024), 3-5 for a recent summary.
15. Hamerow 2016.
16. Carver 2005, 2017. For the detailed discussion of all the artefacts (including the ship), Bruce-Mitford (ed.) 1975,1978, 1983 (out of print and not yet available online).
17. Semple 2013.
18. Fern (ed.) 2015.
19. Inhumation 19 (Fern 2015, 207).
20. Carver and Fern in Carver 2005, 285-287.
21. Müller-Wille, M 1976.
22. Carver 2005, 182-199.
23. The case for a tree-trunk coffin secured by iron clamps is presented in Carver 2005, 192-9 as an alternative to a bier or bed, with parallels on pp292-300. See also Evison 1980; Evans 1983, 922-3; East 1984; Blackmore et al 2019, 303-4 (Prittlewell), and Fenwick and Tanner 2023, 52 and Fig 7.
24. For a summary of Mound 1 see Carver 2017, Chapter 5.
25. Carver 2000.
26. Caruth and Hines 2024. See *Saxon* 76 (2023), 7-8.
27. Mango 2009, 232-3; also Marlia Mundell Mango et al 1989 (then known as the Bromeswell bucket), p299 for the depiction of the mythical hunt of the Calydonian boar and the lion by Meleager and Atalanta; p.304-5 for the use of such buckets by senior officers in the baths. See Carver 2017, 117-119 for a synopsis. The bottom of the bucket and fragments of the decorated sides were excavated in 2024 and the bucket was confirmed as having contained a cremation.
28. A very fine excavation and publication: Blackmore et al. 2019. Date at p. xxvii.
29. Mango 2019, 184: the Prittlewell type of flagon may have been brought home by pilgrims or mercenaries. “Some of the Sergius flagons may have been carried by

military men who were devoted to the soldier saint". Mango also observes that saints' lives of the seventh century refer to ships and merchants and trade networks including metalwork across the Mediterranean and up to Britain. Metalwork cargoes have been found in four shipwrecks of the seventh century, one of which contained a drop handled basin of the general type found at Prittlewell and elsewhere, (p186).
30. Gittos 2025.
31. Reynolds, 2009. Reynolds shows how the social rejection of individuals in pre-Christian Anglo-Saxon communities changed in the later seventh and eighth century when public execution sites were placed at key points in the landscape: Reynolds 2013, 704. See comprehensive new research by Andrew Reynolds at Foundry Field near Burnham Market. Carver 2017, 164 for an interpretation of the Sutton Hoo execution cemetery.
32. Bede *Life of Cuthbert*, p76.
33. Bassett 1989.
34. HE IV.1, IV.2; Hines and Bayliss 2013, 553.

CHAPTER 3

1. Multicoloured glass beads were made by blending twisted cables of glass into spheres, lozenges or cylinders held on a stick. "Traffic light" is a term used to describe those made of red, yellow and green glass but there is a multitude of variations of colour and technique. (Lucidly explained by Sue Heaser and applied at her Suffolk workshop; see https://exarc.net/issue-2022-4/at/anglo-saxon-beads-redefining-traffic-lights).
2. Hills and Lucy 2013, 79-83.
3. See Fern et al. 2019, Chapter 5 for a detailed review.
4. Evans 2005, Fig 114, 115; See Carver 2017, fig 5.6, 5.7, 7.9, 7.10 for images.
5. Carver 2019, 99-102.
6. Scull et al.2024a, 82.
7. Blakelock in Scull et al. 2024a, 178-187, quote: p187.
8. Scull et al. 2024a, 236.
9. Andrew Woods in Scull at al 2024a, 418-419.
10. Woods, ibid,; see also Carver 2019, 654 for the secular (as opposed to spiritual) response to Christianity in East Anglia.
11. Helen Geake, personal communication.
12. Adams 2016, 108; Bruce-Mitford, 1978, Inv.10 and 17, pp 475, 467.
13. An idea inspired by the 'proverbial' figures on gold linguist staffs from west Africa. (Garrard 1989,78).
14. Adams 2010, 101-2.
15. Fern et al. 2019, 280.
16. Fern et al 2019, 271, 279, 354.
17. Fern et al. 2019, 205.
18. See Ch 1; argued in Carver 2019, 102.
19. Hinton 2000; Leahy 2011, 450-1.
20. Evans 1978, 307; Evans 2005, 244.
21. Hall 2018. The scientific investigation used electron micro-probe analysis.
22. Fern et al. 2019, 181.
23. Walton Rogers 2007, 63.
24. Walton Rogers 2007, 206.
25. Hills 2001; Walton Rogers 2007, 236; Rowan English (2024) has assembled a corpus of 752 ivory rings deposited in Anglo-Saxon graves mostly in the fifth century. One example was determined

by ZooMS to be from an African elephant and two others by strontium isotopes as likely to be African in origin (p310-1).

26. List of textiles from Mound 1: Twill from tunic, trousers or cap: SH1, SH20; Otterfur cap SH3, SH21; Yellow piled cloak(s) SH10; Coarse cloak or blanket SH2, SH4; Braided cross-gartering with shoes SH6; Shoe-laces SH23; Fine tape for binding SH13; Fine tape for binding scabbard SH16; Cloth for wrapping weapons SH8; Cushion cover or bag SH9; Pillow cases SH11, SH12 Decorated hanging or cover SH7; Fine rug, hanging or tapestry SH17, SH18, SH19; Coarse floor covering SH25 [or table] (Crowfoot, E 1983, 457-462).
27. Walton Rogers 2007, 86, 230, 239-40. See Carver 2017, 193 for a reconstruction of the dressed up occupant of Mound 1.
28. Geake 1997, 1999; Walton Rogers 2007, 187-9; Owen-Crocker 2004, 144-148.
29. Owen-Crocker 2004, 145.
30. Owen-Crocker 2004, 150-4; and see Chapter 2.
31. Owen-Crocker 2004, 134-7.
32. Owen-Crocker 2004, 129.
33. Research and publication by Penelope Walton Rogers, 2005
34. Geake 1997, 156; 1999, 203-4; Owen-Crocker 2004, 145
35. Such as the Calendars BL Cot Julius A VI; the Psalters Harley 603, Bodleian Junius 11 or the Prudentius Psychomachia, See Carver 2019, 586-588.
36. Wilson 1976; Leahy 2011, 441-444, Fig 24.1; see also Christensen 1986a. The Ship's Company has reconstructed its own wood-workers' tool-kit based on Anglo-Saxon exemplars; see Chapter 5.
37. Carver et al. 2009, 95.
38. Examples were defined at Sutton Hoo in Mound 1 and Mound 17 Carver 2005, 195-6 and see 292-5 for well-preserved carved examples from Germany; p132-4 for Mound 17; and Fenwick 1984, 37 for nearby Burrow Hill, Butley.
39. Fenwick and Tanner 2023.
40. Carver 2005, 153-177.
41. Lau 2014, abb.4.
42. Ramqvist 1992, p46-7, 153.
43. For other examples, see Carver and Fern in Carver 2005, 283-313.
44. Blackmore et al. 2019, 94-99.
45. Blackmore et al, 2019, 104-112, 272
46. West 1985, 167-170; Summary in Tipper 2012, 1-12.
47. Hope-Taylor 1977.
48. Hope-Taylor 1977, 148-154. summarises the archaeological argument for the development of timber architecture at Yeavering.
49. A suggestion owed to Rosemary Cramp. (Carver 2019, 163).
50. Directed by Sarah Semple, Durham University. The radiocarbon dates so far for the Great Halls span 575-655CE cal. at 95%, as opposed to Hope-Taylor's alignments with Bede from 592 (Aethelfrith) to 670 (Oswiu). The Great Enclosure, assigned by Hope-Taylor to Edwin's reign, always anomalous, was shown by re-excavation to belong to the pre-Anglian period at the site [lecture to the Society of Antiquaries in February 2024].
51. Millet and James 1983 for what follows.
52. Scull et al 2024b, 207, 209, 219. The hall (Structure 2528) with a ground plan measuring 23x11.5m, was first identified by aerial photography in 2015. It had an annexe at each

end and a row of (buttress) pits each side [reminiscent of Yeavering A4]. A large adjacent rubbish area excavated in alternative squares produced vast quantities of meat bones mainly beef and pork, dress accessories and fragments of glass drinking vessels. The Temple (Structure 3760) measuring *c.* 5 x 10 m, had four substantial postholes in the centre suggesting a raised roof like the 'Ceremonial Building' at Uppäkra, Skåne, Sweden, where numerous gold votive plaques (*guldgubber*) were found (Larsen 2004). Interim reports will be found in *Saxon 76*, 1-2. *Saxon* 78, 1-3.

53. Scull et al. 2024b, 225.
54. Hamerow and Brennan 2015; Thomas and Knox 2017; Scull et al 2024a, 2024b.
55. Scull and Thomas 2020, 58, 60-63.
56. Loveluck and Tys 2006, Brookes 2007; summarised in Scull and Naylor 2016, 229-230. Carver 1995a raised the possible ideological associations of ship and boat burial.
56. Blair 2018, 174-6.
57. Carver 2019, 646-7.

CHAPTER 4

1. Cunliffe 2008, 35, 159-160; Johnstone 1988, 85-6.
2. Carver 2019, 1-13.
3. Carver 1990, 122, and refs; especially Taylor 1956, Binns 1980.
4. St Brendan's hide boat was imagined, built and sailed in the Atlantic by Tim Severin 2005.
5. Thier 2003; Carver 2014, 24.
6. McGrail 1978, 1997.
7. Robinson et.al 2015, 202-215; Knight et al. 2024 (both on open access). See also https://www.academia.edu/The_Must_Farm_Logboats_Why_Was_Oak_Used_Primarily_in_the_Construction_of_Logboats_in_Bronze_Age_Britain.
8. This dug-out 'canoe' was 'landed' while 'fishing off Covehithe' by Dunwich fisherman, Rodney Collett, in June 1998. It was deposited on beach at Dunwich, from where it was transferred to a 'mere' (on Dunwich marshes, N of Dunwich car park) by Stuart Bacon, who also took samples for radiocarbon dating (S1). Dated (paid for by Sizewell Nuclear Power Station) to 775-892 CE. The dugout was transferred to the new Deep Sea Explorations Marine Finds Laboratory at Bentwaters during November 2002 (S1). *East Anglian Daily Times*, 19 June 1998, 9, ill. https://heritage.suffolk.gov.uk/Source/SSF5480.
9. Johnstone, 1988, 49-50; Crumlin-Pedersen 1991, 178; National Museum of Finland.
10. Crumlin-Pedersen 1991, 254-5.
11. Filmer-Sankey and Pestell 2001, 199-203; p200.
12. Johnstone, 1988, 116, 212; Crumlin-Pedersen 1991, 261.
13. Wright and Wright 1947, Plate XV for dimensions. The same method of using raised cleats to attach ribs to hull planks was used in Oseberg and Gokstad (Evans.1975, 370).
14. https://www.canterburytrust.co.uk/dover-bronze-age-boat.
15. Crumlin-Pedersen and Trakadas 2003.
16. Marsden 1994.
17. The New Guy's House ship 2nd century found near London Bridge, and the County Hall ship (fourth century) had similar construction Marsden 1994.

18. Johnstone 1988, 88-89
19. Milne 1996.
20. John Makepeace, unpub. *wics* (beach markets) MA diss, University of York.
21. Loveluck and Tys 2006; Ludowici et al. 2010.
22. Bonde and Stylegar 2016.
23. Research by Crumlin-Pedersen 2010, 65-8; Indruszewski 2011; Bockius 2017, Maps 1-4.
24. Crumlin-Pedersen 1968.
25. Peets et al. 2011, 2013. Lõagas et al 2023.
26. Price et al. 2020.
27. ERR News (Estonian Public Broadcasting:.https://news.err.ee) 2011.
28. Nordeide et al 2020.
29. Carver 1995b.
30. Bischoff 2021.
31. Bischoff 2021, 292-3.
32. Christensen 1986b.
33. For the Skudelev and Hedeby ships and their reconstructions, Crumlin-Pedersen 2010, 107-112; and see Fig.4.32 in that book for three of the Skudelev ships in the museum harbour.
34. Nordeide et al. 2020.
35. Rule 1982, 37-9.
36. Schofield 1988.
37. Bill 2020; and see Chapter 2.
38. Bonde and Stylegar 2016.
39. Myrhe 1987; Bill 2020.
40. Hines 1984, 1992; Näsman 1986; Heen-Pettersen 2019.
41. Baug et al. 2019; Heen-Pettersen 2019.
42. Mango, 1989, 2009, 2019; Geake 1997, 1999; Gittos 2024.
43. Gittos 2024, 9, 22, 32.
44. Gittos 2025, 34.
45. Damian Robinson, personal communication.
46. Bass and van Doornink 1982.
47. Images of these ships, including reconstructions, will be found on the internet.
48. Kocabaş & Özsait-Kocabaş 2021
49. Pulak et al 2015.
50. Cvikel 2020; Cohen and Cvikel 2020; Natan et al. 2021.
51. Morris 2004, 19-23; The Bible was lost until 1887 when it turned up as the Codex Amiatinus now in the Laurentian Library in Florence. Bruce-Mitford, 1969; McClure and Collins 2008, 339.
52. Jenkins 1949, 66-69.
53. Balsam is a resin with pain-relieving properties; a calabash is a bottle-shaped container formed by the dried fruit of the calabash plant.
54. Jenkins 1949.
55. What follows is owed to Newell 2020.
56. Crumlin-Pedersen 2010, 65-68.
57. Blair 2018, 123.

CHAPTER 5

1. The 2021 film was produced by Netflix, directed by Simon Stone and entitled *The Dig*. It was based on the book of the same name by John Preston and starred Ralph Fiennes as Basil Brown and Carey Mulligan as Mrs Pretty.
2. *Ipswich Journal* 24 November 1860.
3. Basil Brown's Diary, 20 July 1938; in Bruce-Mitford 1974, 150.
4. Carver 2005, 153-177.
5. Evans 1986, 23-24. See Evans' chapter in the British Museum report on the ship burial (SHSB I), Evans 1975, for the definitive study of the ship.
6. Charles Phillips claimed that scarf joints fastening the keel to the stem and stern were found between ribs 3 and 4 forward,

and ribs 23 and 24 aft. " Each was secured by three large vertical iron nails 6 ¼ in. long riveted over roves like all the other clench nails in the ship" (Phillips 1940). His notes and paper in Antiquaries Journal (also 1940) were less conclusive. Scarf joints were necessary, but may have employed treenails (thanks to Joe Startin for this research).

7. Digital copies of photographs by Lack and Wagstaff are now held by the National Trust at Sutton Hoo, who may be contacted for access to them. This is the source of Figures 5.2 -5.3 reproduced here.
8. SHSB I, Figure 325.
9. Carver 2005, 472. Tracks of armoured vehicles and infantry trench were found in the 1983 campaign.
10. Phillips 1940. Evans 1975,.fig 325; Evans 1986, fig 14. See Chapter 2, Fig 2.12 here for the plan with numbered frames and the location of evidence for tholes (oarlocks).
11. McGrail and Hutchinson, Maritime Aspects of Sutton Hoo Sutton Hoo Research Committee Bulletin No.2 (1984), 13.
12. Gifford and Gifford 1996; *Sæ Wylfing* was half scale (12.5m in length) could carry a full sail of 23m2 in a 16-knot wind making 7 knots on the Deben (Gifford and Gifford 1999, at pp80-85).
13. Letter from Malcom Hodd to Martin Carver dated 11 September 2014.
14. These are available from the Ship's Company archive. See list below.
15. Joe Startin comments of this event "this is what I think of as the Sutton Hoo Ship's Company 'coming out'", personal communication.
16. Tanner, Whitewright, and Startin, 2020
17. The WITAN (lit. 'wise ones') was the advisory council of an Anglo-Saxon King. Originally constituted to assemble academic allies, our WITAN soon expanded to included modern maritime experts and influencers.
18. *Project Designs* were generated as follows: by Martin Carver (in Ship's Company Archive): 2014 (June) Feasibility study: building a full-scale reconstruction of the Sutton Hoo Mound 1 ship; 2015 (July) The Sutton Hoo (Mound 1) Ship: a scope of work for its experimental design reconstruction and trials.; 2018 (October) Presentation to the Symposium; Post-Symposium thoughts on a way forward; 2021 (September) Project Design; 2022 (October) Flagship of Early England: the Reconstructed Sutton Hoo Ship. Progress Report and Future Plans; 2023 (April) Project Plan for the Sutton Hoo Experimental Ship, 2017-2034; 2017 Whitewright, J. Sutton Hoo Ship Reconstruction: Phase One Project Design. Unpublished Project Design completed on behalf of Sutton Hoo Ships Company and Woodbridge Riverside Trust.
19. The three volumes of their Sutton Hoo Ship Burial (1975, 1978, and 1983) running to 2431 pages.
20. See Carver, 2017
21. Carver and Loveluck (eds) 2021
22. Bruce-Mitford 1974, 198-213; Bruce-Mitford 1978, 138-231
23. For Anglo-Saxon canals, possibly early, see Blair 2007
24. Crumlin-Pedersen and Vinner 1986; 1995; 2010; (with Trakadas) 2003; (with McGrail) 2006; McGrail

1986; Mudie 1986.
25. Crumlin-Pedersen 1995, 303, 306.
26. Crumlin-Pedersen and Trakadas 2003.
27. Knud V. Valbjørn in Crumlin-Pedersen and Trakadas 2003, 57-60.
28. Max Vinner in Crumlin-Pedersen and Trakadas 2003, 103.
29. Max Vinner in Crumlin-Pedersen and Trakadas 2003, 103-118.
30. Evans 1975, passim; Bill 1994 for the distribution of rivet types.
31. Evans 1975, 434.
32. Clusters of rivets gave evidence of repair.
33. Carver 2023.
34. As encouraged by Evans 1975, 434.
35. The Sutton Hoo Ship's gin is made by Dunster Distillery (dunsterdistillery.com).
36. For metrology in buildings see Hope-Taylor 1977, on the Yeavering foot; Blair 2018, 70 et seq. on the perch, and Carver et al 2016, 241 on the ratios used in an eighth century monastic building for spacing ratios pre-empting the Fibonacci series but observable in the nautilus shell.
37. Bischoff 2021, 293-4.
38. Joe Startin, personal communication.
39. Many thanks to Jacq Barnard, champion rower, for these insights.
40. Beacons, lookouts and military communications: Baker and Brookes 2015.
41. Carver 1995c; 2014, 2015.

REFERENCES

Abbreviations

ASC Whitelock, Dorothy (ed) 1961 *The Anglo-Saxon Chronicle* (London: Eyre and Spottiswoode).

IJNA *The International Journal of Nautical Archaeology.*

SHSB I, II, III Bruce-Mitford, Rupert (ed.) *The Sutton Hoo Ship Burial* Vol I Excavations (1975); Vol II Regalia (1978); Vol III Other Finds (1983) (British Museum: London).

SHSC The Sutton Hoo Ship's Company.

Adams, Noël 2010 Rethinking the Sutton Hoo Shoulder Clasps and Armour in Christopher Entwistle and Noël Adams (eds) *'Intelligible Beauty': Recent Research on Byzantine Jewellery* (British Museum Research Publication 178, London), 83-112.

Adams, Noël 2016 Of Men and Mushrooms in Adám Bollók, Gergely Csiky and Tivadar Vida (eds) *Between Byzantium and the Steppe: Archaeological and Historical Studies in Honour of Csanád Bálint on the Occasion of his 70th Birthday* (Institute of Archaeology Research Centre for the Humanities Hungarian Academy of Sciences, Budapest), 87-114.

Baker, John and Stuart Brookes 2015 Signalling intent: Beacons, Lookouts and Military Communications in Maren Clegg Hyer and Gale Owen-Crocker (eds) *The Material Culture of the Built Environment in Anglo-Saxon England* (Liverpool University Press, Liverpool), 216-34.

Bass, George F. and Frederick H. van Doorninck, Jr 1982 Yassi Ada. *A Seventh-Century Byzantine Shipwreck* (Texas A&M University Press, College Station).

Bassett, Steve (ed.) 1989 *The Origins of Anglo-Saxon Kingdoms* (Leicester University Press: London and New York).

Baug, Irene, Dagfinn Skre, Tom Heldal, Øystein J. Jansen 2019 The Beginning of the Viking Age in the West *Journal of Maritime Archaeology* 14, 43-80.

Bede, The Venerable 735 *The Ecclesiastical History of the English People* trans. Bertram Colgrave, ed. Judith McClure and Roger Collins (2008, Oxford University Press, Oxford).

Bede *Life of Cuthbert*, Book 3 in *Lives of the Saints*, trans J.F. Webb (1970, Penguin, Harmondsworth).

Berry, Jessica, David Parham, Catrina Appleby (eds) 2019 *The Poole Iron Age Logboat* (Archaeopress, Oxford).

Bill, Jan 1994 Iron Nails in Iron Age and Medieval Ships in Christer Westerdahl (ed.) *Crossroads in Ancient Shipbuilding* (Proceedings of the Sixth International Symposium on Boat and Ship Archaeology, Roskilde 1991) (oxbow, Oxford), 55-63.

Bill, Jan 2020 The Ship Graves on Kormt - And Beyond in Dagfinn Skre (ed.) Rulership in 1st to 14th Century Scandinavia: Royal Graves and Sites at Avaldsnes and Beyond (De Gruyter, Berlin, Boston), 305-392. https://doi.org/10.1515/9783110421101-005

Binns, Alan L. 1980 *Viking Voyagers* (Heinemann, London).

Bischoff, Vibeke, 2021 The Oseberg Ship: Reflections on the Choice of Methodology When Testing Experimental Archaeological Reconstructions *Archaeonautica* 21, 289-294.

Blackmore, Lyn, Ian Blair, Sue Hirst and Christopher Scull 2019 *The Prittlewell Princely Burial. Excavations at Priory Crescent, Southend on Sea, Essex, 2003* (MOLA Monograph 73, London).

Blair, John 2007 Transport and Canal-Building on the Upper Thames, 1000-1300 in John Blair (ed.) *Waterways and Canal-building in Medieval England* (Oxford University Press, Oxford), 254-294.

Blair, John 2018 *Building Anglo-Saxon England* (Princeton University Press, Princeton NJ).

Bockius, Ronald 2013 The Nydam Ship Finds (Denmark) and the Crystallization of North European Shipbuilding Tradition during the Roman Iron Age in Andreas Rau (ed.) *Jernalderen i Nordeuropa. Nydam Mose 4: Die Schiffe. Beiträge zu Form, Technik und Historie.* (Jysk Arkaeologisk Selskabs Skrifter 72, Århus and Schleswig), 211-299.

——— 2017 The Nydam Ship Finds (Denmark) and the Crystallization of North European Shipbuilding Tradition during the Roman Iron Age in Jerzy Gawronski, André van Holk and Joost Schokkenbroek (eds) *Ships and Maritime Landscapes* (Proceedings of the Thirteenth International Symposium on Boat and Ship Archaeology, Amsterdam) (Barkhuis, Eelde), 251-259.

Bonde, Niels and Frans-Anne Stylegar 2016 Between Sutton Hoo and Oseberg - Dendrochronology and the Origins of the Ship Burial Tradition *Danish Journal of Archaeology* 5, 19-33. http://dx.doi.org/10.1080/21662282.2016.1245885

Brather, Sebastian 2010 Silver, Weights and Scales around the Baltic, 8th to 11th Centuries in Babette Ludowici, Hauke Jons, Sunhild Kleingärtner, Jonathan Scheschewitz and Mattias Hardt (eds) *Trade and Communication*

Networks of the First Millennium AD in the Northern part of Central Europe. Central Places, Beach Markets, Landing Places and Trading Centres (Neue Studien zur Sachsenforschung) (Niedersächsisches Landesmuseum, Hannover), 143-164.

Brookes, Stuart 2007 Boat Rivets in Graves in Pre-Viking Kent: Re-assessing the Anglo-Saxon Boat Burial Traditions *Medieval Archaeology* 51, 1-18.

Brownlee, Emma 2022 Bed Burials in Early Medieval Europe *Medieval Archaeology*, 66.1, 1-19.

Bruce-Mitford, Rupert, 1969 The Art of the Codex Amiatinus: Jarrow Lecture 1967 *Journal of the British Archaeological Association* 32, 1-25. https://doi.org/10.1080/00681288.1969.11894883

Bruce-Mitford, Rupert 1974 *Aspects of Anglo-Saxon Archaeology. Sutton Hoo and Other Discoveries* (Gollancz, London).

Bruce-Mitford, Rupert (ed.) 1975, 1978, 1983 *The Sutton Hoo Ship Burial* (British Museum, London).

Caruth, Jo and John Hines 2024 *The Anglo-Saxon Cemeteries at RAF Lakenheath, Eriswell, Suffolk: Excavations 1997-2008* (East Anglian Archaeology 182) (Archaeological Service, Suffolk County Council, Bury St Edmunds).

Carver, Martin 1990 Pre-Viking Traffic in the North Sea in Sean McGrail (ed.) *Maritime Celts, Frisians and Saxons* (CBA Research Report 71, York), 117-125.

——— 1995a Ship Burial in Early Britain: Ancient Custom or Political Signal? in Ole Crumlin-Pedersen and Birgitte Munch Thye (eds) *The Ship as Symbol in Prehistoric and Medieval Scandinavia* (National Museum of Denmark, Copenhagen), 111-124.

——— 1995b On - and Off - the Edda in Olaf Olsen, Torsten Madsen and Flemming Rieck (eds) *Ship-Shape: Essays for Ole Crumlin-Pedersen* (The Viking Ship Museum, Roskilde), 305-312.

——— 1995c The North Sea Highway: Cultural Arena or Political Barrier? in Jan Magnus Fladmark (ed.) *Sharing the Earth. Local Identity and Global Culture* (Routledge, London), 177-190.

——— 2000 Burial as Poetry: The Context of Treasure in Anglo-Saxon Graves in Elizabeth Tyler (ed.) *Treasure in the Medieval West* (Boydell, Woodbridge), 25-48.

——— 2005 *Sutton Hoo. A Seventh-Century Princely Burial Ground and its Context* (British Museum, London). Available at http://martincarver.com/publications/sutton-hoo-report

——— 2009 with Catherine Hills and Jonathan Scheschkewitz *Wasperton. A Roman, British and Anglo-Saxon Community in Central England* (Boydell, Woodbridge).

——— 2014 Travels on the Sea and in the Mind in Stacy S. Klein, William

Schipper and Shannon Lewis-Simpson (eds), *The Maritime World of the Anglo-Saxons. Essays in Anglo-Saxon Studies* 5 (Arizona Center for Medieval and Renaissance Studies, Tempe AZ), 21-36.

——— 2015 Commerce and Cult: Confronted Ideologies in 6th-9th Century Europe *Medieval Archaeology* 59, 1-23.

——— 2016 (with Justin Garner-Lahire and Cecily Spall) *Portmahomack on Tarbat Ness. Changing Ideologies in North-East Scotland, Sixth to Sixteenth Centuries* (Society of Antiquaries of Scotland, Edinburgh). https://doi.org/10.9750/9781908332165

——— 2017 *The Sutton Hoo Story. Encounters with Early England* (Boydell, Woodbridge).

——— 2019 *Formative Britain. An Archaeology of Britain, Fifth to Eleventh Century AD* (Routledge, Abingdon and New York).

——— 2021 with Chris Loveluck (ed.) with contributions from Stuart Brookes, Robin Daniels, Gareth Davies, Christopher Ferguson, Helen Geake, David Griffiths, David Hinton, Edward Oakley and Imogen Tompsett The Early Medieval, AD 400-1000 in Jesse Randlsey and Fraser Sturt (eds) *People and the Sea: A Maritime Archaeological Research Agenda for England* (CBA Research Report 171, York), 113-137.

——— 2023 Joined-up Synthesis in Multi-Disciplinary Projects in Alessandra Molinari and Chris Wickham (eds) *Hard Sciences in History and Archaeology of the Early Middle Ages: Towards New Paradigms* (*Archeologia Medievale* 50), 67-76.

Christensen, Arne-Emil 1986a Tools Used for Boat-Building in Ancient and More Modern Times in Crumlin-Pedersen and Vinner (eds) (The Viking Ship Museum, Roskilde), 150-155.

——— 1986b “Viking” a Ship Replica from 1893 in Crumlin-Pedersen and Vinner (eds) (The Viking Ship Museum, Roskilde), 68-77.

Cohen, Maayan and Deborah Cvikel 2020 Rigging of the Ma’agan Mikhael B Shipwreck (7th-8th Century AD): New Finds *IJNA* 49.2, 291-302.

Crowfoot, Elizabeth 1983 The Textiles in Angela Care Evans (ed.) Rupert Bruce-Mitford *The Sutton Hoo Ship-Burial* Volume 3 (British Museum, London), 409-479.

Crumlin-Pedersen, Ole 1968 The Gredstedbro Ship; The Remains of a Late Iron Age Vessel Found in 1945 in South Jutland. *Acta Archaeologica* 39, 262-267.

——— 1991 *Slusegårdgravpladsen III. Gravfomer og Gravskikke bådgravene* (Jysk Arkaeologisk Selskabs Skrifter 14, Højbjerg).

——— 1995, Experimental Archaeology and Ships - Bridging the Arts and the Science *IJNA* 24.4, 303-306.

——— 2010 *Archaeology and the Sea in Scandinavia and Britain. A Personal Account* (The Viking Ship Museum, Roskilde).

Crumlin-Pedersen, Ole and Sean McGrail, 2006, Some Principles for the Reconstruction of Ancient Boat Structures *IJNA* 35, 53–57.

Crumlin-Pedersen, Ole and Athena Trakadas (eds) 2003 *Hjortspring. A Pre-Roman Iron-Age Warship in Context* (Ships and Boats of the North 5) (The Viking Ship Museum, Roskilde).

Crumlin-Pedersen, Ole and Max Vinner (eds) 1986 *Sailing into the Past* (The Viking Ship Museum, Roskilde).

Cunliffe, Barry 2008 *Europe Between the Oceans, 9000 BC–AD 1000* (Yale University Press, New Haven and London).

Cvikel, Deborah 2020 The Late-Antique Ma'agan Mikhael B Shipwreck *Near Eastern Archaeology* 83.1, 30-37.

Dickinson, Tania 1993 An Anglo-Saxon Cunning-Woman from Bidford-on-Avon in M.O.H. Carver (ed.) *In Search of Cult: Archaeological Investigations in Honour of Philip Rahtz* (Boydell, Woodbridge), 45-54.

East, Katherine 1984 The Sutton Hoo Ship Burial: A Case against the Coffin *Anglo-Saxon Studies in History and Archaeology* 3, 79-84.

English, Rowan S. 2024 Elephant Ivory Rings in Early Medieval Graves Reconsidered *Early Medieval Europe* 32.3, 306-336.

Evans, Angela Care 1975 The Ship in R. Bruce-Mitford (ed.) *The Sutton Hoo Ship Burial*, Vol I, 345–435 (British Museum, London).

——— 1978 A Note on the Pattern-Welding of the Sword-Blade in Rupert Bruce Mitford, *The Sutton Hoo Ship Burial Vol II, Arms Armour and Regalia* (British Museum, London), 307.

——— 1983 The Iron Cleats in Angela Care Evans (ed.) *The Sutton Hoo Ship-Burial Volume III* (British Museum, London), 913-923.

——— 1986 *The Sutton Hoo Ship Burial* (British Museum, London).

——— 2005 Seventh-Century Assemblages, in Martin Carver, *Sutton Hoo: A seventh-Century Princely Burial Ground and its Context*, (British Museum, London), 201-282.

Evison, Vera 1980 The Sutton Hoo Coffin in Philip Rahtz, Tania Dickinson and Lorna Watts (eds) *Anglo-Saxon Cemeteries 1979* (British Archaeological Reports 82, Oxford), 357-62.

Fenwick, Valerie 1984 Insula de Burgh: Excavations at Burrow Hill, Butley, Suffolk 1978–81 *Anglo-Saxon Studies in Archaeology and History* 3, 35-54.

Fenwick, Valerie and Pat Tanner 2023 Sutton Hoo: Re-Imaging the Ship and Chamber *Antiquaries Journal* 103, 36-62.

Fern, Christopher J.R. (ed.) 2015 *Before Sutton Hoo : The Prehistoric Remains and Early Anglo-Saxon Cemetery at Tranmer House, Bromeswell, Suffolk*

(East Anglian Archaeology 155, Bury St Edmunds).
Fern, Chris, Tania Dickinson and Leslie Webster (eds) 2019 *The Staffordshire Hoard, An Anglo-Saxon Treasure* (Society of Antiquaries Research Report 80, London).
Filmer-Sankey, William and Tim Pestell 2001, *Snape Anglo-Saxon Cemetery, Excavations and Surveys 1824-1992* (East Anglian Archaeology 95) (Suffolk County Council, Ipswich).
Garrard, Timothy F. 1989 *Gold of Africa. Jewellery and Ornaments from Ghana, Côte d'Ivoire, Mali and Senegal in the Collection of the Barbier-Mueller Museum* (Preste, Munich).
Geake, Helen 1997 *The Use of Grave Goods in Conversion-Period England, c.600-c.850* (British Archaeological Reports 261, Oxford).
Geake, Helen 1999 Invisible Kingdoms: the Use of Grave-goods in Seventh-Century England *Anglo-Saxon Studies in Archaeology and History* 10, 203-215.
——— 2003 The Control of Burial Practice in Anglo-Saxon England in Martin Carver (ed.) *The Cross Goes North. Processes of Conversion in Northern Europe AD 300-1300* (Boydell, Woodbridge), 259-269.
Gifford, Edwin and Joyce Gifford 1996 The Sailing Performance of Anglo-Saxon Ships as Derived from the Building and Trials of Half-Scale Models of the Sutton Hoo and Graveney Ship Finds *Mariner's Mirror* 82, 131–153.
——— 1999 The Art of Anglo-Saxon Shipbuilding in Jane Hawkes and Susan Mills (eds) *Northumbria's Golden Age* (Sutton, Stroud), 73-86.
Gittos, Helen 2025 Sutton Hoo and Syria: The Anglo-Saxons Who Served in the Byzantine Army? *The English Historical Review* 139, 1323-1358. https://doi.org/10.1093/ehr/ceae213
Hall, Neil 2018 Iron Working in Anglo-Saxon England: New Evidence to Show Fresh Iron Smelting of Ironstone Ores from the 6th–10th Centuries CE *Journal of Archaeological Science* 19, 344-351.
Hamerow, Helena 2016 Furnished Female Burial in 7th Century England: Gender and Sacral Authority in the Conversion Period *Early Medieval Europe* 24.4, 423-447.
Hamerow, Helena and Naomi Brennan 2015. An Anglo-Saxon Great Hall Complex at Sutton Courtenay/Drayton, Oxfordshire: A Royal Centre of Early Wessex? *Archaeological Journal* 172, 325–50.
Hamerow, Helena, David A. Hinton and Sally Crawford (eds) 2011 *The Oxford Handbook of Anglo-Saxon Archaeology* (Oxford University Press, Oxford).
Heen-Pettersen, Anne Margrethe 2019 The Earliest Wave of Viking Activity? The Norwegian Evidence Revisited *European Journal of Archaeology* 22.4, 523-541.
Hill, David 1981 *An Atlas of Anglo-Saxon England* (Blackwell, Oxford).

Hills, Catherine 2001 From Isidore to Isotopes: Ivory Rings in Early Medieval Graves, in Arthur Macgregor and Helena Hamerow (eds) *Image and Power in Early Medieval British Archaeology: Essays in Honour of Rosemary Cramp* (Oxbow, Oxford), 131-146.

Hills, Catherine and Sam Lucy 2013 *Spong Hill Part IX: Chronology and Synthesis* (McDonald Institute for Archaeological Research, Cambridge).

Hills, Catherine, Kenneth Penn and Robert Rickett 1984 *The Anglo-Saxon Cemetery at Spong Hill, North Elmham, Part III: Catalogue of Inhumations* (East Anglian Archaeology Report 21) (Norfolk Museums Service, Gressenhall).

Hines, John 1984 *The Scandinavian Character of Anglian England in the Pre-Viking Period* (British Archaeological Reports British Series 124, Oxford).

Hines, John 1992 The Scandinavian Character of Anglian England: An Update in Martin Carver (ed.) *The Age of Sutton Hoo: The Seventh Century in North West Europe* (Boydell, Woodbridge), 315-330.

Hines, John and Alex Bayliss (eds) 2013 *Anglo-Saxon Graves and Grave Goods of the 6th and 7th Centuries A.D.: A Chronological Framework* (Society for Medieval Archaeology Monograph 33) (Routledge, Abingdon).

Hinton, David, 2000 *A Smith in Lindsey. The Anglo-Saxon Grave at Tattershall Thorpe, Lincolnshire* (Society for Medieval Archaeology Monograph 16) (Routledge, Abingdon). https://doi.org/10.4324/9781351196758

Hope-Taylor, Brian 1977 *Yeavering: An Anglo-British Centre of Early Northumbria* (Department of the Environment Archaeological Report 7, HMSO, London).

Indruszewski, George, 2011 The Origin of the "Clinker Construction" Method in Roman and Post-Roman Shipbuilding in Europe. *Jahrbuch des Römisch-Germanischen Zentralmuseums Mainz* 56.2, 539-74.

Jenkins, Claude 1949 Christian Pilgrimages AD 500-800 in Arthur Newton (ed) *Travel and Travellers of the Middle Ages* (Routledge, London).

Johnstone, Paul 1988 *The Sea-Craft of Prehistory* (Routledge, London).

Knight, Mark, Rachel Ballantyne, Matthew Brudenell, Anwen Cooper, David Gibson and Iona Robinson Zeki 2024 *Must Farm Pile-Dwelling Settlement: Volume 1. Landscape, Architecture and Occupation* (McDonald Institute for Archaeological Research, Cambridge).

Kocabaş, Ufuk and Işıl Özsait-Kocabaş 2021 Hull Characteristics of the Yenikapı 16 Galley *Archaeonautica* 2021, 79-82.

Lau, Nina 2014 Kammergrab und Gräberfeld von Pilgramsdorf (Pielgrzymowo) - Ein Fundplatz zwischen kulturellem Kontext und überregionalen Einlüssen in Angelika Abregg-Wigg, and Nina Lau (eds) *Schriften des Archäologischen Landesmuseums, Ergänzungsreihe* 9 (Wachholtz, Neumünster), 199-228.

Leahy, Kevin 2011 Anglo-Saxon Crafts in Hamerow et al. (Oxford University Press, Oxford), 440-459.

Larsen, Lars 2004 *Continuity for Centuries: A Ceremonial Building and its Context at Uppåkra, Southern Sweden* (Uppåkrastudier 10, Almqvist & Wiksell, Lund).

Lõagas, Lembi, Heidi Luik, Raili Allmäe, Alar Rosentau et al. 2023 *The Salme Ship Burials: Two Eighth-Century Mass Graves on Saaremaa Island, Estonia. Fieldwork and Catalogue* (Archaeological Research Collection, Tallinn University).

Loveluck, Chris and Dries Tys 2006 Coastal Societies, Exchange and Identity Along the Channel and Southern North Sea Shores of Europe, AD 600-1000 *Journal of Maritime Archaeology* 1, 140-69.

Ludowici, Babette, Hauk Jöns, Sunhild Kleingärtner, Jonathan Scheschkewitz, Matthias Hardt (eds) 2010 *Trade and Communication Networks of the First Millennium AD in the Northern Part of Central Europe* (Neue Studien zur Sachsenforschung 1) (Niedersächsisches Landesmuseum, Hannover).

Mango, Marlia Mundell 2009 Tracking Byzantine Silver and Copper Metalware, 4th to 12th Century in Marlia Mundell Mango (ed.) *Byzantine Trade, 4th-12th Centuries. The Archaeology of Local, Regional and International Exchange* (Publications of the Society for Byzantine Studies 14, Ashgate, Farnham), 221-238.

——— 2019 East Mediterranean Flagon and Basin in Blackmore et al. *The Prittlewell Princely Burial* (MOLA Monograph 73, London), 178-186.

Mango, Marlia Mundell, Cyril Mango, Angela Care Evans and Michael Hughes 1989 A 6th-Century Mediterranean Bucket from Bromeswell Parish, Suffolk, *Antiquity* 63, 295-311.

Marsden, Peter 1994 *Ships of the Port of London. First to Eleventh Century* (English Heritage. Archaeology Report 3, London).

McClure, Judith and Roger Collins (eds) 2008 Bede *The Ecclesiastical History of the English People* trans. Bertram Colgrave (Oxford University Press, Oxford).

McGrail, Sean 1978, *Logboats of England and Wales* (British Archaeological Reports 51(i), Oxford).

——— 1986 Experimental Boat Archaeology - Some Methodological Considerations in Crumlin-Pedersen and Vinner (eds) (The Viking Ship Museum, Roskilde), 8-17.

——— 1987 *Ancient Boats of North-West Europe* (Longman, Harlow).

Millett, Martin and Simon James 1983 Excavations at Cowdery's Down,

Basingstoke, 1978-1981 *Archaeological Journa*l 140, 151-279.
Milne, Gustav 1996 Blackfriars Ship 1: Romano-Celtic, Gallo-Roman or *Classis Brittanicae*? *IJNA* 25, 234-238.
Morris, Richard 2004 *Journeys from Jarrow* (Jarrow Lecture).
Mudie, Colin 1986 Designing Replica Boats. The Boats of St Brendan, Sinbad and Jason in Crumlin-Pedersen and Vinner (eds) (The Viking Ship Museum, Roskilde), 38-59.
Müller-Wille, Michael 1976 *Das Bootkammergrab von Haithabu* (Berichte über die Ausbrabunge in Haithabu, 8) (Wachholtz, Neumünster).
Myrhe, Björn 1987 Chieftain's Graves and Chieftain's Territories in South Norway in the Migration Period *Studien zur Sachsenforschung* 6, 169-197.
Näsman, Ulf 1986 Vendel Period Glass from Eketorp II, Öland, Sweden *Acta Archaeologica* 55, 66-116.
Natan, Eyal, Yael Gorin-Rosen, Agnese Benzonelli and Deboral Cvikel 2021 Maritime Trade in Early Islamic-Period Glass: New Evidence from the Ma'agan Mikhael B Shipwreck *Journal of Archaeological Science: Reports* 37, 102903.
Newell, A. K. 2020 *The First Muslim Navy: Sailing on the Sea like Kings on Thrones* [online]. Available at https://islamciv.com/2020/02/27/the-first-muslim-navy
Nordeide, Saebjørg, Niels Bonde, Terje Thun 2020 At the Threshold of the Viking Age: New Dendrochronological Dates for the Kvalsund Ship and Boat Bog Offerings (Norway), *Journal of Archaeological Science: Reports* 29, 102192.
Ordnance Survey 1966 *Map of Britain in the Dark Ages* (2nd edition) (Ordnance Survey, Southampton).
Owen-Crocker, Gale 2004 *Dress in Anglo-Saxon England* (Boydell, Woodbridge).
Peets, Jüri, Raili Allmäe and Liina Maldre 2011 Archaeological Investigations of Pre-Viking Age Burial Boat in Salme Village at Saaremaa *Archaeological Fieldwork in Estonia* 2010, 29-48.
Peets, Jüri, Raili Allmäe, Liina Maldre, Ragnar Saage, Teresa Tomek, Lembi Lõugas 2013 Research Results of the Salme Ship Burials in 2011-2012 *Archaeological Fieldwork in Estonia* 2012, 43-60.
Phillips, Charles, 1940 The Sutton Hoo Burial Ship. *Mariner's Mirror* 26, 345-355.
Price, Neil S. (ed.) 2001 *The Archaeology of Shamanism* (Routledge, London).
——— 2002 *The Viking Way: Religion and War in Late Iron Age Scandinavia* (Aun 31) (Uppsala University Department of Archaeology & Ancient History, Uppsala).

Price T. Douglas, Jüri Peets, Raili Allmäe, Liina Madre and Neil Price 2020 Human Remains, Context, and Place of Origin for the Salme, Estonia, Boat Burial *Journal of Anthropological Archaeology* 58, 101149.

Pulak, Cemal, Rebecca Ingram and Michael Jones 2015 Eight Byzantine Shipwrecks from the Theodosian Harbour Excavations at Yenikapı in Istanbul, Turkey: An Introduction *IJNA* 44.1, 39-73. doi.org: 10.1111/1095-9270.12083

Ramqvist, Per H. 1992 *Högom. The Excavations 1949-1984* (Department of Archaeology University of Umeå, Umeå).

Reynolds, Andrew 2009 *Anglo-Saxon Deviant Burial Customs* (Oxford University Press, Oxford).

——— 2013 Judicial Culture and Social Complexity: A General Model from Anglo-Saxon England *World Archaeology* 45.5, 699-713.

Robinson, Iona, Mark Knight and Kerry Murrell 2015 *Must Farm Paleochannel Investigations 2009-2012. Post Excavation Assessment* (Cambridge Archaeological Unit, Cambridge).

Rosenberg, Gustav 1937 *Hjortspringfundet* (Nordiske Fortidsminder 31) (Nordisk Forlag, København).

Rule, Margaret 1982 *The Mary Rose: The Excavation and Raising of Henry VIII's Flagship* (Conway Maritime Press, London).

Schofield, Fred 1988 *Humber Keels and Keelmen* (Terence Dalton, Lavenham).

Scull, Chris and John Naylor 2016 Sceattas in Anglo-Saxon Graves *Medieval Archaeology* 60.2, 205-241.

Scull, Chris and Gabor Thomas 2020 Early Medieval Great Hall Complexes in England: Temporality and Site Biographies *Anglo-Saxon Studies in Archaeology and History* 22, 50-67.

Scull, Chris, Stuart Brookes and Tom Williamson (eds) 2024a *Lordship and Landscape in East Anglia AD 400-800. The Royal Centre at Rendlesham, Suffolk, and its Contexts* (Society of Antiquaries, Research Report 84, London).

Scull, Chris, Linzi Everett and Faye Minter 2024b Excavations at Rendlesham, Suffolk, 2021-2023: Investigating an Early Medieval Royal Settlement *Medieval Archaeology* 68.2, 203-228. https://doi.org/10.1080/00766097.2024.2419190

Semple, Sarah 2013 *Perceptions of the Prehistoric in Anglo-Saxon England. Religion, Ritual and Rulership in the Landscape* (Oxford University Press, Oxford).

Severin, Tim 2005 *The Brendan Voyage: Across the Atlantic in a Leather Boat* (Gill and Macmillan, Dublin and London).

Speake, George 1989 *A Saxon Bed-Burial on Swallowcliffe Down*

(English Heritage Archaeological Report 10, London).

Tanner, Pat, Julian Whitewright and Joe Startin 2020 The Digital Reconstruction of the Sutton Hoo Ship *IJNA* 49.1: 5-28.

Taylor Eva Germaine Rimington 1956 *The Haven-Finding Art. A History of Navigation from Odysseus to Captain Cook* (Hollis and Carter, London).

Thier, Katrin 2003 Sails in the North - New Perspectives on an Old Problem *IJNA* 32.2: 182-190.

Thomas, Gabor and Alexandria Knox 2017 *Early Medieval Monasticism in the North Sea Zone: Recent Research and New Perspectives. Proceedings of a Conference Held to Celebrate the Conclusion of the Lyminge Excavations 2008-2015* (Anglo-Saxon Studies in Archaeology and History 20, Oxford).

Tipper, Jess 2012 Experimental Archaeology and Fire: the Investigation of a Burnt Reconstruction at West Stow Anglo-Saxon Village (East Anglian Archaeology 146, Suffolk County Council, Bury St Edmunds).

Walton Rogers, Penelope 2005 The Textiles from Mounds 5, 7, 14 and 17 in Martin Carver, *Sutton Hoo: A Seventh Century Princely Burial Ground and its Context* (British Museum, London), 262-268.

——— 2007 *Cloth and Clothing in Early Anglo-Saxon England AD 450-700* (Council for British Archaeology, York).

West, Stanley 1985 West Stow. The Anglo-Saxon Village (East Anglian Archaeology 24, Suffolk County Planning Department, Ipswich).

Wilson, David 1976 Craft and Industry in David Wilson (ed.) *The Archaeology of Anglo-Saxon England* (Methuen, London), 253-282.

Wright, Edward V. and Chester W. Wright 1947 Prehistoric Boats from North Ferriby, East Yorkshire *Proceedings of the Prehistoric Society* ns 12, 114-38.

PARTICIPANTS

During the period covered by this book.

TRUSTEES

Andrew FitzGerald (2017-) Treasurer (2017-2022)
Philip Leech, (2017-2021) (Chair 2018-2021)
Annie Leech (2017-2021)
Peter Clay (2017-2022)
Martin Carver (2017-) (Chair 2017-18, 2021-2023)
Joe Startin (2017-)
Simon Steel (2017-)
Julian Whitewright (2017-2022)
Angela Care Evans (2021-)
Nicola Stacey (2021-2024)
Damian Robinson (2021-)
Jonathan Lea (Treasurer 2022-)
Mark Jones (2022-2023)
Sharon Kindleysides (2022-)
Sean McMillan (2023-) (Chair 2023-)
Helen Geake (2023-)

CREW

Jacq Barnard (2017-) Project Manager
Tim Kirk (2017-2025) Master Shipwright
Laurie Walker (2021-) First Shipwright, (2025-) Master Shipwright
Carl Moore (2023-) Assistant Shipwright
Alec Newland Treewright
David Keeble Volunteer co-ordinator
Shipbuilding Crew Jo Wood, David Rowley, John Orr, David Turner, Mike Pratt, David Steptoe, Simon Charlesworth
Andy Mills, photographer
Catherine Hoy, artist

CONSULTANTS

Norman Macritchie (Health and Safety)
Damian Goodburn (splitting timber)
Paul Handley (naval architect)

Toby Jones (nautical archaeologist)
Pat Tanner (digital modelling)
Richard Symes (procurement of timber)
Alex Pole (Ironwork)
Adrian Overbury (Marine surveyor)
Dan Snow (History Hits)
Julian Whitewright (Nautical Archaeologist)

WITAN advisors (2021-2023)
Prof. Jan Bill (Oslo), Prof. Helena Hamerow (Oxford), Prof. Francis Leneghan (Oxford), Dr Catherine Hills (Cambridge), Prof. Simon Keynes (Cambridge), Prof. Rosalind Love (Cambridge), Dr Rory Naismith (Cambridge), Prof. Marcos Martinón Torres (Cambridge), Dr Chris Evans (Cambridge), Prof Andrew Reynolds (UCL), Prof. Chris Scull (Cardiff and UCL), Sean McMillan (Spirit Yachts, Ipswich), Keith Wade (Ipswich Archaeological Trust), Geoffrey Dyball (Ipswich Maritime Trust), Chris Wiltshire (Ipswich Archaeological Trust) Angus Wainwright (National Trust), Allison Girling (National Trust), Laura Howarth (National Trust), Richard Barber (Publisher), Tim Taylor (Director, Time Team), Robert Simper (author), Bryony Abbot (Sutton Hoo Society), Brian Knibbs (Woodbridge Riverside Trust), David Adelson (Woodbridge Town Council).

DONORS in CASH or in KIND
We are grateful for the many donations large and small, known and unknown, which have made the reconstruction of the Sutton Hoo Ship a reality.

INDEX

Pages with illustrations are in bold